Town Planning in Practice: An Introduction to the Art of Designing Cities and Suburbs

Sir Raymond Unwin

TOWN PLANNING IN PRACTICE

BY BARRY PARKER AND RAYMOND
UNWIN, "THE ART OF BUILDING A
HOME." ILLUSTRATED, 10/6 NET.
LONDON : LONGMANS, GREEN & CO.

Illus. **145.**—*Regensburg. Moltke Platz.*

TOWN PLANNING

IN PRACTICE · AN IN-
TRODUCTION TO THE ART
OF DESIGNING CITIES AND
SUBURBS · *By* RAYMOND UNWIN

WITH 300 ILLUSTRATIONS

T. FISHER UNWIN · LONDON: ADELPHI
TERRACE · LEIPSIC: INSELSTRASSE 20   1909

MY WIFE AND I
INSCRIBE THIS BOOK
TO THE MEMORY OF
MY FATHER

PREFACE

WHEN a Bill conferring town planning powers on municipal bodies was promised by the Government, it occurred to me that it would probably be of use if some of the maps, photographs, and other material which I had collected during some years' study and practice of what I have ventured to call the art of town planning could be put together and published. Hence this book. The spare time at my disposal has only enabled me to deal in an introductory and imperfect manner with the different points raised; but I am hopeful that those who do me the honour to read the text will find it at any rate sufficient to help them to glean from the illustrations many of the valuable suggestions which I believe them to contain. I have made free use of ideas gathered from many sources which it is impossible for me to acknowledge in detail; but I would like here to express my indebtedness to those with whom I have collaborated, particularly to Mr. Barry Parker; also to Mr. Edwin L. Lutyens, whose suggestions in connection with the Hampstead Garden Suburb work have been invaluable.

My thanks are due to many whose writings on the subject I have found helpful—Mr. Horsfall, Dr. Stübben, Mr. C. Mulford Robinson, Professor Geddes, Mr. Phené Spiers, Professor Schultze-Naumburg, Mr. Halsey Ricardo, Mr. Reginald Blomfield, to mention the names of a few only of those of whom I think with gratitude in this connection.

I would like also to record my appreciation of the way in which my requests for permission to use valuable illustrations and other material have throughout been met. These are, I hope, all acknowledged in their places. I am particularly indebted to Dr. Stübben and to the editor and publisher of "Der Städtebau," also to Herr Berlepsch-Valendas, and to the officials of many German towns, who have given me the greatest assistance at different times, and have always been willing to help an Englishman to understand their town-planning methods and to profit by their experience.

Last, and by no means least, my acknowledgments are due to many of the members of my own staff who have co-operated with me in various ways. Without Mr. Wade's charming and imaginative pictures and the very useful illustrative sketches made by Mr. Mottram, or wanting the numerous diagrams prepared by Mr. Hollis and others, the book would have been but imperfectly illustrated.

R. U.

WYLDES, HAMPSTEAD, N.W.
    June, 1909.

CONTENTS OF THIS BOOK

ALPHABETICAL LIST OF ILLUSTRATIONS

FOLDED MAPS.

I.—OF CIVIC ART AS THE EXPRESSION OF CIVIC LIFE

THE last century has been remarkable, not only in this country but in some others, for an exceedingly rapid and extensive growth of towns. In England this growth has produced most serious results. For many years social reformers have been protesting against the evils which have arisen owing to this rapid and disorderly increase in the size of towns and their populations. Miles and miles of ground, which people not yet elderly can remember as open green fields, are now covered with dense masses of buildings packed together in rows along streets *Illus.* 2. which have been laid out in a perfectly haphazard manner, without any consideration for the common interests of the people. It is not to any design adopted for the benefit of the whole that we are indebted for such semblance of order or convenience as may be found here and there in these new areas. The very complete system of country roads following usually the lines of old tracks, and made for convenience of access to and from the town, has undoubtedly formed a connecting frame for the network of streets which has sprung up along and between them. A part of these developments, too, has taken place on estates of large size, where there has been a limited possibility of comprehensive planning and where it has been to the advantage of the individual owner to consider the convenience of a tolerably large area. But for these two circumstances, the confusion of our town plans would have *Illus.* 1. been even worse than it is. To-day it is hardly necessary to urge the desirability of a proper system of town planning. The advantage of the land around a growing town being laid out on a plan prepared with forethought and care to provide for the needs of the growing community seems self-evident; and yet it is only within the last few years that any general demand for such powers of town planning has been made. The corporations and other governing bodies have looked on helplessly while estate after estate around their towns has been covered with buildings without any provision having been made for open spaces, school sites, or any other public needs. The owner's main interest, too often his only one, has been to produce the maximum increase of value or of ground rent possible for himself by crowding upon the land as much building as it would hold. The community, through its representative bodies, having watched the value of land forced up to its utmost limit, has been obliged to come in at this stage and purchase at these ruinous values such scraps of the land as may have been left, in order to satisfy in an indifferent manner important public needs. In this way huge sums of public money have been wasted.

In the year 1889 Mr. Ebenezer Howard published a little book entitled " To-morrow," in which all this was very forcibly stated, and in which he suggested that it would be comparatively easy to try the experiment of developing a town on the precisely opposite and obviously rational method of first making a plan, and, by the

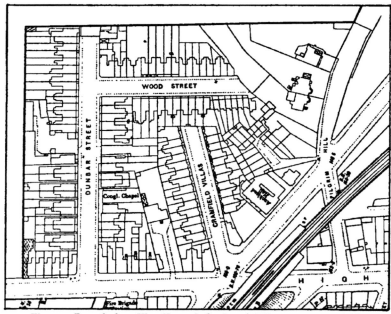

Illus. 1.—Example from West Norwood, London, of futile arrangement resulting from lack of town planning powers. Reproduced from the Ordnance Survey Map, with the sanction of the Controller of H.M.'s Stationery Office.

exercise of foresight, providing in that plan for all public needs likely to arise, and then securing the development of the town along the lines of this plan. This scheme was so obviously rational and desirable that in a comparatively short time it attracted the attention of a sufficient number of reformers to create a strong Garden City Association ; and as a result of their efforts in popularising the idea, in the year 1903 an estate was purchased of about 3,800 acres at Letchworth in Hertfordshire, by the First

Garden City Company, upon which there has now come into being the nucleus of a considerable town.

Fold Plan VII.

This movement was too theoretical and experimental to appeal very widely to the English people, but another book was forthcoming of quite a different character. "The Example of Germany," by Mr. Horsfall, first published in 1904 (University Press, Manchester), showed how in Germany the same problem of rapid increase of towns had been dealt with on lines much akin to those advocated by Mr. Howard. Unfortunately, the English people do not in very large numbers read books in foreign languages; and until the publication of Mr. Horsfall's book turned general attention to the matter it was known to only a few in this country that for many years in Germany, and indeed in many other countries, orderly planning and designing of town development formed a part of the ordinary routine of municipal government. Since the publication of Mr. Horsfall's book the facts have become generally known. International congresses of housing reformers and architects, the exchange of international courtesies, between municipal bodies, and the work of various associations and individuals, have contributed to spread the knowledge that powers for planning and controlling the development of their cities more or less on the lines of those possessed by Germany are enjoyed and successfully used by the municipalities of most countries except America, France, and England up to the present time. This is the kind of evidence which the Englishman likes, and on the strength of this the demand for town planning powers has become so general and so influentially backed by municipal corporations that the Government has already passed through the House of Commons a Bill conferring upon municipalities some, at any rate, of the necessary powers; and it is confidently expected that such a Bill will become law during the present year.

Although we have only just realised the importance of the comprehensive and orderly planning of our towns, it must not be supposed that nothing has hitherto been done to cope with the evils raised by their rapid growth. On the contrary, much good work has been done. In the ample supply of pure water, in the drainage and removal of waste matter, in the paving, lighting, and cleansing of streets, and in many other such ways, probably our towns are served as well as, or even better than, those elsewhere. Moreover, by means of our much abused building bye-laws, the worst excesses of overcrowding have been restrained; a certain minimum standard of air-space, light, and ventilation has been secured; while in the more modern parts of towns a fairly high degree of sanitation, of immunity from fire, and general stability of construction have been maintained, the importance of which can hardly be exaggerated. We have, indeed, in all these matters laid a good foundation and have secured many of the necessary elements for a healthy condition of life ; and yet the remarkable fact remains that there are growing up around all our big towns vast districts, under these very bye-laws, which for dreariness and sheer ugliness it is difficult to match anywhere, and compared with which many of the old unhealthy slums are, from the point of view of picturesqueness and beauty, infinitely more attractive.

Illus. 2.

Illus. 260 and 260 a, 237, 238.

The truth is that in this work we have neglected the amenities of life. We have forgotten that endless rows of brick boxes, looking out upon dreary streets and squalid backyards, are not really homes for people, and can never become such, however complete may be the drainage system, however pure the water supply, or however detailed the bye-laws under which they are built. Important as all these provisions for man's material needs and sanitary existence are, they do not suffice. There is needed the vivifying touch of art which would give completeness and increase their value tenfold ; there is needed just that imaginative treatment which could transform the whole.

Professor Lethaby has well said, " Art is the well-doing of what needs doing." We have in a certain niggardly way done what needed doing, but much that we have done has lacked the insight of imagination and the generosity of treatment which would have constituted the work well done ; and it is from this well-doing that beauty springs. It is the lack of beauty, of the amenities of life, more than anything else which obliges us to admit that our work of town building in the past century has not been well done. Not even the poor can live by bread alone ; and substantial as are the material boons which may be derived from such powers for the control of town development as we hope our municipalities will soon possess, the force which is behind this movement is derived far more from the desire for something beyond these boons, from the hope that through them something of beauty may be restored to town life. We shall, indeed, need to carry much further the good work begun by our building bye-laws. We shall need to secure still more open ground, air-space, and sunlight for each dwelling; we shall need to make proper provision for parks and playgrounds, to control our streets, to plan their direction, their width, and their character, so that they may in

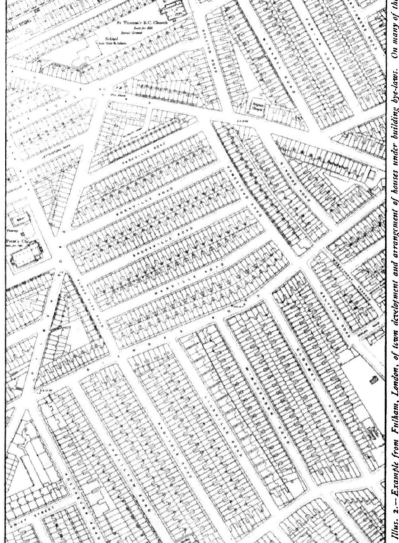

Illus. 2.—*Example from Fulham, London, of town development and arrangement of houses under building bye-laws. On many of the areas there are 40 fairly large houses to the acre, excluding roads. Over the whole area shown the number of houses to the acre is 20, and in this case the acreage includes the roads and the sites of churches, schools, works, playgrounds, &c. Reproduced from the Ordnance Survey Map with the sanction of the Controller of H.M.'s Stationery Office.*

Illus. 3.—Karlsruhe, Markt Platz. View looking towards the Schloss.

Illus. 3a.—Karlsruhe, Markt Platz. Opposite view to above. This market-place is symmetrically planned on the axis line of the town. See Fold Map IV.

the best possible way minister to the convenience of the community. We shall need power to reserve suitable areas for factories, where *Fold Plan* they will have every convenience for their work and cause the *VII.* minimum of nuisance to their neighbours. All these practical advantages, and much more, may be secured by the exercise of powers for town planning; but above all, we need to infuse the spirit of the artist into our work. The artist is not content with the least that will do ; his desire is for the best, the utmost he can achieve. It is the small margin which makes all the difference between a thing scamped and a thing well done to which attention must be directed. From this margin of well-doing beauty will spring.

In desiring powers for town planning our town communities are seeking to be able to express their needs, their life, and their aspirations in the outward form of their towns, seeking, as it were, freedom to become the artists of their own cities, portraying on a gigantic canvas the expression of their life.

Beauty is an elusive quality, not easily defined, not always easily attained by direct effort, and yet it is a necessary element in all good work, the crowning and completing quality.   It is not a quality that can be put on from outside, but springs from the spirit of the artist infused into the work. We are too much in the habit of regarding art as something added from without, some species of expensive trimming put on. Much of the restless, fussy vulgarity we see about us springs from this mistake. So long as art is regarded as a trimming, a species of crochet-work to be stitched in ever increasing quantities to the garments of life, it is vain to expect its true importance to be recognised. Civic art is too often understood to consist in filling our streets with marble fountains, dotting our squares with groups of statuary, twining our lamp-posts with wriggling acanthus leaves or dolphins' tails, and our buildings with meaningless bunches of fruit and flowers tied up with impossible stone ribbons. William Morris said : " Beauty, which is what is meant by Art, using the word in its widest sense, is, I contend, no mere accident of human life which people can take or leave as they choose, but a positive necessity of life, if we are to live as Nature meant us to—that is, unless we are content to be less than men." The art which he meant works from within outward ; the beauty which he regarded as necessary to life is not a quality which can be plastered on the outside. Rather it results when life and the joy of life, working outwards, express themselves in the beauty and perfection of all the forms which are created for the satisfaction of their needs.

*

Such exuberance of life will, indeed, in due course find expression in the adornment of its creations with suitable decoration, and such adornment may become their crowning beauty ; but the time for this is not yet. While the mass of the people live in hovels and slums and our children grow up far from the sight and pleasure of green fields and flowers ; while our land is laid out solely to serve the interests of individual owners, without regard to the common needs, this is no time to think of the crowning beauty of ornament. We need to begin at the other end. Our immediate business is to lay a firm foundation.

Remembering then that art is expression and that civic art must be the expression of the life of the community, we cannot well have a more safe practical guide than Mr. Lethaby's saying that "Art is the well doing of what needs doing." Does the town need a market-place, our rule would teach us to build the best, most convenient, and comely market-place we can design ; not to erect a corrugated-iron shed for the market and spend what would have done this work well in "decorating" the town park with ornamental railings. First, let our markets be well built and our cottage areas well laid out ; then there will soon grow up such a full civic life, such a joy and pride in the city as will seek expression in adornment. This is not the place to consider in detail the many causes which have led to the rapid growth of town populations. The concentration of industry, the decay of agriculture, the growing contrast in the conditions of life offered in the country and the town, have all had their influence in leading people in such vast numbers to forsake the lonely cottage on the hillside or the sleeping village in the hollow in favour of the dirty street in the town slum. The impulse partly springs from the desire for higher wages and the attraction of varied amusement and flaring gas lamps ; but it equally arises from the desire for a greater knowledge, wider experience, and fuller life generally which men realise they can only find in closer association with their fellows. But whatever their motives in leaving their villages, the people have broken many old ties of interest and attachment ; it should be our aim to secure that in going to the city they may find new ties, new interests, new hopes, and that general atmosphere which will create for them new homes and new local patriotism. Hitherto our modern towns have been too much mere aggregations of people ; but it must be our work to transform these same aggregations into consciously organised communities, finding in their towns and cities new homes in the true sense, enjoying that fuller life which comes from more intimate intercourse, and finding in the organisation of their town scope and stimulus for the practice and development of the more noble aims which have contributed to bring them together.

Aristotle defined a city as a place where men live a common life for a noble end.   The movement towards town improvement of which town planning forms but one branch must have for its aim the creation of such a city as shall at once express the common life and stimulate its inhabitants in their pursuit of the noble end.   With the expression of the common life, as we have already seen, town planning is intimately concerned, and whether our cities will indeed become great works of art will principally depend on the prevalence of the aim towards a noble end to which Aristotle referred.   It is, indeed, from this expression that civic art must draws its inspiration and guidance.   We are told by many authorities that expression is one of the fundamental elements in all art, and that the creation of great art results when some great idea is finely rendered.   It is probable that in the art of city building great work will again be done when there is a fine common life seeking expression, and when we have so mastered the technique of our art as to have established a tradition capable of giving adequate form to such expression.

Before attempting to consider in detail the various practical problems of town planning, it will be useful if we can understand something of the reasons which exist for the general lack of beauty in our towns, and further if we try to arrive at some principles to guide us in determining in individual cases what treatment is likely to lead to a beautiful result and what to the reverse. We have become so used to living among surroundings in which beauty has little or no place that we do not realise what a remarkable and unique feature the ugliness of modern life is.   We are apt to forget that this ugliness may be said to belong almost exclusively to the period covered by the industrial development of the last century.   We do not find evidence of it before that period, in our own towns or in those of a character to be compared with our own in other countries.   It is not that in other respects older towns excelled modern ones ; it is not that they were less overcrowded, that their streets were finer, better kept, or cleaner.   On the contrary, excessive overcrowding existed in old towns ; the streets were usually very narrow, and at many periods were both dirty and insanitary.   Nor does there appear to have been generally very much conscious planning of the streets.   Often there is little apparent order or arrangement in the placing of the buildings ; and yet, in spite of this, a high degree of beauty almost always marked the effect produced. So much so, that both in this country and in many others wherever one finds a street or part of a street dating from before what may be called the modern period, one is almost sure to see something pleasing and beautiful in its effect. The result, no doubt, is due largely to a greater degree of beauty in the individual buildings ; many of these, in fact most of them, were quite simple and unadorned, yet there seems to have been such an all-pervading instinct or tradition guiding the builders in past times, that most of what they did contained elements of beauty and produced picturesque street pictures. Something also is due to the hand of time, which, through the sagging of timbers, has softened the lines of the buildings, and through the weathering of the surfaces has mellowed the textures of the materials used in them. The influence of the tradition we have mentioned was not confined to the buildings themselves, but seems to have extended to the treatment of streets and *places* as well as to such minor details as steps, entrance gates, walls, and fences, which often enhance the beauty of the picture. To a very great degree this tradition appears to have acted unconsciously and almost as a natural force ; for the absence of symmetry or orderly arrangement is often as evident as the picturesqueness of the architectural grouping is pleasing. In these old towns and streets we read as in an open book the story of a life governed by impulses very different from our own ; we read of gradual growth, of the free play of imaginative thought, devoted without stint to each individual building ; while the simplicity of treatment, the absence of decoration or ornament in the majority of cases, and the general use and skilled handling of the materials most readily accessible, tell of the usual avoidance of what could be called extravagance. Nevertheless, we are impressed by the generous use of material and labour revealed in the dimensions of the beams, in the thickness of the walls, and in the treatment of all necessary features, which suggests that two prominent elements in the tradition which influenced builders in old times were that the work should be well done, and that it should be comely to look upon when finished. While obviously the cost was carefully considered, it was not deemed legitimate to sacrifice proper construction, good design, or good finish in order to attain the last possible degree of cheapness. How different is the spirit in which the modern suburb is built up ! A similar absence of planning or conscious design in the laying out, and an almost equal freedom to the individual builder to do as he likes mark the modern method ; but with what a different result ! There is little thought bestowed on

Illus. 32-35, 42-45, *and* 50-55.

the individual building, or on its adaptation to the site and surroundings, no imaginative fitting of it into a picture.   Instead, some
stock plan of a house which is thought to be economical is reproduced in row after row without regard to levels, aspect, or anything *e.g., view of*
but just the one point, can the building be done so cheaply that it *Northamp-*
can be made to yield a good return on the outlay ?   Is it any wonder, *ton from L.*
then, that our towns and our suburbs express by their ugliness the *& N.W. Ry.*
passion for individual gain which so largely dominates their
creation ?   How, then, it may be asked, are we to make any
progress, for the passing of a Town Planning Bill will not change
the character of the life which we see expressing itself in our dreary
suburbs ?   And, indeed, if this desire for individual gain represented the only impulse of the citizens, it is little that we could
hope to do.   But happily this is not the case.   There is much that
is great and splendidly co-operative in the life of our towns, and
our social instinct is already highly developed by the mutual help-
fulness of common life.   Therefore, though town planning powers
will not change the individualistic impulses which prevail, they will
for the first time make possible an adequate expression of such
corporate life as exists.   Here, as elsewhere, action and reaction
will take place ; the more adequate expression of corporate life in
the outward forms of the town will both stimulate and give fresh
scope to the co-operative spirit from which it has sprung.

The conscious art of town building is practically a new one for us
in England.   We shall need to begin somewhat tentatively, and at
first we may well be content if we can introduce order to replace
the present chaos, if we can do something to restrain the
devastating tendency of personal interests and to satisfy in a
straightforward and orderly manner the obvious requirements of
the community.

Though the study of old towns and their buildings is most useful,   ?
nay, is almost essential to any due appreciation of the subject, we
must not forget that we cannot, even if we would, reproduce the
conditions under which they were created ; the fine and all-
pervading tradition is gone, and it will take generations for any
new tradition comparable to the old one to grow up.   While, therefore, we study and admire, it does not follow that we can copy ; for
we must consider what is likely to lead to the best results under
modern conditions, what is and what is not attainable with the
means at our disposal.

The informal beauty which resulted from the natural and apparently
unconscious growth of the medieval town may command our

highest admiration, but we may feel that it arose from conditions of life which no longer exist, and that it is unwise to seek to reproduce it. Possibly other forms of beauty will be found more adapted to our present conditions. The very rapidity of the growth of modern towns demands special treatment. The wholesale character of their extension almost precludes the possibility of our attaining that appearance of natural growth which we have admired in the medieval town, where additions were made so gradually that each house was adapted to its place, and assimilated into the whole before the next was added. We already see in the modern suburb too much evidence of what is likely to result from any haphazard system of development. Modern conditions require, undoubtedly, that the new districts of our towns should be built to a definite plan. They must lose the unconscious and accidental character and come under the rules of conscious and ordered design. We find that in the few instances in which towns were laid out as a whole in ancient times the plans usually follow very simple rectangular lines, and are quite different in character from those which developed by slow, natural growth. A short examination of the different types of town plans will perhaps be the most helpful way of approaching our subject.

II.—OF THE INDIVIDUALITY OF TOWNS, WITH A SLIGHT SKETCH OF THE ANCIENT ART OF TOWN PLANNING

MANY Englishmen, as tourists, have become familiar with foreign towns as well as with those in their own country; but the tourist in examining town maps does not regard them as designs. Let any one so regard them and he will be astonished at the variety of types which he will find. It is only necessary to turn over the pages of Baedeker's or Baddeley's Guides *Illus. 4.* to Great Britain to realise this. If we compare, for example, the plan of Chester, obviously based on the rectilinear lines of a regular

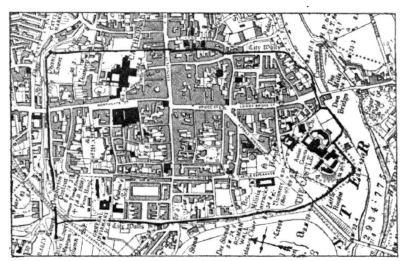

Illus. 4.—Plan of Chester, showing development based on lines of early Roman Camp. Reproduced from the Ordnance Survey Map, with the sanction of the Controller of H.M.'s Stationery Office.

oblong Roman camp, with that of Conway, following the irregular *Illus. 5.* strategic lines of its fortifications; of Hereford, so much influenced by the three main roads which meet in its High Town; or of *Illus. 6.* Edinburgh, containing within itself the contrast between the narrow, *Illus. 7.* irregular streets of its old town and the formal lay-out in the large manner of its more modern north-western quarter, we must be struck by the wide differences between them, and the marked individuality which characterises these different town plans. If the survey be extended further and plans of foreign cities and of those founded at different periods be compared, the variety increases

Illus. 8.

*Fold Maps
I. and II.*

Illus. 9.

Illus. 10.

greatly and the individuality becomes still more marked.   Contrast, for example, the plan of Moscow with that of Nuremburg or Turin, or either of them with that of Washington.   To the lover of cities this individuality is a very real quality, and one of the dangers of town planning schemes, against which we should guard, is the tendency to efface this individuality and to drill all town plans into a similar type and pattern.   This tendency can only be avoided by a very thorough appreciation of the individuality—one might almost say the personality—of towns.   There are in each certain settled characteristics arising from the nature of the scenery, the colours of local building materials, the life of the citizens, the character of the industries prevalent in the district, and numerous other circumstances, which taken all together, go to make up that

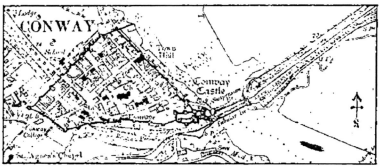

*Illus. 5.—Plan of Conway, showing irregular walled town.
Reproduced from the Ordnance Survey Map, with the sanction of the Controller of
H.M.'s Stationery Office.*

Illus. 14, 15,
19, 42, 104,
105, 114, 119,
123, 125, 148,
150, 188, 189.

flavour which gives to the town its individuality.   For purposes of comparison and study, it may be necessary to classify cities and towns as we classify races and peoples ; but we must not, when so doing, forget that classification is only a rough and superficial aid to study, nor must we let it in any way obscure the varying characters of the individual cities.

It is to be hoped that some competent authority will take in hand the complete history of town development and town planning, with a classification of the different types of plan which have been evolved in the course of natural growth or have been designed at different periods by human art.   We can here only give sufficient examples of various types of plan and a sufficient sketch of the historical development of town planning to render generally intelligible the references which may be made in considering the details of the work of the town planner.

The first broad classification would divide towns into those which have been definitely designed and those which have grown gradually without being based on any prearranged plan. In both of these divisions we shall find such subdivisions as fortified or walled towns and unfortified or open ones; while among designed towns we shall find a main subdivision of those laid out on regular

Fold Maps I. and III.

Illus. 10, 47.

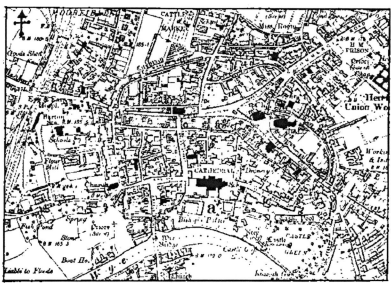

Illus. 6.—*Plan of Hereford, showing town plan influenced by junction of three main roads. Reproduced from the Ordnance Survey Map, with the sanction of the Controller of H.M.'s Stationery Office.*

lines and those definitely designed but on irregular lines. The former we can again classify according to whether the plans are based upon rectilinear lines, variations of what is known as the checker-board design—probably the oldest and most common type— on circular, diagonal, or radiating lines, or on various combinations of these, forming geometrical figures.

Of the towns which have grown there would be found characteristics common to those which have clustered round some centre—some castle, palace, church, or harbour, for example—and others characteristic of those which have sprung up at the junction or

Illus. 11, 13, and 37.

Illus. 61, 70, 71.

Illus. 47 and Fold Map IV., 56 and 63.

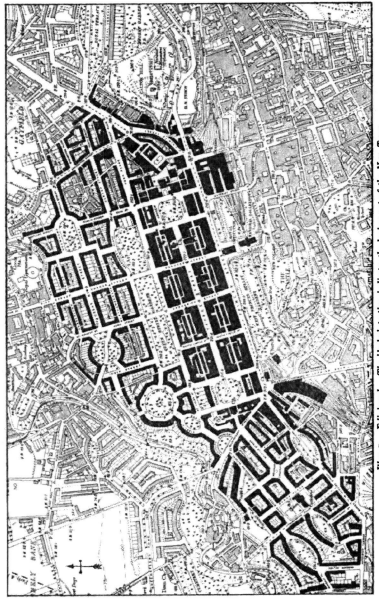

Illus. 7.—Edinburgh. The blacked portion indicates the laying out of the New Town.
Reproduced from the Ordnance Survey Map, with the sanction of the Controller of H.M.'s Stationery Office.

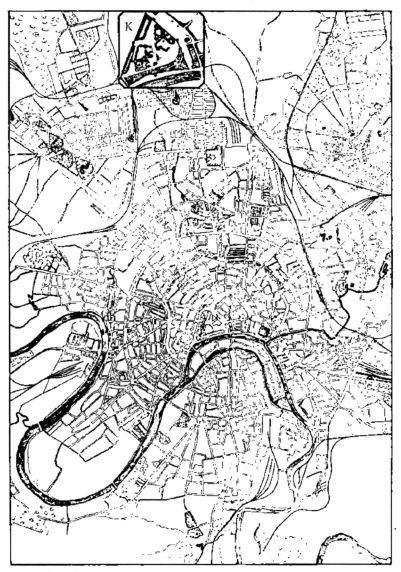

Illus. 8.—Plan of Moscow, which clearly shows radiating and ring roads.

crossing of main highways, or where such ways cross rivers by fords or bridges. Other peculiarities may characterise towns which have developed around some special industrial site, near iron, coal, or other mineral deposits ; or those which have developed near spots of exceptional beauty, near medicinal springs or holy wells, and have become places of resort for health or pleasure. All these circumstances which determine the development of a town

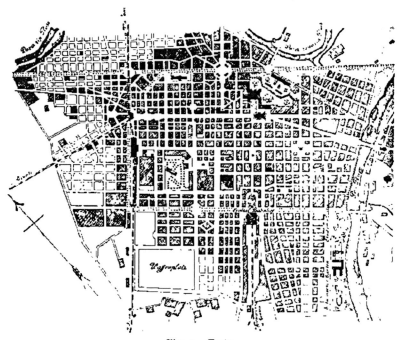

Illus. 9.—Turin.
Reproduced by kind permission of Dr. Stübben.

profoundly affect its plan and might form subdivisions in any complete classification ; while in each type there is the natural classification of period—the ancient, medieval, and the modern towns ; though it will be found that many of the types were prevalent at the same period, and not a few have been common at most periods. There is ground here for interesting study and very valuable historical work to be done. We find that towns have been designed as a whole, on comprehensive lines, in almost

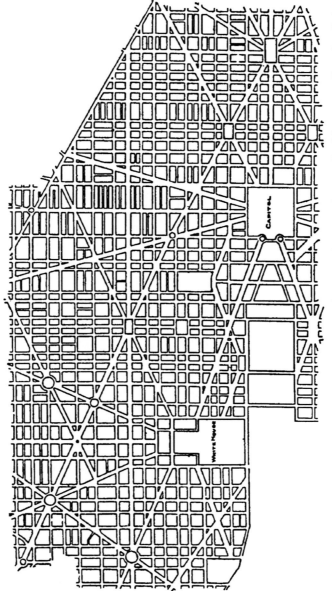

Illus. 10.—*Plan of the City of Washington. The basis of this plan is a rectangular system of streets relieved by numerous diagonals radiating at angles of 30 degrees or 60 degrees.*

Reproduced by kind permission from the Reports of the City Parks Association, Philadelphia.

3

all ages. Probably even in prehistoric times certain forms have been typical of certain tribal settlements, just as to-day, for example, we see that the Swazi kraal nearly always takes the customary form, the circular huts being generally arranged in a circle.

Illus. 11. Professor Flinders Petrie has described in his book "Illahun" the ancient town of Kahun, recently excavated, which was built about 3,000 B.C. to accommodate the workmen and others engaged in the building of the pyramid of Illahun. It is interesting as showing the earliest known town laid out on a definite plan. It

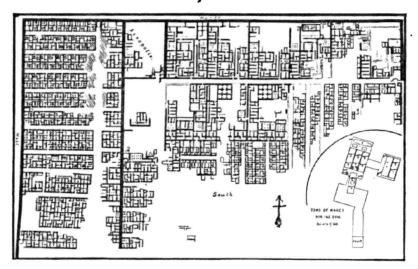

Illus. 11.—*Kahun. Date about 3000 B.C.*
Reproduced by kind permission of Professor Flinders Petrie.

will be seen from the illustration given, which is taken from Professor Flinders Petrie's book, that the town was laid out on regular lines and consisted of a few large houses and a number of smaller ones for workmen, the latter containing four or five rooms each. A small acropolis on the higher part of the ground served as the centre of the little community, probably both as a place of worship and seat of government. It is interesting, among other things, to find that the roads are arranged with a drain in the centre, this being the earliest known example of street drainage. It will be seen from this that nearly five thousand years ago town

Illus. 14.—M. Hulot's conjectural restorati
Reproduced by kind perm

Illus. 15.—M. Hulot's conjectural restorati
Reproduced by kind perm

...on of Sélinonte. View from the south.
...ission of M. Hulot.

...on of Sélinonte. View from the east.
...ssion of M. Hulot.

[To face page 26.

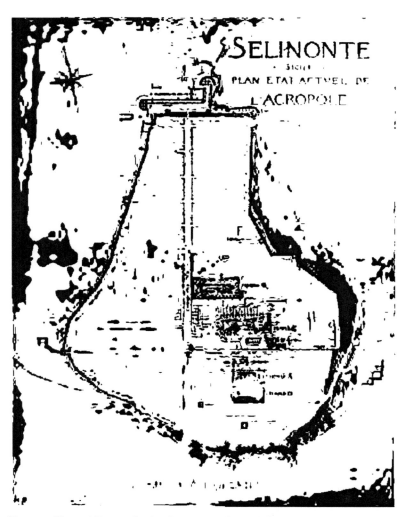

Illus. 12.—Plan of Sélinonte, showing the actual condition of the Acropolis at the present time. Reproduced by kind permission of M. Hulot.

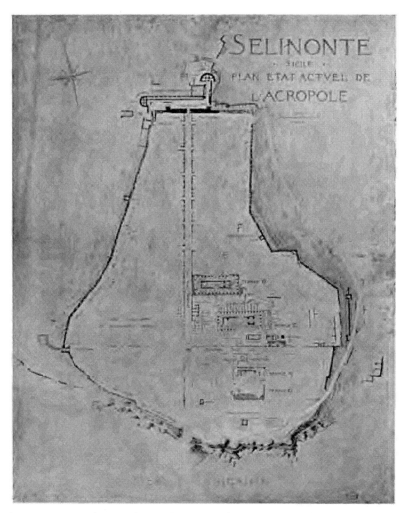

Illus. 12.—*Plan of Sélinonte, showing the actual condition of the Acropolis at the present time. Reproduced by kind permission of M. Hulot.*

Illus. 13.—*Plan of Selinonte, showing conjectural restoration of the plan of the Acropolis and part of the city made by M. Hulot, based on a study of the existing remains. Reproduced by kind permission of M. Hulot.*

planning on simple and orderly lines was practised by the ancient
Egyptians; and when we consider the disorderly, haphazard
character of the temporary settlements or little towns which grow
up near great engineering works in our own country, we may
well feel humbled that after the lapse of so many ages instead of
doing better we do worse than these ancients.

Another interesting example of town planning on regular lines has
been recently brought into notice by the joint work of M. Gustav
Fougères, antiquarian, and M. Jean Hulot, architect, the winner
of the Grand Prix de Rome, who, as part of the work imposed on
the winners of this Blue Ribbon of architectural students, has made
a most careful study and survey of the ruins of the ancient Doric *Illus. 12.*
colony of Sélinonte in Sicily, and has embodied the results in a
most beautiful set of drawings, which were exhibited in England *Illus. 13.*
under the auspices of the Royal Institute of British Architects,
during the summer of 1908. By the kind permission of the
authors I am able to reproduce some of the drawings, showing the
plans of this fortified city and its re-creation, based on careful study
of the existing remains and of the historical data. It will be seen
that the city consists of an acropolis regularly laid out and enclosed
by walls, and a much larger outer city on the landward side, also
probably fortified. Interest for us centres in the smaller city or
acropolis, the plan of which appears to date from 575–560 B.C.
I cannot do better than quote from the translation of M. Fougères'
paper, made by Mr. J. W. Simpson, F.R.I.B.A., and read at the
opening of the exhibition.

"Sélinonte, or Selinus, was a Greek colony in the South of Sicily, *Illus. 14 and*
founded 628 B.C. by the Dorians of Megara Hyblæa, a town *15.*
situate to the north of Syracuse. The history of Selinus was as
short as it was brilliant. The city existed but two centuries,
unceasingly at war with its neighbours of Segesta. . . . The
city thus fortified was divided as to its length by a great street
running straight from north to south, and seven metres wide; and
as to its width, by seven or eight transverse streets, cutting the
first at right angles, and dividing the houses into nearly equal
blocks. All this American town plan, which we believe attribut-
able to Hermocrates, is of the highest interest. It is the oldest
example known of the application to the lay-out of towns of the
geometric principles of the architect Hippodamus of Miletus, a
contemporary of Pericles, and author of the plans of the Piræus, of
Thurii, and of Rhodes. Hippodamus, a follower of Pythagoras,
was the Greek "Haussmann" of the fifth century B.C. Strongly

imbued with the idealistic spirit of his time, he desired to substitute clear, reasoned, and scientific conceptions for the caprices of chance. He dreamed of regular and geometric cities, preferring his theoretic plans to the tortuous mazes gradually formed by force of time, and saw therein a triumph of reasoned order over the wanton riot of Nature. The Germans have discovered at Priene, in Asia Minor, a type of city built throughout according to these principles ; but this late example dates only from the third century B.C. That of Selinus, almost contemporary with Hippodamus, must henceforward be regarded as classic.

" The houses which line these streets are also of the end of the fifth century B.C. They are of extreme simplicity and of a uniform model. Towards the street the front wall, with a massive plinth, is pierced by two doorways, one large and one small. On each side of the entrance corridor a shop opens to the street, being shut off from the interior, as at Delos and Pompeii. The corridor leads to a small internal court, surrounded by a rough peristyle and provided with a well. All around the peristyle are narrow rooms. The type is, in fact, that of the small houses at Delos. . . . There remain the temples, the glory of Selinus, whose colossal ruins still astound the traveller ; of these eleven now exist, divided into three groups. In the Acropolis are six Temples of the tutelary divinities of the city." . . .

In the second edition of " The Architecture of Greece and Rome," by W. J. Anderson and R. Phené Spiers, there is an interesting account of the early cities of Greece and Rome, and the excavations and remains of these cities prove beyond question that many of them were laid out on definite and regular lines. At the same time, it seems to have been characteristic of the Greeks that they usually took advantage of natural features and were very ready to modify or upset the regularity of their arrangement in order the better to make use of hillsides or rocky eminences to give grandeur and emphasis to their temples and other buildings. The treatment of the southern range at Gergantum is a good instance of this tendency of which the Acropolis at Athens is perhaps the best known and most splendid example. The same characteristic marked the arrangement of the temples at Eleusis, at Olympia, at Ephesus, and at many other places. It seems that the private buildings and dwelling-houses of the Greeks were comparatively insignificant, whereas their public buildings and *places* are usually laid out on a scale of magnificence that astonishes us.

The plan of Ephesus is a good example, with its fine treatment of

Illus. 16.

Illus. 16.—*Conjectural Restoration of the Acropolis at Athens, by M. Lambert.*
Reproduced by kind permission of Mr. R. Phené Spiers, F.S.A., F.R.I.B.A.

29

Illus. 16a.—Karlsruhe. Corner treatment in the Rondell Platz. See Fold Map IV.

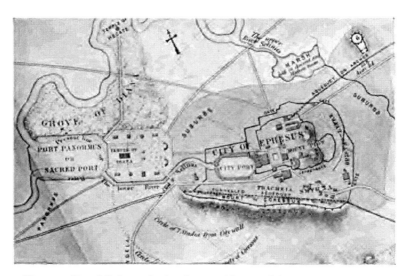

Illus. 17.—Plan of Ephesus, showing the general lay-out of the city in connection with the great Temple of Diana and the City and Sacred Port.

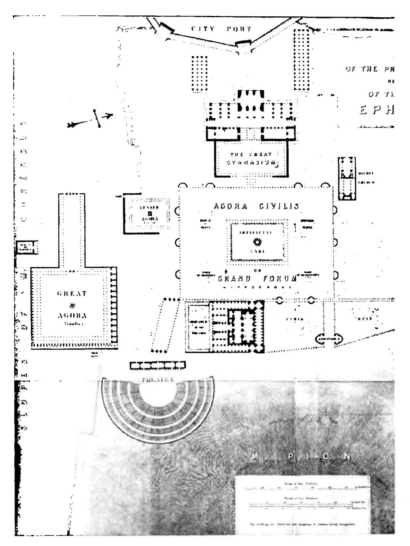

Illus. 18.—*Ephesus. Detailed plan of the Agora and other public buildings.*

Illus. 19.—View from the Coressus, showing conjectural re-creation of that portion of the City of Ephesus given in Illustration 18.

35

the outer and inner ports leading up to the great Agora, itself the
centre of a group of public buildings, squares, theatres, race-courses *Illus.* 17.
and gymnasia, which convey to us some idea of the greatness of *Illus.* 18.
the civic life which could express itself with such magnificence. *Illus.* 19.
Where the conditions of the site allowed, it appears that, in the
later periods at any rate, it was customary to lay out the streets of
the town on square and regular lines, opening out in places into
the great squares, or agoræ, leading up to the temples and other
public buildings.

Many conjectural restorations of Greek cities have been made by the
students of the Grand Prix de Rome in Paris, and these show groups
of buildings often situated in wide enclosures with groves of trees,
the whole forming a magnificent combination of the art of building
with natural beauty of scene and foliage, a parallel to which can
hardly be found except perhaps in some of the great Buddhist
sanctuaries of the East.

No very definite line can be drawn between the Greek and the
Roman cities, the remains of one often overlying the other, as at
Ephesus, which was measured by Edward Falkener and later by
J. T. Wood, who confirmed the accuracy of the former survey.
Wood states that although the actual remains found are Roman,
in many cases they were built on Greek foundations, some of
which he found, and it may therefore be fairly assumed that the
general lines of the plan agree with the Greek city of Ephesus as
laid out in the fourth century. Falkener, in his book "Ephesus,
the Temple of Diana," published in 1862, draws attention to the
fact that the Ionians laid out their streets in straight lines, with
the cross streets at right angles to them, and considers that it was *Illus.* 20.
from the Ionians that the Greeks derived this plan of laying out
their towns.

In Asia Minor and Syria there are interesting ruins of many old
cities of Greek or Roman origin, most of the remains found being
Roman. Many of these furnish examples of colonnaded streets,
which, like the agorae of the Greek cities, impress us with the
greatness of the public life to which they bear witness. Unfortunately very little has yet been done by excavating to discover
the details of the arrangement of these cities, but in some
instances sufficient remains above ground to give evidence of
extensive town planning having been carried out. Some of the
earliest records of these colonnaded streets are those describing
the city of Antioch, where Antiochus Epiphanes is said to have
laid out a street with a double colonnade more than two miles in

length, with other streets crossing at right angles.   This would be about the year 170 B.C.

Illus. 21.

The ruins of Palmyra are described by Robert Wood in a book published in 1753 ; and many fine drawings and plans of the same city are included in a book published by Cassas in Paris in 1799, entitled " Voyages Pittoresques de la Syrie et de la Phoenicie," from which our illustrations are taken.   Cassas draws attention to the

Illus. 22.

curious bends in the main colonnaded street, and to the masterly

Illus. 23.

way in which these bends have been treated by means of triumphal

Illus. 24.

arches, so that looking along the street from either direction the

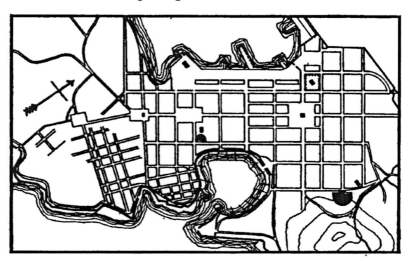

Illus. 20.—*Piræus, showing plan of the town as laid out by the Greeks.   It will be noticed that some of the temples are orientated.*
Reproduced by kind permission from " Der Städtebau."

arch set square with the line of the street terminates the vista. He suggests that these bends may have arisen owing to the existence of buildings, or to the fact that the road, intended apparently to connect two great temples, could not run in a straight line from one to the other and finish squarely with both. Whatever be the reason, the treatment of these bends is very impressive.   It is interesting also to compare the fine architectural method of providing shade and shelter along the footways of this road with the mean glass and iron structures which we nowadays erect in the few cases where any shelter at all is provided.

Palmyra.   View of the best preserved portions of the Grand Colonnade, showing the portio

Illus. 21.—General plan of the whole of the Grand Colonnade of Palmyra.   The length of this colon

from the building marked " C " on the left of the plan to the pedestals marked " D."

'e from the Triumphal Arch on the left to the Temple of Neptune on the right is about 3,500 ft.

[To face page 32.

Illus. 22.—Palmyra. View of the Grand Colonnade taken opposite the circular building looking towards the Temple of the Sun at the extreme left of the plan.

Illus. 23.—Palmyra. Enlarged plan of Triumphal Arch and portion of Grand Colonnade.

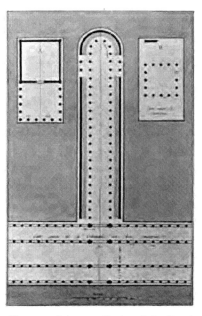

Illus. 24.—Palmyra. Portion of the Grand Colonnade, showing the Stadium and detailed plan of two temples.

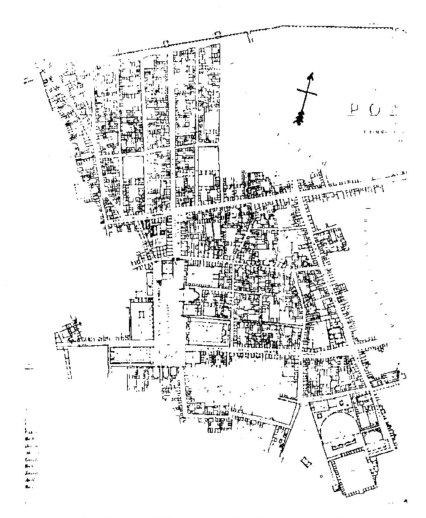

Illus. 25.—Plan of the excavated portion of the town of Pompeii.
Reproduced, by kind permission of Messrs. George Bell & Sons, from Dyer's "Pompeii."

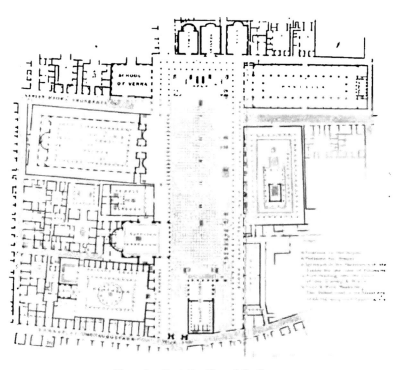

Illus. 26.—*Pompeii. Plan of the Forum.*
Reproduced, by kind permission of Messrs. George Bell & Sons, from Dyer's "Pompeii."

We must admire also the treatment of the road junctions, at one of
which four immense pedestals, each carrying a group of four columns
with their entablature, emphasise the crossing. Anderson and Spiers *Illus.* 21.
tell us that in some cases where colonnaded streets were used, as
at Antouret, Bosra, and Gersa, the intersection of two cross roads is
marked by a four-arched gateway vaulted over.

In these streets the central space or roadway was open to the sky,
the side avenues or footways being covered in with a terraced roof,
often extending over the shops and offices on each side, which, in
some cases at any rate, were of two storeys. Although the buildings
themselves and the roofs have mostly disappeared, the indications
on the columns and arches remaining are sufficient to prove their
existence. The central avenue of the main street at Palmyra is *Illus.* 23.!
37 feet wide, flanked on each side by a row of columns 31 feet
high. There were originally 454 columns in this street, of which
116 were still standing erect in Cassas' time. The side avenues or
covered walks were 16 feet wide. Archways exist at the entrance
of some of the minor cross roads, and at the east end of the main
street is an immense triple gateway the central arch of which is
23 feet 6 inches wide and 45 feet high, and the two side arches for
pedestrians are 11 feet 6 inches wide and 23 feet high.

It is to be hoped that some of these towns will be excavated and
that we shall know more of the plans on which the remaining
and less important portions of them were laid out. Many further
examples are pointed out and interesting particulars given in the
book already mentioned by Anderson and Spiers, to which the
reader is referred and to which I am indebted for the information
here given.

In the work of the Romans we find less respect and consideration
for the site than was characteristic of the Greeks. [Where the
Greek would adapt his arrangement to the site, the Roman would
adapt the site to his arrangement, carving away the rocks and
levelling the ground to obtain a clear field for his work. In
general the lay-out of the Roman town seems to have been on
regular lines and similar in many ways to that of the Greeks,
the forum taking the place of the Greek agora. The same
importance does not seem to have been attached to the orientation
of the temples by the Romans as by the Greeks.]

For the general character of Roman town planning I cannot do
better than quote from Anderson and Spiers :—

" On the foundation of a new town, the first consideration would *Illus.* 25.
appear to have been the two chief thoroughfares, and these were laid

out at right angles to one another, running as a rule north to south
and east to west.   In order to be as central as possible, the forum
occupied an angle of two of the streets, but there were always
buildings between the street and the forum, the entrance to the
central area of the latter being at one of the narrow ends, so as to
interfere as little as possible with the covered porticus round it.
The forum of Pompeii, which may be taken as a typical example,
was about 500 feet long, north to south, and 150 feet wide, in both

26.

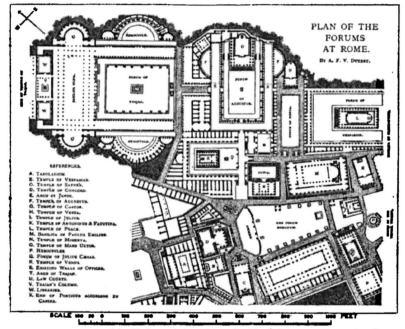

Illus. 27.—Reproduced by kind permission of Mr. R. Phené Spiers, F.S.A., F.R.I.B.A.

cases including the peristyle.   At the north end, projecting about
100 feet into the forum, was the Temple of Jupiter and an entrance
gateway, the Arch of Tiberius, at the north-east corner.   On the
east side were in succession the provision market, the sanctuary
of the city Lares, a small Temple of Vespasian, the building of
Eumachia (which was probably a cloth market), and the Comitium,
or voting-place.   On the south side were three municipal buildings,
and on the west side the Basilica, to the north of which was the

Illus. 28.—View of curved street in Pompeii.

Illus. 28a.—Karlsruhe. Corner treatment in the Rondell Platz. The Markt Platz and Schloss Tower in the distance. See Fold Plan IV.

Temple of Apollo in a court surrounded by a peristyle in two storeys, and, farther north, another market and latrines. Excepting the temple of Jupiter, the only other monumental features in the forum itself were statues raised on pedestals to various emperors and distinguished citizens."

Rome itself rapidly outgrew the capacities of the original forum, *Illus.* 27. and others of greater extent were added by the Emperors. Apparently the original Forum Romanum may have been partly the result of natural growth, as it was unsymmetrical in shape ; the subsequent forums, however, were in the main laid out on strictly symmetrical lines ; and extensive excavations into the hillside were made to render this possible ; so much so that the height of the retaining wall round the Forum of Augustus was in some places over 100 feet.

The older Forum Romanum, as also the forum at Pompeii, may be taken as representing the general character of the more typical centres of the Roman towns better than those architectural creations which were added from time to time by Roman emperors.

It will be noticed in the plan of Pompeii that although there is a general sense of regularity in the lay-out of the streets, the town pretty obviously grew gradually and was not laid out on very exact lines ; irregular streets are not wanting, and the photograph of one of these illustrates the beautiful curved line resulting from the way that the *Illus.* 28. Romans, in this instance at any rate, adapted their road to the contours of the hillside, instead of driving straight over or through it. The paving of this street is interesting as showing the double gutter at the sides and the convexity of the road surface which we have adopted in modern times as preferable to the more ancient arrangement of a central gutter which we noticed in the Egyptian town of Kahun.

We have an interesting example in Silchester of a Roman town laid *Illus.* 29. out in our own country. The plan, which is taken from the Ordnance Survey, shows a quite regular arrangement of streets, within, however, a line of fortifications of irregular shape.

The old part of Chester also shows even now the clearly marked *Illus.* 4. lines of its origin as a Roman camp or town. The two main streets run approximately east to west and north to south ; the Northgate Street and the Water Gate are very characteristic, and these streets have given a general squareness and regularity to many of the other streets in the town.

Dr. Stübben gives two interesting plans of Aosta, one showing *Illus.* 30. the ancient Roman town within the walls so far as it is known, the *Illus.* 31.

other the modern town ; if these are compared, it will be seen how much the Roman origin has influenced the later planning and development.

Illus. 9. Turin is another instance of a town laid out on very formal and four-square lines, largely as a result of its Roman origin. It is conspicuous among Italian cities for its broad, straight streets and spacious squares.

The plan of the old town is known to be substantially that of the colony founded by the Emperor Augustus, which formed a rectangle of about 2,210 feet in length and 1,370 feet in width.

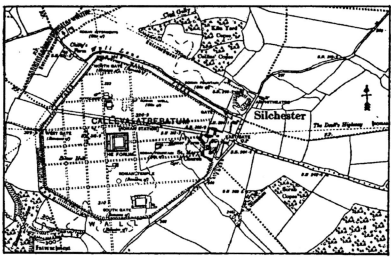

Illus. 29 —Plan showing the remains of the Roman town of Silchester. Reproduced from the Ordnance Survey Map, with the sanction of the Controller of H.M. Stationery Office.

Some diagonal streets have been introduced for convenience. The plan is peculiarly interesting as showing more variety than is usually found in a town so entirely laid out on four-square lines with straight streets.

If we compare with these towns, characterised in the main by formal systems of lay-out, one or two typical medieval towns, such as *Illus.* 150. Rothenburg or the little town of Buttstedt, for example, the contrast is most striking. Looking at the plan of Rothenburg, it is easy to *Fold Maps.* *III.* recognise the line of the inner thirteenth-century town, and to see how the direction of its fortification influenced the planning of the

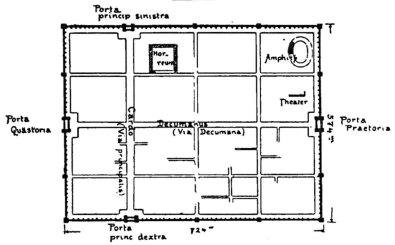

Illus. 30.—*Plan of the ancient Roman town of Aosta.*
Reproduced by kind permission of Dr. Stübben.

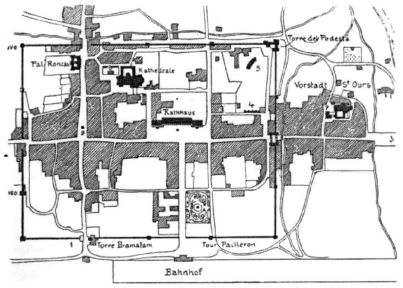

Illus. 31.—*Aosta, showing the town plan developed from the Roman lay-out.*
Reproduced by kind permission of Dr. Stübben.

streets, both in the inner portion and also in the extended area of the town which was developed and filled in to the present line of fortifications probably in the fourteenth century. This affords a good example of a plan developed apparently in the main by natural growth, but at the same time characterised by very distinct framework lines and a marked sense of scale or proportion in the main *places* and streets, so that although there is nothing of regularity in any of it, a very definite sense of design is produced, the central portions and the main streets being well emphasised and the minor portions subordinated and falling into place.

It is interesting to notice also how the irregularly shaped *places* are still so planned that in the main the views from all the streets opening into them are closed with picturesque groups of buildings, and how, also, the *places* to some extent adapt themselves in shape and size to the main buildings overlooking them ; so that the Rathaus has the wide space facing its side, while the Church of St. Jacob has the comparatively deep *place* facing its end, and a wide, shallow *place* facing its side. Both the church and the Rathaus, though detached from other buildings, are so placed that it is not possible from any point to get a view of the *Illus.* 32, 33, buildings entirely detached from their surroundings. The photo-
34, 35. graphs given testify to the picturesqueness and beauty which have resulted from this gradual development of the town on irregular lines. Camillo Sitte deduces from the fact that in most such medieval towns the irregularities appear to have so much system and art in them that there must have been much more of conscious planning and designing in the laying out of these towns than we have been accustomed to think. This may well be the case, and that the general lines in their irregularity and want of symmetry suggest natural growth may at least to some extent be due to the fact that probably the setting out of the buildings was done largely on the ground by the eye, and not transferred from a paper plan by means of an accurate survey with careful alignment ; but whether the designing was conscious, as Sitte and his school think, or the unconscious result of the influence of the guiding tradition in which the whole building profession was steeped, is very difficult to determine.

*Illus.*150-159. A much simpler example is to be seen in the town of Buttstedt, where the same marvellously happy result has sprung from natural growth or from very cunning design. The tendency for a road to grow up following the lines of walls or fortifications is fairly evident in such plans as that of Rothenburg, and we can often recognise

Illus. 32.—*Rothenburg, Standpoint I. on Plan, looking towards the Markusthurm on the inner ring of the early smaller town.*

Illus. 33.—*Rothenburg, Standpoint II. on Plan. Spital Gasse, looking towards the town and the Siebersthurm.*

Illus. 35.—Rothenburg, Standpoint IV. on Plan. Weisserthurm, from the Würzberger Gasse.

Illus. 34.—Rothenburg, Standpoint III. on Plan. Spital Gasse, looking towards the Spitalthor.

Illus. 36.—*Montpazier. Covered way round the market-place.*
Reproduced from Parker's " Domestic Architecture of the Middle Ages" (p. 154).

Illus. 36a.—*Karlsruhe. View of the Schloss Platz and Schloss. Fold Map IV.*

in roads ringing a town such an origin, although the walls or
fortifications may long since have been obliterated.   Reference has
already been made to Conway as an instance in our own country of *Illus.* 5.
a completely walled town, the lines of whose generally straight roads
have been influenced by fortifications.   Here, however, we do not
find within the walls any roads following their line, though there
are such roads on two sides without.

Although it appears that in medieval times towns mainly grew or
were developed on irregular lines, there are not wanting examples
of that period which were definitely laid out on regular lines.   Some
of these we know to have been planned by English engineers or

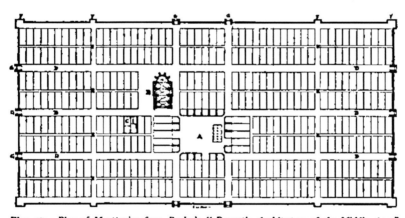

Illus. 37.—*Plan of Montpazier from Parker's " Domestic Architecture of the Middle Ages."*
    A. *Market-place.*   D. *The principal streets.*
    B. *Church.*   E. *The lanes.*
    C. *A double house of the original plan.*   F. *The towers.*
                      G. *The gates.*

architects, particularly those in the south-west of France which
were laid out during the time of the English conquest in the
fourteenth century.

A diagrammatic plan of Montpazier is given showing the general *Illus.* 36.
lay-out, together with a sketch taken from Parker's " Domestic *Illus.* 37.
Architecture of the Middle Ages."   It will be seen that the
general scheme is entirely regular.   Two large *places* are formed in
one of which the cathedral is placed, and the other is the market-
place or central square of the town.   The sketch shows the covered
way round the market-place which formed such a beautiful feature
in this and other similar towns, causing a break in the long straight

streets and affording an arched frame to the vista of these streets, at the ends of which appear the gatehouses to the main roads.

38.
39.
Aigues Mortes is another example of a walled town in southern France, with the streets laid out on fairly regular lines, while Ragusa forms an interesting Dalmatian example in which occurs a fine series of *places* with a regular network of streets. It will be noticed that in many cases the line of these streets is slightly broken at the junctions, the continuation on the opposite side of the road not

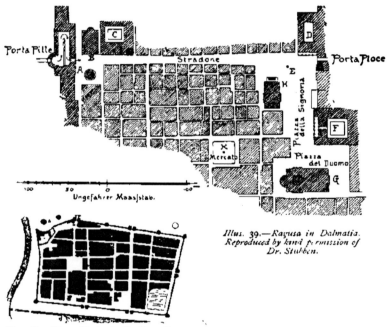

Illus. 39.—Ragusa in Dalmatia.
Reproduced by kind permission of
Dr. Stübben.

Illus. 38.—Aigues-Mortes in Southern France.
Reproduced by kind permission of Dr. Stübben

being exactly opposite to the previous line of the road. In this way many of the street vistas would be closed by buildings.

40.
At Winchelsea we have in our own country an example of a town planned as a whole at the same period and on very similar lines. The new town of Winchelsea was laid out in the year 1277, after the destruction of the old one by the encroachment of the sea. It is interesting here to notice that although the site and the line of the wall would suggest the usual irregular development, the town is

laid out on square lines, one of the central spaces or plots between four roads being reserved as a site for the church. Leyland in his "Itinerary," after describing the destruction of the old town, proceeds :—

"Whereupon A.D. 1277, the King sent thither John Kirkeby Bishop of Ely and Treasorer of England, and vewid a plot to

Illus. 40.—Winchelsea.
Reproduced from the Ordnance Survey Map, with the sanction of the Controller of
of H.M. Stationery Office.

make the new Toune of Winchelsey on, the which was at that time a ground wher conies partily did resorte. Sir John Tregose a Knight was the chief owner of it, and one Maurice and Bataille Abbay. The King compoundid with them : and so was there vii score and tenne Acres limittid to the New Toune, whereof parts is in the King Mede withoute the Toune, and part in Hangging of the Hille.

" Then in the tyme of the yere aforesayde the King set to his Helpe in beginning and waulling New Winchelsey and the Inhabitantes of

Olde Winchelsey took by a little and a little and builded at the
New Toune. So that within the vi or vii yere afore expressid the
New Towne was metely well furnishid and dayly after for a few
yeres encreasid.

"In the Toune as withyn the walles be 2 Paroche Chirches and there
were 2 Colleges of Freres."

This regularly planned town, however, must be regarded as
exceptional ; the characteristic beauty and picturesqueness of the
Gothic town are due in no small degree to its irregular plan,

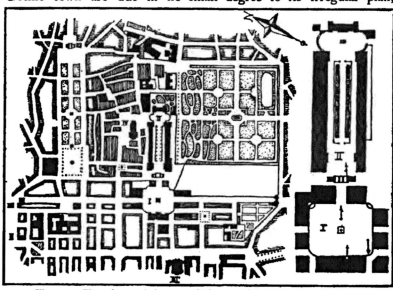

Illus. 41.—Plan of part of the town of Nancy with enlarged detail of places.
I. Place Stanislas.   III. Cathedral.
II. Place de la Carrière.   IV. Church of St. Epore.
Reproduced by kind permission of MM. Berger-Levrault et Cie.

combined with a style of architecture which displays great freedom
in the proportion and outline of its masses, and a richness and
picturesqueness in its details contrasting in a high degree with the
Greek and Roman architecture, so much more stiff and limited in its
lines, and consisting as regards its masses mainly of groups of cubes.
The Renaissance of classical learning and art, followed by the introduction of classical traditions and feeling into architecture in the
sixteenth and seventeenth centuries, influenced the planning of
towns. The regularity and symmetry of the buildings soon spread

Illus. 42 —Nancy. Place Stanislas, looking towards the Place de la Carrière.

Illus. 43.—*Nancy. Archway leading to the Place de la Carrière.*

Illus. 44.—*Nancy. View from the Place Stanislas looking towards the Cathedral.*

Illus. 45.—*Nancy.   Place de la Carrière.*

to the streets and *places* which were laid out at this period. Indeed, the Renaissance brought with it the power and courage to handle town planning on a large scale, and developed what one may call a grand manner in the schemes of laying out. The town of Nancy is *Illus.* 41. a good example, and its plan affords in itself a contrast between the old Gothic and the newer Renaissance types.

Around the old town, which is marked by irregular street lines and informal *places*, there has developed a very handsome scheme of town extension on Renaissance lines, including *places* of formal shape and some of them of great size. The Place Stanislaus in the *Illus.* 42. heart of this new town, with the Hôtel de Ville on the south side, the Bishop's Palace on the east, and the theatre on the west, is one of the finest of these. Connected with this by a triumphal archway *Illus.* 43. is the Place de la Carrière, with the Palais du Gouvernment at the *Illus.* 44. northern end. From this end of the *place* direct access is given to *Illus.* 45. the series of *places* round the church in the old town, while on the east there is an opening into a large formal park or garden. The bulbous forms favoured by a later school of landscape gardeners appear to have invaded a portion of this park, but the main formal lines on which it was laid out remain intact. In Paris and in very many other French towns will be found quarters laid out on comprehensive lines during this period.

Dr. Stübben, to whom all town planners are so greatly indebted, and to whom I gratefully acknowledge my own obligations for more information than I can specify and for permission to use illustrations from his great work "Der Städtebau," published in 1907, tells in that work how, after the troubles of the Thirty Years' War were over, the foundation of new towns and town districts in Germany became a favourite occupation of princes, who associated it with the building of their castles. These towns and districts are generally laid out on the straight, formal lines typical of the Renaissance work. The plans of Mannheim and Karlsruhe are *Illus.* 46. given as examples ; in each case the older parts of the town are shaded more darkly. Mannheim is exceedingly regular in its lines ; nevertheless variety occurs owing to the different widths of the streets and to a certain number of diagonals. The relation of the whole town to the castle, or Schloss, is evident. A wide ring-strasse, or avenue, surrounds the town on three sides, and we notice from the plan that the regular system has been departed from, outside *Illus.* 47. *Fold Map.* this ring, in the more modern parts of the town. Karlsruhe is *IV.* interesting from the largeness of the conception in which the castle *Illus.* 3, 3a, 36a,94a,103b, forms the great central feature ; the main lines of the roads radiate 114a, 198a.

4

out from this, and are cut by a long, straight road formerly known as the Lange Strasse, now the Kaiser Strasse. Here, again, the main system of framework has been departed from in various ways.

Illus. 48. Freudenstadt offers an interesting example of a different plan for

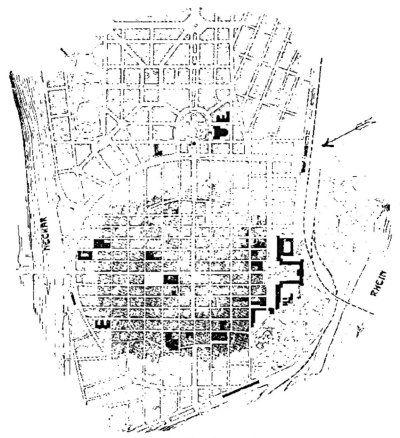

Illus. 46.—Plan of Mannheim.
Reproduced by kind permission of Dr. Stübben.

Illus. 49. laying out a town. Here the tendency is to enclose the corners, the main streets going out from the sides of the large square which forms the central feature of the town. This was originally intended for the site of a castle; to-day a portion of it is occupied by the

Illus. 47.—Plan of Karlsruhe.
Reproduced by kind permission of Dr. Stübben.

market-place, and the remainder by gardens and various buildings. It is interesting to note that even the church, which occupies one of the corners, has been planned to suit the site, in the shape of the letter L, the pulpit being in the corner and commanding both wings of the building.

The town of Magdeburg, though without a central square, is planned on somewhat similar lines as to the treatment of the corners. Herr Stübben suggests that this system offered advantages for defence, and that this may have been the reason for its adoption. It has the effect of producing a large number of closed street

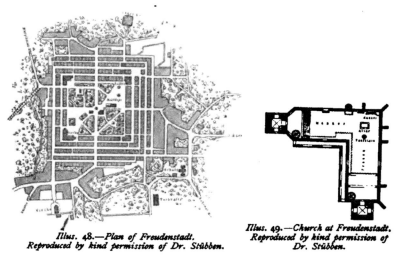

Illus. 48.—Plan of Freudenstadt.
Reproduced by kind permission of Dr. Stübben.

Illus. 49.—Church at Freudenstadt.
Reproduced by kind permission of
Dr. Stübben.

pictures which are generally wanting in plans based on straight lines.

Illus. 7 and 50-55. Edinburgh affords a fine example in our own country of this large manner of Renaissance town planning, dating from about 1768. The magnificent Princes Street from its commanding position overlooking the gorge, through which the railway now passes, and the gardens which have been laid out in it, is in itself one of the finest streets of the kind to be seen anywhere. Behind it, George Street and Queen Street, with numerous squares, *places*, gardens, and crescents, afford an example of the stateliness of the orderly laying out of towns on generous lines. We do not find in this suburb that exclusive provision for one class of people which is such a

Illus. 50.—Edinburgh.   View across Princes Street from Hanover Street to the Old Town.

Illus. 51.—Edinburgh.   Charlotte Square.
Photo kindly taken by Mr. F. C. Mears.

Illus. 53.—Edinburgh. Moray Place, looking S.E.
Photo kindly taken by Mr. F. C. Mears.

Illus. 55.—Edinburgh. Albyn Place, North Side.
Photo kindly taken by Mr. F. C. Mears.

Illus. 52.—Edinburgh. Moray Place, looking N.E.
Photo kindly taken by Mr. F. C. Mears.

Illus. 54.—Edinburgh. Ainslie Place, from Glenfinlas Street.
Photo kindly taken by Mr. F. C. Mears.

marked feature of many modern suburbs. On the cross roads small tenements were amply provided for.

To the same style, though a century earlier in date, belongs Sir Christopher Wren's plan for rebuilding the centre of London after *Illus.* 56. the great fire. I cannot do better than quote the description of this plan given by Mr. Elmes in his "Life of Sir Christopher Wren." "In order therefore to a proper reformation Dr. Wren pursuant to the Royal Command immediately after the fire took an exact survey of the whole area and confines of the burning, having traced with great trouble and hazard the great plain of ashes and ruins, and designed a plan or model of a new city in which the deformities and inconveniences of the old Town were remedied by enlarging the streets and lands, and carrying them as near parallel to one another as might be : avoiding if compatible with greater conveniences, all acute angles, by seating all the parochial churches conspicuous and insular, by forming the most public places into large piazzas the centres of eight ways ; by uniting the Halls of twelve chief Companies into one regular space annexed to the Guildhall ; by making a commodious Quay on the whole bank of the river from Blackfriars to the Tower. Moreover in contriving the general plan the following particulars were chiefly considered and proposed.

"The streets to be of three magnitudes ; the three principal leading straight through the city, and one or two cross streets to be at least 90 feet wide; others 60 feet and lanes about 30 feet, excluding all narrow dark alleys without thoroughfares and courts. The Exchange to stand free in the middle of a piazza and be as it were the nave or centre of the town, from whence the 60 feet streets as so many ways should proceed to all principal parts of the city ; the building to be contrived after the form of the Roman Forum with double porticoes. Many streets also to radiate upon the bridge. The streets of the first and second magnitude to be carried on as straight as possible and to centre in four or five piazzas.

"The Key or open Wharf on the banks of the Thames to be spacious and convenient, without any interruption and with some large docks for deep laden barges.

"The Canal to be cut up Bridewell 120 feet wide, with sashes [sluices or floodgates] at Holborn Bridge and at the mouth to cleanse it of all filth, and stores for coal on each side. The churches to be designed according to the best forms for capacity and hearing, adorned with useful porticoes and lofty ornamental

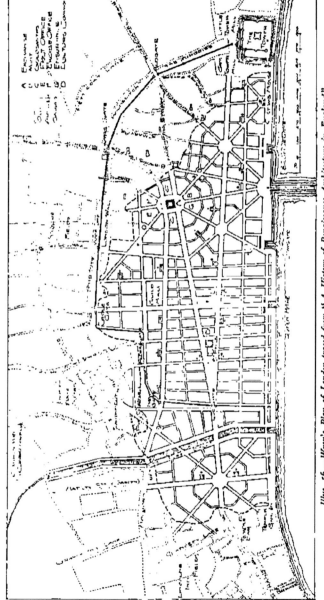

Illus. 56.—*Wren's Plan of London traced from "A History of Renaissance Architecture in England."*
By kind permission of Mr. Reginald Blomfield, A.R.A.

towers and steeples in the greater parishes. All church yards, gardens and unnecessary vacuities and all trades that use great fires or yield noisesome smells to be placed out of the town.

"The model or plan formed on these principles, delineated by Dr. Wren, was laid before the King and the Honourable House of Commons, and is thus explained :—

"From that part of Fleet Street which remained unburnt about St. Dunstan's Church, a straight street 90 feet wide crosses the valley, passes by the south side of Ludgate Prison and thence in a direct line ends gracefully in a piazza at Tower Hill, but before it descends into the valley where now the great sewer [Fleet Ditch] runs, about the once middle of Fleet Street, it opens into a round piazza the centre of eight ways, where at one station are these views, first straight forward into and through the city ; second, obliquely towards the right hand to the beginning of the key that runs from Bridewell Dock to the Tower, third obliquely on the left to Smithfield ; fourth, straight on the right to the Thames ; fifth straight on the left to Hutton Street and Clerkenwell ; sixth straight backwards towards Temple Bar ; seventh, obliquely on the right to the walks of the Temple ; eighth, obliquely on the left to Cursitor's Alley.

"Passing forward we cross the valley, once sullied with an offensive sewer, now to be beautified by a useful canal, passable by as many bridges as streets that cross it. Leaving Ludgate Prison on the left side of the street (instead of which gate was designed a triumphal arch to the founder of the new city, King Charles II.), this great street presently divides into another as large which carries the eye and passage to the south front of the Exchange (which we leave as yet for a second journey), and before these two streets, spreading at acute angles, can be clear of one another, they form a triangular piazza the basin of which is filled by the Cathedral Church of St. Paul. But leaving St. Paul's on the left, we proceed as our first way led us, toward the Tower, the way being all along adorned with parochial churches. We return again to Ludgate, and leaving St. Paul's on the right hand, pass the other great branch to the Royal Exchange, seated at the place where it was before, but free from buildings, in the middle of a piazza included between two great streets, the one from Ludgate leading to the south front and another from Holborn over the canal to Newgate, and thence straight to the North front of the Exchange.

"The practicability of the whole scheme without loss to any man or infringement of any property was at that time demonstrated and all material objections fully weighed and answered ; the only, and as it happened insurmountable difficulty remaining was the obstinate averseness of great part of the citizens to alter their old properties and to recede from building their houses on the old ground and foundations; as also the distrust in many and unwillingness to give up their properties, though for a time only, into the hands of public trustees or commissioners till they might be dispensed to them again with more advantage to themselves than was otherwise possible to be effected, for such a method was proposed that by an equal distribution of ground into buildings leaving out churchyards, gardens, &c. (which were to be removed out of town), there would have been sufficient room both for the augmentation of the streets, disposition of the churches, Halls and all public buildings and to have given every proprietor full satisfaction, and although few proprietors should happen to have been seated again directly upon the very same ground they had possessed before the fire, yet no man would have been thrust any considerable distance from it, but placed at least as conveniently and sometimes more so to their trades as before. By these means the opportunity in a great degree was lost of making the new city ·the most magnificent as well as commodious to health and trade of any upon earth, and the Surveyor being thus confined and cramped in his designs it required no small labour and skill to model the city in the manner it has since appeared."

Wren's plan is interesting alike for the masterly grasp of the problems to be dealt with and for the variety in the arrangement and treatment. The streets are all straight, but are not all parallel, the main roads are made to radiate from certain fixed points, to connect conveniently with thoroughfares existing in the parts of London outside the area destroyed by the fire. The plan is, indeed, laid out in the grand manner, and depends for its effect on the largeness of its scale and the length of its vistas, while no attempt is made to reproduce the enclosed *places* and the limited street pictures so characteristic of the medieval towns. We find in Wren's plan no provision for open spaces, gardens, or parks, the necessity for which had not apparently been realised then as it is now.

57. Mr. F. Madan, of the Bodleian Library, Oxford, has in his possession an interesting sketch plan made by an Italian architect about the year 1730, showing a proposed rearrangement of the central part of the City of Oxford carried out on Renaissance lines.

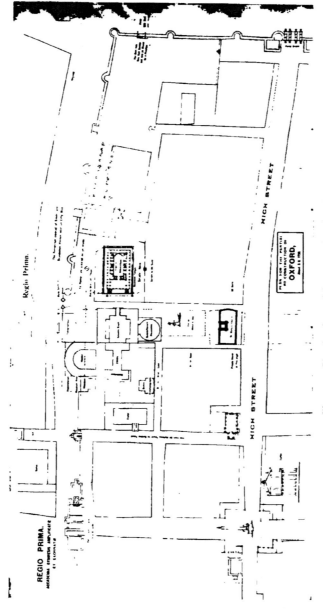

Illus. 57.—Plan for the partial reconstruction of Oxford.

Reproduced, by kind permission of Mr. F. Madan, Bodleian Library, from a photograph made by H. W. Taunt, Oxford.

Illus. 58.—Plan showing the lay-out of streets and squares in the neighbourhood of Regent's Park, London. Reproduced from the Ordnance Survey Maps, with the sanction of the Controller of H.M. Stationery Office.

By the kind permission of the owner and of Mr. Henry W. Taunt, who has photographed and prepared this plan for reproduction in his fine book "Oxford, Past and Present," I am able to give an illustration. Those who know Oxford as it is cannot but be interested in the proposals made for reconstructing portions of the city on the more symmetrical and formal lines characteristic of Renaissance work. The proposed bringing forward of the Ashmolean Museum, to balance the old Clarendon Press on the other side of the Sheldonian Theatre, is an interesting feature, as also are the suggested rearrangements of the lines of Broad Street and the High and the treatment of Carfax.

58.   Many parts of London—such, for example, as the squares and districts around Regent's Park—were laid out by what we may call the Renaissance School of town planners, and similar squares and

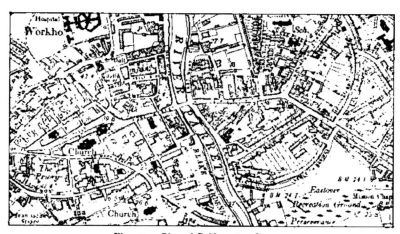

Illus. 59.—Plan of Bridgewater, Somerset.
Reproduced from the Ordnance Survey Map, with the sanction of the Controller of
H.M. Stationery Office.

59.   districts may be found in other towns. Such town planning as
60.   took place was chiefly on the land of individual owners of large estates, and was generally rigid and formal, until the influence of the landscape gardening school began to extend to the planning of streets. Since that period they have been laid out very largely with a view to produce curved lines, without much regard to the architectural effect of the buildings. Eastbourne, Bournemouth, and the
61.   newer parts of Buxton, and many other towns and suburbs which

Illus. 60.—*Castle Street, Bridgewater, laid out about* 1720. *View looking from river.*
See plan.

Illus. 60a.—*Karlsruhe. View of houses facing the Schloss Platz. See Fold Plan IV.*

Illus. 61.—*Bournemouth, showing plan influenced by the ideas of the landscape school.*
Reproduced from the Ordnance Survey Map, with the sanction of the Controller of H.M. Stationery Office.

have grown up on land belonging chiefly to one owner, have been developed on these lines. But when the whole of these examples are considered, they are still exceptional in character, and in the main we in this country were found entirely unprepared for the enormous growth of town population which the last century wit- *Illus. 1 and 2.* nessed, and towns have been allowed to grow in a haphazard manner, each individual owner developing his own land on the lines which suited his own interest or fancy. Too often the only consideration has been to find a plan which would give the maximum number of building sites at the minimum cost. In the main it is true to say that the newer portions of our English towns represent a hopeless jumble of unrelated groups of streets.

Meantime the reconstruction of Paris, which took place between 1852 and 1870, gave a new impetus to town planning on the Continent. With this reconstruction is always associated the name of Georges Eugène Haussmann, who was born in 1809, and who became Pre-fect of the Department of the Seine. But the actual work, as is clearly set forth in Haussmann's autobiography, was carried out by M. Deschamps. In 1853, under Haussmann's influence, M. Des-champs was appointed to take charge of the plan of Paris, under the pompous but inexact title of " Conservateur du Plan de Paris," and to him is due the great and masterly town planning work which made Paris what we know it to-day. His work is characterised by straight lines, formal arrangements, and geometrical patterns. Many roads are made to converge at important points, and usually these points are chosen so that some monument or public building stands in full view down each of these roads. The *place*, as understood by Deschamps, was largely a space to facilitate the circulation of traffic at points where many roads meet, and seldom was anything of the nature of an enclosed *place* formed by him. If we examine a plan of Paris of the seventeenth century, we find that it is characterised by certain main, direct thoroughfares, direct but not straight, with a number of informally arranged minor roads, much like other Gothic towns. The plan of Paris as left by Baron Haussmann is a mass of geometrical pattern-work, consisting almost exclusively of straight streets very cunningly disposed to show up all the public buildings from the maximum number of points of view, and so make the greatest possible use of these in glorifying the city. No doubt the strategic convenience for the control of revolutionary mobs may have had something to do with the choice of the straight street style of planning, but a high appreciation of the value of long vistas and of the use to be made of public buildings and monuments

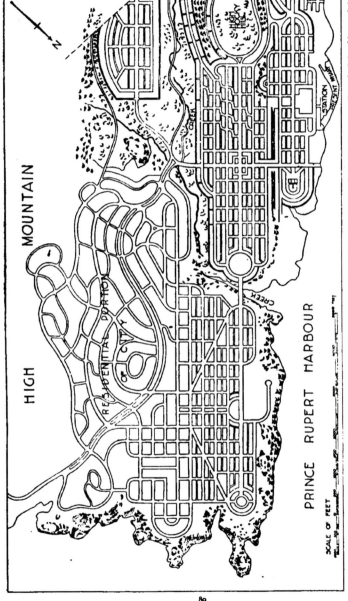

HIGH   MOUNTAIN

PRINCE RUPERT HARBOUR

SCALE OF FEET

Illus. 62.—Plan of the proposed City of Prince Rupert at the western terminus of the Grand Trunk Pacific Railway, British Columbia, as laid out by Messrs. Hall and Brett of Boston, U.S.A. The town is laid out on one or two tolerably level plateaus separated by deep creeks or valleys, and interspersed with high rocky portions which are being reserved as park lands, while a residential portion of the city is arranged on the slopes of a high mountain.
By courtesy of the Surveyor-General to the Government of the Province of British Columbia.

in beautifying a town must have been at the bottom of the way in which the work was carried out.

In America the tradition of a formal lay-out, usually on a rigid gridiron or checker-board pattern, has hitherto been little disturbed by any other style. Towns once started on this pattern have continued to grow to an enormous extent, until vast areas are covered by this regular, monotonous latticework of streets laid out in parallel lines, cutting up the building areas into rectangular blocks of equal size. The inconvenience and monotony of this arrangement are, however, now compelling the Americans to consider new systems. Diagonal streets are being arranged, and in some cases cut through the existing blocks, so that it will not be necessary on so many occasions

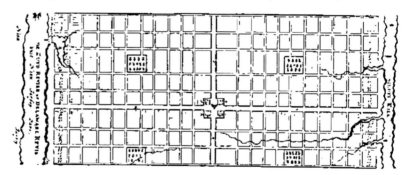

Illus. 63.—William Penn's Plan for the City of Philadelphia.
By courtesy of the City Parks Association, Philadelphia.

to travel two sides of a triangle in order to go from point to point. The Americans, like ourselves, have hitherto been without municipal town planning powers, but the work of town improvement has been taken in hand by Commissioners, well supported, and much good work is being done under the guidance of able men like Mr. Mulford Robinson and Mr. Day. Special attention is being devoted to the provision of parks to break up the monotony of the towns and provide breathing spaces, also to the arrangement of wide boulevards and strips of parkway to link up the parks and so provide walks and drives about the town, passing through belts of park or garden.

Illus. 63. The town of Philadelphia may be taken as illustrating many others. A plan of the town as designed by William Penn is given, the central square of which, marked " A," became the site of the City Hall, while four other squares or parks are shown. This plan

Illus. 64.—*Plan of the main portion of Philadelphia, showing development from Penn's plan with the introduction of certain diagonals, and giving the position of Fairmount Park, Logan Square, and the City Hall, the latter marked " A" on this Plan as also on Penn's Plan.*

By courtesy of the City Parks Association, Philadelphia.

seems in the main to have been followed, and the city has to a large extent grown on the rectangular lines thus laid down, as will be seen by reference to the plan of the modern town, where the City Hall and the Logan and Franklin Squares will enable the portion included in Penn's design to be identified. The regularity of the plan has been in various parts broken by tracks which had been established before the growth of the town reached these points, but has tended to reassert itself after passing these roads. Numerous straight, diagonal roads and parkways are now being planned, and one of these, leading from the City Hall to the Fairmount Park, passing diagonally across Logan Square, is shown as at present marked on the city plan. A complete design for the treatment of this parkway and the Logan Square, prepared for the Fairmount Park Art Association by Horace Trumbauer, C. C. Zantziger, and Paul P. Cret, is also given. In this plan the French treatment of developing along vistas with terminal features has been taken as a model, and numerous subsidiary vistas around the Fairmount Parkway have been planned. An imaginary bird's-eye sketch of this parkway at the Fairmount end will explain the proposal. Another illustration shows a further scheme which is under consideration for the treatment of League Island Park and the surrounding district, and the introduction of radial symmetrical diagonals into the gridiron of the street plan. The modern German school of town planners point out with much truth that this arrangement of diagonals crossing a square trellis system of streets, leaves numerous acute-angled plots which do not lend themselves to the production either of very successful groups of buildings or very useful open spaces. Too often a regular system of streets, once started, is continued quite regardless of the contours of the ground, and not only entails vast expense in levelling, but destroys any interesting character that may spring from a more perfect adaptation of the town plan to the conditions of the site. It will be interesting to compare with the plan of Philadelphia that of Washington, where the design includes a considerable number of diagonals.

In spite of the lack of municipal town planning powers, the civic spirit would appear to be strong enough in many American cities to carry out very extensive and costly improvements, and the numerous careful and exhaustive reports on city developments which are constantly being issued by voluntary associations, architectural societies, &c., are proof that the Americans are seriously taking in hand the beautifying of their towns. Reference to some of these reports will be found in the Bibliography.

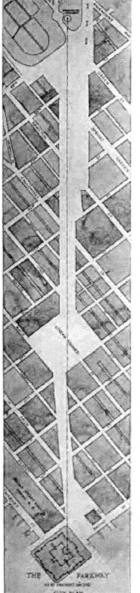

Illus. 65.— *Plan of proposed parkway forming a diagonal from the City Hall to Fairmount Park as at present shown on the City Plan. By courtesy of the City Parks Association, Philadelphia.*

Illus. 66.— *Plan of parkway as proposed by the Fairmount Park Art Association. By courtesy of the City Parks Association, Philadelphia.*

93

Illus. 67.—Bird's-eye view of the proposed lay-out of the Fairmount parkway, as shown on Plan 66.
By courtesy of the City Parks Association, Philadelphia.

The geometrical system adopted by Baron Haussmann in his reconstructions in Paris was practised also by the Germans previous

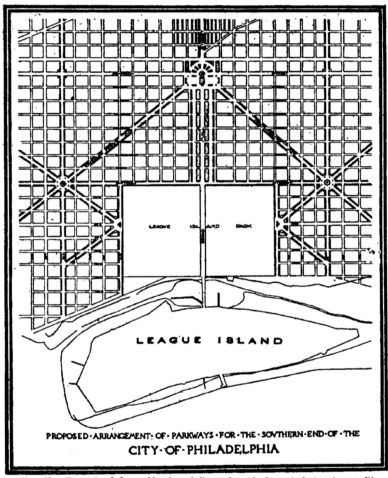

PROPOSED·ARRANGEMENT·OF·PARKWAYS·FOR·THE·SOUTHERN·END·OF·THE
CITY·OF·PHILADELPHIA

*Illus. 68.—Example of the combination of diagonals with the typical American trellis arrangement of streets.
By courtesy of the City Parks Association, Philadelphia.*

to 1889; but since the publication in that year of Camillo Sitte's book, " Der Städtebau," the French translation of which, under the title of " L'Art de bâtir les Villes," was published in 1902, there has been a marked change in the character of German town planning.

Camillo Sitte, by a careful study of plans of medieval towns, came to the conclusion that these were designed on lines which not only provided completely for the convenience of traffic, but were in accordance with the artistic principles upon which the beauty of towns must depend.

Impressed by the picturesque and beautiful results which sprang from devious lines and varying widths of streets, and from irregular

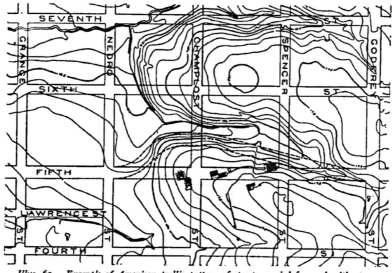

Illus. 69.—Example of American trellis pattern of streets carried forward without any regard to the contours.
By courtesy of the City Parks Association, Philadelphia.

places planned with roads entering them at odd angles, the Germans are now seeking to reproduce these, and to consciously design along the same irregular lines. It is, indeed, maintained by Sitte and others that much of the irregularity characteristic of the medieval town which we have been apt to consider the result of natural and unconsidered growth was, on the contrary, deliberately planned by the ancients in accordance with artistic principles then well understood. Be this as it may, there can be little doubt that the true artistic tradition in the Middle Ages was so steadily maintained and so widely prevalent as to constitute almost an instinct in the people,

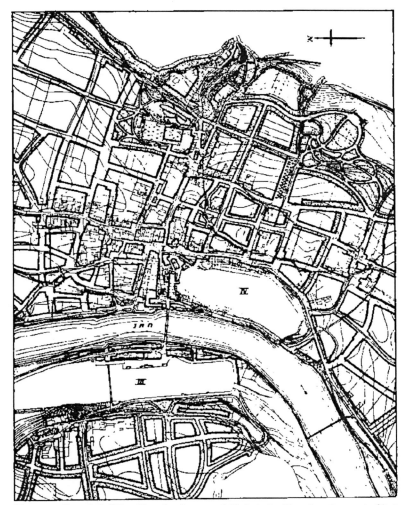

Illus. 70.—*General Building Plan for the town of Kufstein by Herr Otto Lasne, Architect.*
I. *Ober-Stadtplatz.* III. *Railway Area.*
II. *Unter-Stadtplatz.* IV. *Festa Geroldseck.*
By kind permission of the Editor of " Der Städtebau."

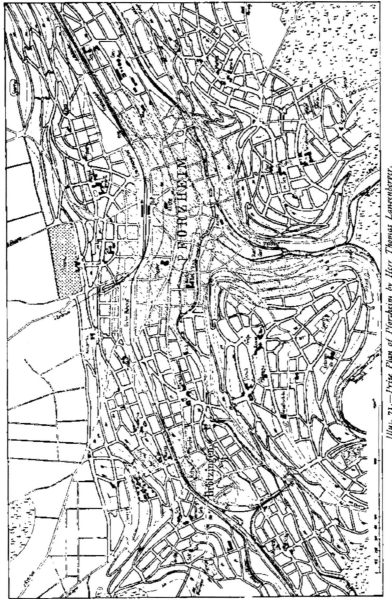

PFORZHEIM

Illus. 71.—Prize Plan of Pforzheim by Herr Thomas Langenberger.
By kind permission of the Editor of "Der Städtebau."

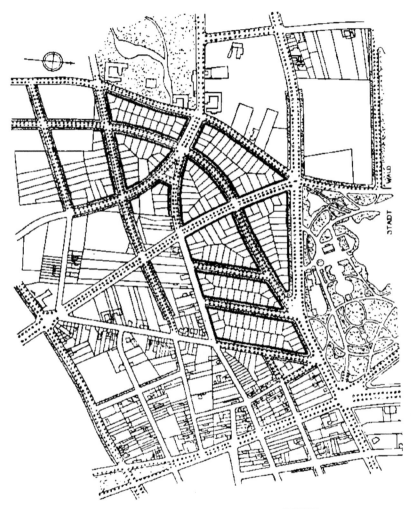

Illus. 72.—*A site plan of the villa colony of Stadt-Wald, a western suburb of Cologne, showing in some spaces the original property lines, and in others the land as rearranged by the municipality in suitable plots.*
By courtesy of the Municipal Authorities of Cologne.

o

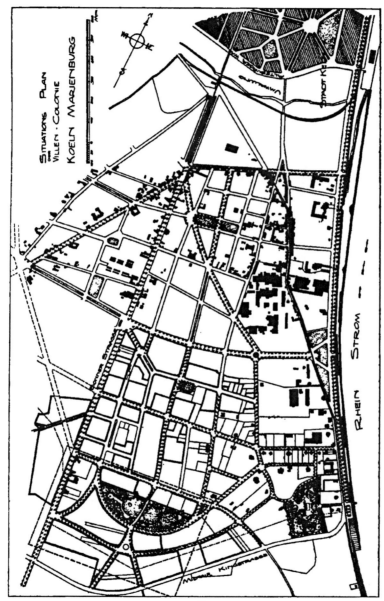

SITUATIONS PLAN
VILLEN · COLONIE
KOELN MARIENBURG

RHEIN STROM

*Illus. 73.—Part of the town plan of Cologne, showing the old line of fortifications, and the lay-out of one of the southern suburbs.
By courtesy of the Municipal Authorities of Cologne.*

102

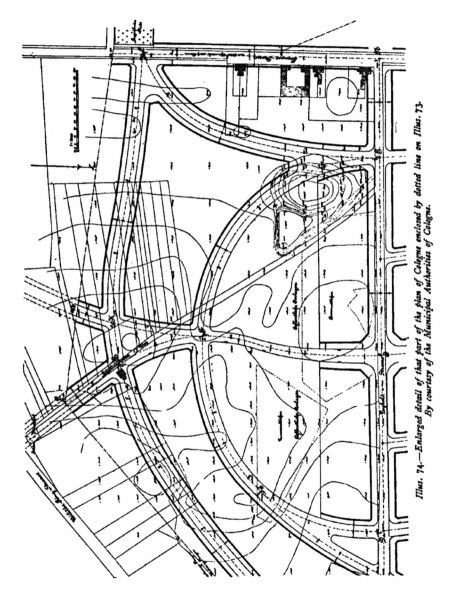

Illus. 74.—Enlarged detail of that part of the plan of Cologne enclosed by dotted line on Illus. 73.
By courtesy of the Municipal Authorities of Cologne.

which would lead them in dealing with irregularities arising from natural growth to do just the right thing in each case. The difference between this instinct which made the best of irregularities, and the conscious artistic designing of these irregularities, may seem a small one, but it is of importance when upon it is based the claim that the conscious designing of the modern town planner should be carried out on the same irregular lines.

Illus. 70.
Illus. 71.
Fold Map III.
If, for example, a modern German town plan such as that for Kufstein, or the prize plan for the town of Pforzheim, be compared with the plans of medieval towns such as Rothenburg or Bruges, it will at once be apparent how closely the modern school in that country are basing their work upon medieval models.

Illus. 72–74.
If, further, these same plans be compared with earlier work, such as may be seen in Cologne, Antwerp, Dusseldorf, and many other towns, it will be equally evident how entirely the character of their work has changed since those plans were made, so much so as to constitute a complete change of style, a change as complete as in the field of architecture would be a Gothic revival following upon a period of Renaissance work.

The examples illustrated will give some idea of town planning as practised in Germany, and it is particularly evident from them how the earlier geometrical and more regular planning has given place to much more carefully considered but altogether irregular systems.

Illus. 80, 81.
The contrast is seen in the two examples of a portion of Stuttgart as planned in 1860 to 1870, and as finally revised in 1902. Several intermediate plans were made for this rather difficult area, each showing a more marked development of irregularity and adaptation to the contours than the one preceding it. It is noticeable also that considerable individuality of style distinguishes the work of

Illus. 78, 79.
Illus. 75.
Illus. 76.
Illus. 70.
different men. If the plans for Zschertnitz, for example, are contrasted with the sweeping lines which mark the plan of Grünstadt, and this again is compared with Flensburg, this variety will be evident; while the plan of Kufstein, with its very carefully worked out building lines designed to produce picturesque street pictures and closed vistas, shows perhaps better than any other the extent to which the modern German School of town planners are trying to embody in their present work suggestions which they derive from their older towns. The three illustrations from

Illus. 72–74.
Cologne serve to show the thoroughness of their work. The plans are worked out with increasing detail, and very large scale drawings of the streets and junctions are prepared before the work is executed. Some plans are specially prepared to show the division of the areas

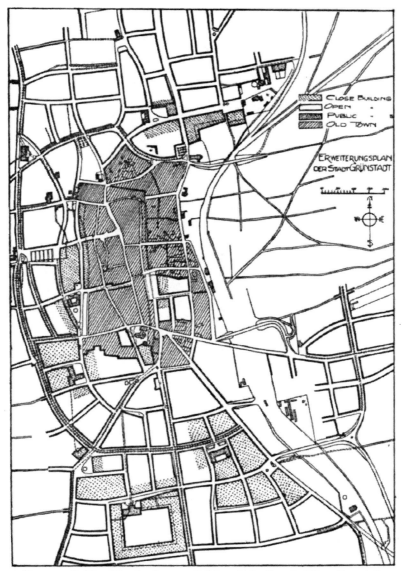

Illus. 75.—*Building Plan for the town of Grünstadt, by Herr A. Pützer, Darmstadt.
By kind permission of the Editor of " Der Städtebau."*

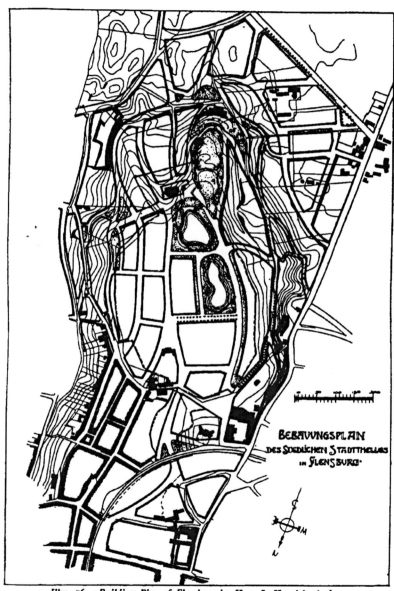

BEBAVVNGSPLAN
DES SODLICHEN STADTTHEILES
IN FLENSBVRG·

Illus. 76.—Building Plan of Flensburg by Herr J. Henrici, Aachen.
By kind permission of the Editor of " Der Städtebau."

Baulinienplan für den Vorort Pfersee bei Augsburg.

Architekt: Peter Andreas Hansen, München.

Illus. 77.
By kind permission of the Editor of " Der Städtebau."

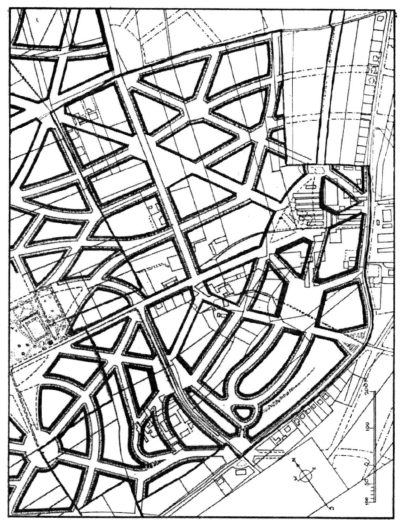

Illus. 78.—Municipal Building Plan for Zschertnitz, near Dresden.
By kind permission of the Editor of " Der Städtebau."

Illus. 79.—Building Plan for Zschertnitz, near Dresden, by Dr. Cornelius Gurlitt and Herr H. Frühling, Dresden. This is an alternative plan for the area shown on Illus. 78.

By kind permission of the Editor of " Der Städtebau."

Illus. 72.
Illus. 73.

into plots, others to indicate the intended arrangement of planting, the treatment of open spaces, or the distribution of different classes of buildings. The Cologne examples may perhaps be classed as representing the period of transition from the geometrical to the modern systems.

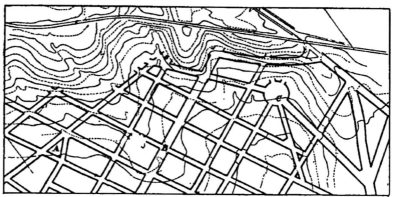

Illus. 80.—Building Plan for a portion of Stuttgart as planned between 1860 and 1870.

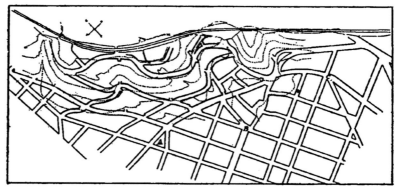

Illus. 81.—Building Plan for nearly the same portion of Stuttgart as planned by Prof. Theodor Fischer in the year 1902, showing greater adaptation to contours and less regular treatment. The letters A, B, C, indicate identical points on both plans. By kind permission of the Editor of " Der Städtebau."

Fold. Maps
I. and II.

The plans of Nuremberg are of special interest, showing one of the most beautiful German cities which has of recent years grown rapidly, and for which a town plan was completed as recently as 1907, covering a large area on all sides of the town. A portion of

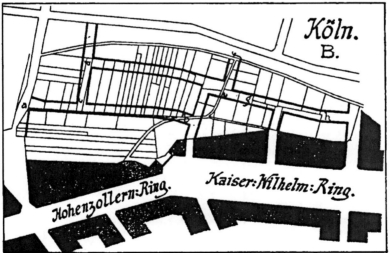

Illus. 82.—Town Plan of Cologne.
A.—*Showing geometrical planning disregarding property boundaries.*
B.—*Showing Camillo Sitte's suggested method of planning to avoid disturbing the property lines.*
By kind permission of the Editor of " Der Städtebau."

Fold Map II.

this plan is illustrated, and shows how the design has been adapted to the sporadic development which had already taken place on the area covered. However much we individually may like or dislike the particular style and the detail treatment adopted by the Germans, we cannot but feel the highest admiration for the skill and the thoroughness displayed in their town planning work ; no labour seems too much for them, no number of revisions too great to be made so that they may bring their plans up to date and in accordance with the best style that is known and approved by the skilled town planners of their country ; and, while there is much in their work that one would not wish to see copied in English towns, there can be no question as to the immense benefit to be derived from a careful study of that which has been accomplished in a field where they have been working earnestly for many years and where we are in comparison mere beginners.

While, however, the importance of most of the principles which Camillo Sitte deduced from his study of medieval towns may be as great as the modern German school thinks, it does seem to me that they are in danger of regarding these principles as the only ones of great importance ; nor do they appear to realise how far it is possible to comply with these principles in designs based upon more

Illus. 78, 79.

regular lines. Some of the irregularity in their work appears to be introduced for its own sake, and if not aimlessly, at least without adequate reason ; the result being that many of their more recent plans lack any sense of framework or largeness of design at all in scale with the area dealt with.

Fold Map III.

If we examine the plan of Rothenburg, we see how, especially in the original old town, the scale of the principal *places* and streets is sufficiently large for them to dominate the town, and to provide for it a frame and centre points which render the whole really simple and easily comprehensible to the stranger, but in any such plan as

Illus. 71.

that of Pforzheim one feels the same simplicity is lacking. In the case of towns arranged on land having such complicated contours as characterise the neighbourhood of Pforzheim, it is, of course, impossible to criticise the plan fairly without an intimate knowledge of the ground. The system of roads appears to be most admirably adapted to the contours ; nevertheless this kind of plan, which is characteristic of much modern German work, seems lacking in the simplicity of framework and order of design which are needful to enable the plan of the town to be readily grasped. It would be very easy for a stranger to get lost in such a town. The same remarks

Illus. 75.

apply to the town of Grunstadt, which covers a far smaller area.

The continual repetition of small, irregular *places* and road junctions suggests a degree of artificial imitation of accidentally produced features hardly likely to lead to successful results in the hands of modern builders; who have completely lost touch with the tradition which apparently proved so successful a guide to our forefathers.

One point of great interest in the description which we have quoted *Illus. 56.* of Sir Christopher Wren's plan of London may well be again mentioned here, namely, his proposal that the boundaries of all existing properties should be disregarded, and that the individual parcels of land should all be temporarily given into the hands of public trustees or commissioners so that they might be rearranged and the area divided, each person receiving back, not his own plot exactly, but as nearly as possible the equivalent of it in the shape of a plot of land arranged to suit the new roads and new groupings of buildings proposed. It is interesting to find thus early suggested by Wren a form of solution for this difficult problem in connection with town planning which has been adopted in Germany. The city of Frankfort possesses compulsory powers for thus rearranging boundaries of plots under what is known as the *lex Adickes*. Other cities have to depend on promoting voluntary arrangements for the exercise of indirect pressure to secure this rearrangement of plots. Where land is held in small lots, some such power of rearranging boundaries seems necessary for good planning to be possible ; but there is much discussion among town planners in Germany on this point. Camillo Sitte and those who follow him argue that the necessity chiefly arose owing to the particular geometrical type of planning which was in vogue previous to his day, and that a freer type of planning, in which greater consideration could be shown for the existing conditions of the site for existing roadways and property boundaries, would render needless very much of the rearrangement of properties which the geometrical school of town planning found so necessary. It is further argued that the consideration of these existing conditions would lead to a type of plan having in it something of the interest and variety which characterise the towns of the Middle Ages. To illustrate this point refer to Illustrations Nos. 82 *Illus. 82A.* (A and B), the first of which shows a portion of the ground adjacent to Kaiser Wilhelm Ring in Cologne as laid out by the geometrical town planners, in a scheme which it is obvious could not be carried out without an entire rearrangement of the plot boundaries which are shown. The scheme also cuts up the ground into a number of triangular pieces not very convenient for building sites, and produces a star-shaped junction at the point A, which would not be an

6

attractive feature. The second illustration, No. 82 B, shows the same
ground with roads laid out on lines suggested by Camillo Sitte in
such a way that almost the whole of the existing property lines
could be utilised without rearrangement. The general character of
the planning is much more like that characteristic of the medieval
town, and now being practised by the modern school of German
town planners, the geometrical planning shown in the first illustration which was common a few years ago having been largely super-
seded by the new school in Germany and in some other countries.

Before the architect can properly weigh the arguments on both sides
of this and, indeed, many other questions which town planning raises,
he must think out for himself the abstract question of formalism as
opposed to informalism, and must adopt for his own guidance some
theory by which he can weigh the relative importance of carrying
out some symmetrical design, and, on the other hand, of maintaining
existing characteristics of the site with which he is dealing. Some
preliminary consideration of this rather difficult subject will be found
in the next chapter.

III.—OF FORMAL AND INFORMAL BEAUTY

WE can hardly have examined the many different town plans referred to in the last chapter without realising that in spite of their great variety they fall into two clearly marked classes, which we may call the formal and the informal, and that there are to-day two schools of town designers,

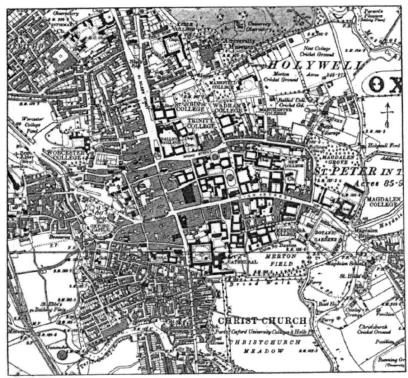

Illus. 83.—Plan of Oxford.
Reproduced from the Ordnance Survey Map, with the sanction of the Controller of H.M. Stationery Office.

the work of one being based on the conviction that the treatment should be formal and regular in character, while that of the other springs from an equally strong belief that informality is desirable. From the views given of both types of town we shall almost certainly agree that a high order of beauty has been attained by each method, for although our personal preference may lean strongly to one or the other type, there will be few who will not admit great beauty in many of the examples of its opposite. We are all sensible of the beauty of such towns as Oxford and Rothenburg, where hardly any lines are straight, any angles square, or any views symmetrical, but we are alike impressed by the formal parts of Paris, Nancy, or Copenhagen, with their straight streets, regular squares and sky-lines, and symmetrical pictures.

In this country we are, perhaps, more familiar with the two schools in the sphere of garden design; the landscape school representing

Fold Plan III.
Illus. 200–205.
Illus. 86.
Illus. 41–45.
Illus. 84 *and* 85.

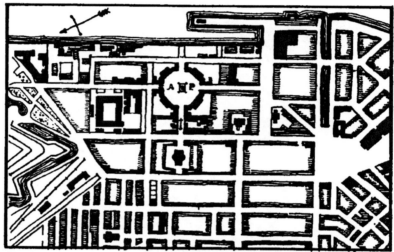

Illus. 84.—Plan of portion of Copenhagen, showing the formal lay-out round the Amalienberg Platz, marked A. P.

the devotees of informality, while the other school is known by the title "formal," which describes its work.

The former school, as its name implies, bases its work on the admitted beauties to be found in landscape scenes. Finding little or nothing of formality in wild nature, it rather rashly assumes that formality in garden work is unnatural, and the less intelligent section easily passes from such a doubtful premise to the even more doubtful conclusion that the avoidance of formality will produce the natural. There follows in the train of these ideas, particularly among those who have only attained to the little knowledge of the subject which we are told is dangerous, a vague belief that the beauty of wild nature arises from the fact that it is free, not subject

Illus. 85.—View of the Amalienberg Platz, Copenhagen, taken from the direction indicated by the arrow on Illus. 84.

to any constraint, and that the fault of formalism lies in its imposing order, and introducing fixed rules which must be obeyed. It is true that the beauty of wild nature is usually informal in the *Illus.* 92. sense in which we have used the term, but this does not mean that it is the result of chance, or of freedom from restraint. On the contrary, the forms which we find beautiful in wild nature are the result, so far as we know, of obedience the most perfect to laws the most complex, so much so that we may call the forms inevitable. That is to say, the forces of weather and gravity, the strengths of the materials and the chemical reactions resulting from their play *Illus.* 87. being what they are, the slopes of the hills and valleys, the bend *Illus.* 88. of the river, the curve of the bay, and the forms of the trees and the *Illus.* 89. shrubs could not have been otherwise than as we see them. *Illus.* 91.

How far this complete adaptation to the circumstances and nature of its being may be called an inevitable rightness in any object, and further, how far its beauty is due to this rightness of form, are matters for the philosophers to decide. It seems probable, however, that adaptation to place and function or, as we have called it, rightness of form, if not necessarily resulting in beauty, is at least the basis upon which it is most likely to flourish. Because the interplay of numerous and complex influences in wild nature results in beauty of a type we call informal, we are not therefore justified in assuming either that there is any beauty in mere informality, or that informality in the work carried out by men is in any sense natural ; nor, on the contrary, can we deduce from such a premise either that formality will not produce beauty or that it is in any sense unnatural for man to do his work on formal lines.

While, therefore, we may share with the landscape gardener his admiration for the beauty of wild nature, while we may even, with Ruskin, place that beauty on a level far higher than any attained by man's handiwork, it does not at all follow that in the making of a garden we should adopt his methods, which amount to an attempt to reproduce the effects which have resulted from the interplay of natural forces. Any attempt to copy nature must be futile, for the conditions of natural growth are so complex as to be quite beyond the power of the gardener to understand or reproduce. He can only hope at best to parody, and is much more likely to caricature. The slopes of his hillocks but distantly resemble those formed by the age-long action of wind and weather, and his artificially shaped ponds have little in common with the tarns scooped out by the mountain torrent ;

o

Illus. 93,93*a*; contrast *Illus.* 94. while meandering paths and bulbous-shaped beds or clumps of trees do not even distantly resemble natural objects.

There can be no doubt as to the beautiful effects often produced by the landscape gardener in clearing away obstructions, opening up views, framing them in a suitable setting, and in a hundred other ways. But when he introduces direct imitation of nature, by seeking to eradicate all traces of the gardener's hand, and particularly when he does this by the studied avoidance of any formality in the lines of his work, he is attempting to do what is so far beyond his power to do properly as to justify us in saying that it is improper to do it. Here and there, indeed, illusion may be produced, but even the illusion cannot long be maintained, and is at best a dangerous and a doubtful expedient. Hence it is, probably, that in spite of the many beautiful effects which a skilled landscape gardener does produce, to many the shapes of his beds and the lines of his footpaths are both unconvincing and irritating. Surely the result of highly revering natural beauty will be to convince us that we cannot create it, that we cannot even successfully imitate it. Rather is it the privilege of the gardener's art to design a simple frame and setting for it. We may terrace the hillside to form beds for nature's blooms, and dig trenches and tanks to hold her water, and by so doing secure in abundance the natural beauty of both ; but this beauty will in no way be helped by the disorderly lines of our terraces or the informal shapes of our tanks. The blooms will be as lovely on the straight terrace, and the light on the water as varied in the *Illus.* 90,94*a*, 95–96*a*. shapely tank as in the most informal setting.

The beauty which we find in many landscape gardens arises mainly from the successful accomplishment of definite purposes ; not only does it not depend on the informality of the forms and lines, but in many cases arises in spite of this. Many of these larger considerations in the treatment of grounds have been little understood by the formal school of gardeners, who have been too apt to design gardens as though their beauty were to depend upon the intricacy and variety of elaborate carpet patterns. While the formalist resents the informality of the landscape gardener's work and does not grasp the rightness of many of his aims and the pleasure produced by many of his effects, the landscape gardener, in his turn, ridicules the meaningless and often fussy pattern-making of the formal gardener, and loses sight of the fact that the formalist is at least designing within limits which he may under-stand, and whatever effects he may be aiming to produce he honestly

Illus. 86.—View showing informal development.

Illus. 87.   *Illus. 88.*
Photos kindly taken by Mr. J. B. Pettigrew.

Illus. 89.—*Photo kindly taken by Mr. J. B. Pettigrew.*

Illus. 90.—*Water Garden, Chateau de Chantilly.*

attempts to reach by means of definite design on orderly lines, which design he seeks to make beautiful in itself. The most beautiful gardens of all I believe to be those in which some of the aims of the landscape gardener have been carried out on a simple and orderly plan, where the formal frame or setting has been provided for the display of the informal beauties of trees and blossoms and still or running water. *Illus. 96,96a.*

The landscape school has taught us the importance of careful study of the site and its possibilities, a reverence for the existing natural beauties to be found upon it ; it has taught us the pleasure to be derived from a wide outlook, the homeliness to be produced by simple treatment, the effect of contrast between enclosed spaces and spaces commanding wide views ; while from the formalist we have learned how all these effects may be obtained through the medium of beautiful formal design.   The formalist needs to remember that his design is subordinate to the site, that the undulation of the ground and the presence of natural features of beauty worth preserving will frequently require some departure from the regularity of his treatment.   His formalism must be regarded as a method of carrying out definite aims, and not as an end in itself justifying either the destruction of existing beauty or the creation of formality for its own sake.

The subject is, of course, a wide and difficult one ; many of the words, such as " natural," "formal," &c., used in discussing it have meanings difficult to define.   Both schools of designers include men of such distinguished abilities and produce results of such marked beauty that we need not so much to decide between them as to seek for some third course, not exactly a *viâ media* but perhaps a *viâ latiora* which shall embrace what is valuable in the aims and methods of each ; and I have ventured to indicate tentatively the direction which I feel such wider way may take.   Whether our sympathies lean to the formal or informal school, it is at least safe to avoid attempted deceptions, and to carry out our aims in the most simple and straightforward manner, and above all, to do nothing without having some definite reason for doing it.   Nature and man will be indulgent alike to the formalist and the informalist so long as they are working to satisfy some requirement or to produce some definite effect ; but that which man will not readily forgive and nature cannot easily disguise is mere aimlessness.

Very much the same arguments apply to the two schools of town planning, though of course the analogy is in many ways incomplete. It is only to a certain extent that the growth of towns in past ages, under the influence of an artistic tradition followed largely unconsciously, can be compared to the growth of wild nature; yet there is a good deal in the analogy, and it is not altogether destroyed even if the builders of these towns were much more conscious designers than we have thought, for even in that case it is true of their growth as it is of the growth of wild nature that the principles which guided it are so complex and illusive as to be little understood by us to-day. It is true that the artist, by giving

97 *and* expression to a well-stored memory, may create the design of a picturesque old town street just as he may create the picture of a landscape.   But the building up of a town is not accomplished by the making of such a sketch design.   And even were the artist himself given absolute control of every detail of the work, he would find that modern conditions would upset many of his proportions and that the result when realised would fall far short of his mental picture.   But if we plan our towns on somewhat formal lines there are effects of simple, orderly dignity which we may with some probability count on, for the conditions which we shall need to impose on the builder in order to realise them will be few and of a character fairly easily understood.   How far it might be possible to cultivate a school consciously working for the reproduction of the beauties of an old Gothic town the present efforts of the Germans in this direction may do something to show, but there can be no doubt that much of the interest of the old irregular streets and towns lies in the sense of their free, spontaneous growth, their gradual extension under changing influences, much of which must be lacking in the case of a town built to order and according to a prearranged plan.   We may well doubt whether new towns so built will ever acquire the same sort of picturesqueness which the old spontaneous and uncontrolled growth brought about, and yet may feel that our right course is not to try and imitate the old.   For in considering town planning we must take into account the conditions of the present day, the lack of unanimity as to style among architects and of guiding tradition among builders.

Not only is there a strong analogy between the landscape school of gardening and the informal system of town planning, but in England at any rate, as we have seen, there is a direct historic connection; for undoubtedly the informal and meandering plans of the few towns and suburbs laid out during the last century in this country were the direct outcome of the spreading influence of the

61.   landscape gardener.   See as examples the plans of Bournemouth, Eastbourne, or Buxton.   The analogy between the formal schools

Illus. 91. *Illus.* 92.
Photos kindly taken by Mr. J. B. Pettigrew.

Illus. 93.—*Example of meandering path.* *Illus.* 93a.—*Example of bulbous-shaped beds.*

Illus. 94.—*Example of a straight path in an Earswick Cottage Garden.*
By courtesy of Mr. F. W. Sutcliffe, Whitby.

Illus. 94a.—Karlsruhe. View from the Schloss. See Fold Map IV.

Illus. 95 —*Formal water-tank, Marshcourt.*
Designed by Mr. Edwin L. Lutyens.

Illus. 96 and 96a.—Formal garden and tank, Sonning.
Designed by Mr. Edwin L. Lutyens.

133

in each case is fairly complete. If, then, the conclusions we have arrived at from our short examination of the question as it applies to gardening are at all correct, we may apply to town

Illus. 97.—An imaginary irregular town.

planning the principles suggested at any rate tentatively; for we must admit that in this art we are in England only beginners, and I feel that we cannot attempt yet to define accurately the right limits between formalism and informalism of treatment, and that for the moment what is needed to guide the town planner is not so much strong prejudice in favour of either formal or informal treatment, but rather a right appreciation of the meaning and value of each, and a just estimate in each case as it arises of the reasons in favour of one or the other. If the designer is to go to work in a right spirit, he must cherish in his heart a love for all natural beauty, and at the same time have always in his mind a clear appreciation of the beauty of the definite design which he seeks to develop. His regard for a type of beauty which it is beyond his power to create will cause him to approach his site with

Illus. 98.—An imaginary irregular town.

reverence, will fit him to receive from it all the suggestions which it has to offer. It will help him to realise the importance of incorporating his design with the site and of so arranging his scheme of laying out that it may serve as a means of harmonising his buildings with the surrounding country. It will save him from rashly destroying trees or other existing features which, with care, might be preserved and incorporated in his design. At the same time, his belief in the rightness and the importance of definite design will prevent him from sacrificing it unduly to quite minor features of the site, which, however charming they may be in their present state, may either lose their value in the new conditions to be imposed or may be of less importance than the completion of the scheme. The designer who approaches his work in this spirit may—no, I would say *must*—be left to decide for himself in each case how far the lines of his site must be followed and how far his design must prevail where the one or the other must give way.

Quite apart from theoretic considerations as to the beauty of the result, there are, of course, many practical ones which will help to determine the course to be followed in each case. For example, a certain degree of orderly design in the main lines of a town plan undoubtedly helps materially to the easy understanding and following of it, and in a town so planned a stranger would more readily find his way about, more easily grasp the main lines of direction.

But the practical advantages of such an orderly arrangement of the plan do not require exactitude of symmetry, which often could not be attained without considerable sacrifice of convenience or natural beauty. In such cases it would seem foolish to pay heavily for securing a degree of symmetry only appreciable on a paper plan or from the car of a balloon. The eye with difficulty measures distances and angles, and very great departures from regularity in certain directions may be made without being noticeable. Standing in an enclosed square, for example, a very considerable departure from the right figure would be necessary to be apprehended even if looked for, while a still greater departure would be needed to cause any serious detraction from the beauty of the effect, and in many cases a *place* might have five sides without the fact being readily discovered *See Haupt Markt at Nurnberg. Fold Map.* by the observer. On the other hand, there are irregularities very easily recognised ; a building which should be central with the end of a road will be readily noticed if not in the exact centre. It is dangerous to presume much on the want of power in the eye to detect irregularities ; it is easy for the planner to overlook some small feature which will often be enough to reveal them. The irregularity of the uneven square not noticed from within will be very evident if viewed from an adjacent hill, and may become very unpleasing if it disturbs an otherwise orderly arrangement of roof lines.

On sites much overlooked from high ground, roofs and roof lines become matters of the utmost importance. In fact, the beauty or otherwise of towns, seen from a distance, depends very often much *Illus. 105, 113, 284, 285.* more on the roofs than upon any other part of the buildings. Much observation and long practice alone will teach us what does and does not disturb offensively an otherwise regular design. We have a certain sense of order and derive gratification from that which satisfies this sense, a gratification slight in degree perhaps, and not to be compared in importance with that to be derived from many other sources ; still, it is sufficient for us to resent its being disturbed for no apparent purpose.

Apart from extremes of formalism and informalism, there is room for a wide divergence of individual preference among designers who accept in general the same guiding principles ; some will lean to one side and some to the other ; some arrive at one estimate of the relative importance of different circumstances, some at quite a different one. We shall be wise at present to avoid dogmatising on the theories, to keep very closely in touch with actual requirements, and to be content if we can give comely form and expression in the most simple and practical manner to the obvious needs of those who are to dwell in the towns or suburbs we plan. So only shall we keep on safe ground, or lay the firm foundation of experience and tradition which may perhaps form a basis for finer efforts of the artist's imagination in the future.

Of this I feel very much convinced, that town planning to be successful must be largely the outgrowth of the circumstances of the site and the requirements of the inhabitants, and going back by way of example, to the point raised at the end of the last chapter as to whether and to what extent the existing boundaries of properties should be regarded in the making of a new town plan, it would seem to me that, so long as the sense of property means what it does to the owners and occupiers of land, it would be neglecting one of the most important existing conditions if we were to disregard entirely these boundaries ; that to try and carry through some symmetrical plan at the expense of upsetting the whole of the properties and destroying all the traditions and sentiment attaching to these properties would be to give to our plan a degree of artificiality which in the result would probably vastly outweigh any advantage which it might gain from a more complete symmetry. On the other hand, it would be attaching undue importance to one only among the many conditions with which a town plan must comply if we were to refuse to the town planner any powers to rearrange properties or boundaries. It seems to me, in short, that a theoretic preference for formalism or for informalism, while it may find ample scope for expression within the limits of the conditions, in no sense justifies either the neglect to satisfy the requirements of the case or to respect the conditions of the site. Therefore, while the informalist might welcome the picturesque accidental groupings and the informal arrangement which would result from respecting in his

Illus. 82A *and* B *and Fold Map V.*

plan the existing property boundaries, he would probably seriously err should he allow his love for informality to lead him to follow these boundaries to the detriment of the public convenience or to the destruction of all comprehensive planning of his site. The formalist, on the other hand, would be open to the opposite temptation, of thinking that the maintenance of a formal character in the details of his plans would justify him in riding roughshod over the property boundaries and the sentiments of the individual owners or occupiers of the various plots of land comprised within his area.

IV.—OF THE CITY SURVEY.

THE very limited sketch given in Chapter II. of the types of town plans to be found in different countries and at different periods, showing as it does the immense variety of these types, must make us feel how rash it would be at present to dogmatise on the best form of plan, and how little we can regard as settled. This being so, it will be well for the designer to approach any actual work with due humility. He should remember that it is his function to find artistic expression for the requirements and tendencies of the town, not to impose upon it a preconceived idea of his own; he must first make himself thoroughly acquainted with that for which a form of expression is needed, and only after he has done this will he be in a position to determine that form. He will, no doubt, have very definite ideas and preferences, and will express the requirements in the terms of that form which most appeals to him; in this way his opportunity is splendid enough to satisfy any legitimate ambition; he has no need to go beyond that, no right to usurp the functions of a dictator decreeing what shall be expressed. Is it not enough for the singer that he should finely voice the song of the poet? Must he also dictate what the poet shall say?

The designer's first duty, then, must be to study his town, his site, the people, and their requirements. There is no need to fear that such a course will lead to commonplace designs, that it will check the flights of fancy, will subordinate the main effect to trivial convenience. The fancies of the man who can only work when his mind is free from the consideration of conditions are likely to be of little value, while the work of the one who, lacking high flights of genius, is yet able to grasp and provide for the needs of the case, will at least be safe and serviceable. In this work we cannot rightly say the practical considerations come before the artistic, or the artistic before the practical; they are interdependent, and must be worked out together. But there is this difference between them, that the practical considerations are often fixed, while the artistic expression may take varying form. Drainage will not run uphill to suit the prettiest plan; nor will people, to please the most imperious designer, go where they do not want to go or abstain from going where they must needs go, and from taking generally the shortest route to get there. Lines of drainage and of traffic may indeed be modified, but only within fairly narrow limits; and the planner who pits the form of his plan against the forces which define these limits will but wreck his scheme.

Before any plan for a new town or for a scheme of town development can with prudence be commenced a survey must be made of all existing conditions, and this survey cannot well be too wide or too complete.

Professor Geddes has published some most helpful and stimulating essays on this subject; and although it may not always be practicable to carry the survey to the extent suggested by him, there can be no doubt about its importance, if the development is to grow healthily from the past life and present needs of the town. The greater part of the work must necessarily be done by the sociologist, the historian, and the local antiquary; and as we are dealing with the work of the town planner, we can only here give a summary of the information which it is desirable that such a survey should provide for his use, and must refer the reader to Professor Geddes's writings for a more complete treatment of the subject. The nature of this survey will necessarily differ in the case of the founding of a new town, such as the Garden City at Letchworth, from that required for a town extension scheme, the sociological survey of the existing population and the historical survey of the past development of the town being absent; but even in the founding of a new town historical and sociological considerations are by no means wanting, though they would be of a more general character. If, then, we consider the survey as it relates to the development of an existing city, this will readily be adapted by the reader to the less frequent case of the laying out of a new village or town.

Seebohm Rowntree's survey of York, T. R. Marr's of Manchester, and Charles Booth's great survey of East London may be mentioned as examples of the sociological side of the survey; and, although such an exhaustive study could not always be made, it should be sufficiently thorough to enable maps to be prepared, based on the Ordnance Survey, coloured to indicate such matters as the degree of density of population in the different parts of the town and any insanitary areas or areas of special poverty; the distribution of residential, business, and manufacturing areas, with such subdivisions of each as may seem desirable; and the distribution of parks, public and other open spaces, and the extent of each. For examples of such maps refer to Rowntree's or Marr's books, above mentioned.

In most towns there exists already much material of the nature of an historical survey. In connection with this there should be collected a series of maps, showing as completely as possible the past development of the town; and in addition plans should be prepared showing all public buildings, and all buildings or places of historic value, general interest, or special beauty; while a collection

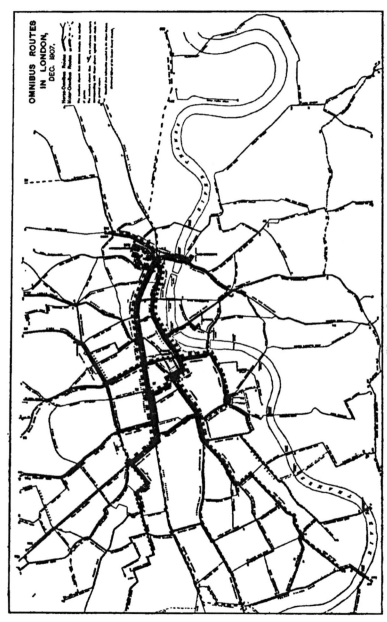

Illus. 99.—Diagram.

Reproduced from the Report of the London Traffic Branch of the Board of Trade, by permission of the Controller of H.M. Stationery Office. The thickness of the lines indicates the number of omnibus routes and therefore approximately of passengers.

of photographs of these taken from points of view exactly indicated on the plans would have great value.

There should also be available for the purpose of comparison and suggestion good plans of neighbouring towns and of towns in this

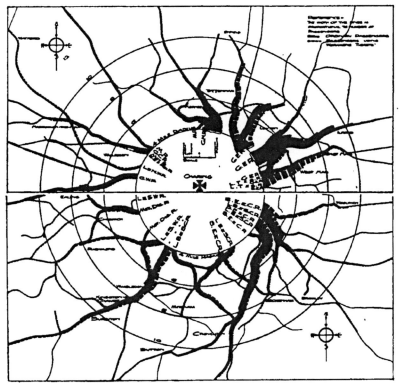

Illus. 100.—*Diagrammatic Plan of London, showing the volume of passenger traffic entering London from the suburbs by railway during the month of October, 1907. The black lines indicate traffic for ordinary passengers, the hatched lines that of passengers using workmen's tickets.*
Reproduced from the Report of the London Traffic Branch of the Board of Trade by permission of the Controller of H.M. Stationery Office.

country and abroad similarly situated to the one under consideration. The geological maps of the Ordnance Survey will be useful, and any other results of local geological investigations should be collected, together with statistics of wind and weather, from which diagrams showing the climatic conditions could be prepared.   Illus. 101.

99 *and* Where the town to be dealt with is at all a large one, there should also be a careful survey made of general traffic ; statistics should be prepared of its distribution and of the relative intensity from different districts of the daily inward and outward flow of population. All existing traffic facilities should be tabulated and their capacities estimated, whether consisting of railways, tramways, water-

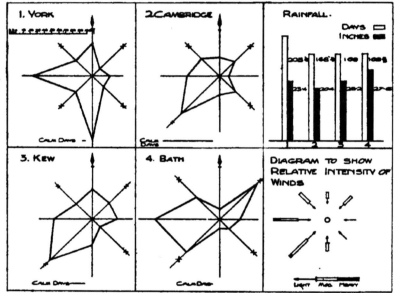

Illus. 101.—*Diagrams showing the relative duration, averaged for three years of different winds in days per annum at four different stations. The length of the line indicates the duration of the wind blowing from the 8 main points of the compass given in days per annum in accordance with the scale given. The number of calm days is indicated by the length of the line to the same scale. Diagrams are also given to show the number of days on which rain fell at the same stations, also the total annual fall in inches. A further diagram indicates how the relative intensity and duration of the different winds may be combined in a diagram.*
The diagrams are based on the annual summary tables issued by the Meteorological Office.

ways, roads, subways, or bridges, and both proposed and desirable extensions noted, so that proper provision could be made for them in the new plan.

Particulars of local industries and of those which show signs of increasing would be needed, with the nature of any special requirements, such as their dependence on water or railway frontage, and the area of land required per hundred employees.

All existing drainage systems and water supplies, with the height and depth to which they are available and their capacity for increased use, should be scheduled.

Any marked tendencies of town growth should be noted, with the indications afforded by them as to the most natural lines for future development.

It is very important also that plans should be prepared showing accurately the different ownerships of the land for which the development is to be arranged. Some reference has been made in Chapters II. and III. to the method adopted by many German towns of rearranging the boundaries of properties. Under the English Town Planning Bill, as it exists at present, powers are given to the local authorities to negotiate with, and institute negotiations between, different owners, also to purchase land where necessary. But it is very important that the town planner should have before him when making his preliminary scheme a map showing accurately the boundaries of the different ownerships, because these ownerships form one of the circumstances of the site, which should be treated with considerable respect, and where they can conveniently be left undisturbed it is obviously an advantage that this should be done. At the same time, particularly where ownerships are in small parcels, cases must frequently arise when the distortion of the plan required to leave all these boundaries undisturbed would be so serious that it would be obviously to the best interests of all to rearrange them. Local requirements, customs, or prejudices affecting the desirable size and shape of building plots for various purposes and so influencing the distance apart of new streets, should be stated, and the widths, character, and treatment of new streets suitable for the locality might be suggested.

Conditions as to building materials and traditional methods of building found in the locality, types of trees and shrubs prevalent or suitable for planting, and any other characteristics which go to make up the individuality, economic, historic, and artistic, of the town should be very carefully noted with a view to preserving and fostering such individuality.

Some estimate might well be made of future requirements in the way of schools and other public buildings, and of parks, playgrounds, and open spaces, so that suitable sites could be provided for them ; while general suggestions as to special spots of natural beauty ; as to the historic or legendary associations attaching to buildings or places ; as to special prospects, of the sea, river front or distant scene, or views of beautiful buildings or groups of buildings, which should be preserved or opened up, could not fail to be of great value.

This, then, shortly summarised, is the City Survey which should be prepared before any plan of new development is made. None of this information can be dispensed with if the best plan is to be obtained. The city which seeks to design its future developments must first know itself thoroughly, must understand its own needs and capacities. On the thoroughness of this understanding will depend both the economic success of all its plans, and the preservation of its individuality of character, by which alone the poetry of its existence can continue to cling to its enlarged self. The sacrifice of this individuality is to a city a vastly more momentous loss than we are to-day apt to realise. We most of us know how some towns appeal to us, how we come to love them, with what affection we remember our visits and with what a sense of joyful reunion we return to them after long absence. All this springs from the individuality of a town and is intimately bound up with the poetry of its existence. Who has heard of the same feelings roused by the modern suburb? We may live there and be happy there after a fashion, but we do not love the place, we can never begin to individualise or personify Kilburn.

This loss of individuality is due partly to the ease of modern long-distance carriage, which takes Welsh slates to Whitby and Ruabon tiles to Rowsley, and delivers them at such a price that the slates displace the red roofs which were one of the glories of the old fishing town, while the tiles drive out the stone slabs which gave character to the Derbyshire village. But what folly it is, surely, that we should allow our cheap transit to reduce all our towns to one dead level of characterless jumble instead of preserving in each its natural characteristic, which for ages has lent an interest and variety to the towns and villages of Britain, hardly to be found elsewhere. This instance is given as the most obvious one, but in many other ways local colour and character may be either destroyed or fostered, and with it the variety, the interest, and the poetry of life. While the need for the survey of economic conditions will be generally acknowledged, it is to be hoped that the equal importance of such a survey as will enable the town planner to preserve the individuality of the town will not be lost sight of.

To make this survey hardly falls within the province of the town planner. It should be made for him, and may very largely be the result of voluntary work on the part of the citizens, and the results should form the basis of his instructions. These results he must

Illus. 102.—*Messrs. Rowntree's Cocoa Works, York.*
Architect, Mr. Fred Rowntree, F.R.I.B.A.

Illus. 103.—*Messrs. W. H. Smith's Bookbinding Factory, Letchworth.*
Architect, Mr. F. W. Troup, F.R.I.B.A.

master, to the interpretation of them he must bring his experience and technical skill, and in the light of them he must make his own survey of the site ; for no general survey can absolve the town planner from the duty of thoroughly studying the site upon which he is to work. Nor will he, if he approaches the work in the right spirit, have any desire to shirk this part of his duties ; for he will regard all the requirements of the community and all the circumstances of the site as together constituting the kindly hand of necessity, guiding him into the right path. Any one to whom all these needs and conditions are so many irksome restraints preventing him from carrying out his own pet ideas had better leave this class of work alone.

The first thing the designer will do is to make sure he has all the needful plans ; these should include a survey of all the trees worth *Illus.* 235. preserving on the site, and a contour plan showing by the contour *Fold Map* lines every five feet of height. Except on sites so level as to be *VI.* quite exceptional, this contour survey will be found not only invaluable to the designer but also a source of economy. It may cost from a few shillings to a pound per acre, according to the size and character of the site, and it is hardly possible that it should not be the means of saving its cost many times over by enabling the roads and sewers to be more accurately adapted to the levels of the ground. If this plan has not formed part of the general survey, the designer's first duty should be to secure its production. It is an essential, alike for the small estate and the large town development scheme, and is such a source of economy that there can be no possible excuse for starting without it.

Having secured all the needful plans and preliminary information and suggestions, the designer will study the site for himself, comparing and considering it in connection with the information and suggestions, and judging for himself the relative importance of each point. He will also have to judge how far the various conditions and tendencies brought to his notice are likely to prove permanent and how far they are likely to undergo modification in the future ; for although it is the present needs for which immediate provision must be made, still in town planning, as in building, the work is of a permanent character and will remain through a long future, so that foresight must be combined with the realisation of past tradition.

As the designer walks over the ground to be planned, he will picture to himself what would be the natural growth of the town or district if left to spread over the area. He will try to realise the

o

direction which the main lines of traffic will inevitably take, which portions of the ground will be attractive for residences, and which will offer inducements for the development of shops, business premises, or industries. As he tramps along there will arise in his imagination a picture of the future community, with its needs and its aims, which will determine for him the most important points ; and the main lines of his plan should thus take shape in his mind before ever he comes to put them on paper.

Fold Map VII. An existing or probable railway station will at once give focus to the lines of traffic, and may be regarded as a centre from which easy access should be provided to all parts of the town or district, a provision the character of which will be affected by all existing highways or waterways. Existing bridges or points where the conditions are favourable for constructing bridges or subways over or under railways, rivers, or canals will suggest themselves as additional centre points in the system of roads, to which they would naturally converge. The grouping of the town or suburb upon the hills or slopes available will also be thought out most readily on the spot ; there, too, will most easily be selected suitable sites for factories, where they will have all the necessary facilities of rail and water carriage, and, if possible, where the prevailing wind will take the noise, dust, smell, and smoke away from the town. If such a site can be found screened somewhat from view from the residential districts and parks of the town, so much the better ; for, unfortunately, it is not yet generally thought necessary to consider the appearance which a factory presents, though there are to be *Illus.* 102, found many notable exceptions of factories and works designed to 103, *and* afford a comely exterior.
103*a*.

The selecting of suitable positions for central squares or *places* round which may be grouped in some dignified order such public buildings as may be required for municipal, devotional, educational, or recreational purposes will be done on the site, and will require much thought. For such purposes places must be chosen that will not only offer adequate architectural possibilities, but will also be suitable in character and position to ·form centre points in the plan, at which it may be reasonable to hope the common life of the city or district will find a focus.

The picture will grow in the designer's mind as the various needs are considered and met ; and all the while he is thinking out the main points of his problem he will be finding spots of natural beauty to be preserved, trees to be guarded from destruction, distant views from the town, and views into it of the fine buildings

*Illus. 103a.—The St. Edmundsbury Weaving Works, Letchworth.
Barry Parker and Raymond Unwin, Architects.*

*Illus. 103b.—Karlsruhe. Houses facing Schloss Platz, showing treatment of the corner of
one of the radiating streets. See Fold Map IV.*

he hopes some day to see rise on their allotted sites, to be kept open. There will be steep places to be avoided or overcome, the cost of roads always to be remembered, and a due relation to be maintained between this and the building areas opened up. But, while the problem seems to become more and more complicated, it is really solving itself; for every fresh need and every circumstance considered is a new formative agency, determining for the designer the lines of his plan ; and his chief aim at first must be to determine and to keep clearly before him the right proportional importance of each and to give it due expression ; and only when, on the ground, all these formative influences have been balanced, can the designer safely commence to draw out his design. There will come a stage when the main lines of the plan as determined on the site exist in a flexible condition in his mind, when he feels the need of something more definite. This is the time for his designing genius to seize upon the ductile mass of requirements, conditions, and necessities, and, anchoring itself to the few absolutely fixed points, brushing aside minor obstacles or considerations where necessary, modifying or bowing to the major ones as each case seems to require, to mould the whole into some orderly and beautiful design.

V.—OF BOUNDARIES AND APPROACHES.

MANY ancient towns derive exceptional beauty from their enclosure by ramparts or walls. To this enclosure is due in no small measure the careful use of every yard of building space within the wall which has led to much of their picturesque effect. To this is due also the absence of that irregular fringe of half-developed suburb and half-spoiled country which forms such a hideous and depressing girdle around modern growing towns. We have no occasion, and it would therefore be a pure affectation, to seek to fortify our towns with walls, nor is it desirable that we should cause undue congestion ; but it is most necessary in some way to define our town areas, and in the case of large towns to define and separate new areas and suburbs. It would seem desirable to limit in some way the size of towns, but how far this may be possible we have yet to learn. When walls were necessary as a means of defence and there was much risk in living outside, we know that towns outgrew even the possibilities of crowding which the standard of the Middle Ages allowed, and that settlements outside the walls were not infrequently made in times of peace, to be abandoned in times of war. If the pressure of this ever present danger proved insufficient to keep the town within its defined limits, we may well doubt whether it will prove possible for us to limit the population of a modern town to a given number, should the town become so prosperous and popular that natural tendency would cause that number to be greatly increased. The attempt would bear some resemblance to King Canute and the flowing tide. There can, however, be little doubt that it is possible to set a limit to the size to which a town shall extend continuously without some break, some intervening belt of park or agricultural land ; and this at least it is most desirable to secure. Thus we may derive useful lessons from the beautiful towns of other lands and other days, not seeking to copy their features, but finding the reasons which gave rise to them and gathering some suggestions which may in turn help to beautify our own cities. Though we shall not copy the fortified wall of the old city, we may take from it a most pregnant suggestion of the value of defining and limiting towns, suburbs, and new areas generally. This may be done in many ways. In numerous continental towns which have outgrown their fortifications or where the changing character of warfare has rendered wider rings of ramparts needful, the removal of inner rings has given an opportunity to replace them by wide boulevards, avenues, or belts of park land, which do to a large extent maintain the break and the

Illus. 104 *and* 105.

Illus. 106, 107 *and* 108.

Illus. 104.—Rothenburg, Standpoint V. on folded Plan III., showing the wall dividing the town from the surrounding country.

155

Illus. 105.—Rothenburg, Standpoint VI. on Fold Plan III., showing the country coming right up to the town.

Illus. 105a.—Rothenburg. Markt Platz from the end of the Hafen Gasse.

Illus. 106.—*Bird's-eye view from point A on Plan, Illus.* 107, *of the garden laid out on the former ramparts of Rheims by Mons. E. Redont.*
By courtesy of L'Association des Cités-Jardins de France.

159

VILLE DE REIMS

PROJET DE TRANSFORMATION DES PROMENADES

Illus. 107.—*Plan of the Gardens which have taken the place of the previous ramparts at Rheims.   Landscape Architect, Mons. E. Redont.
By courtesy of L'Association des Cités-Jardins de France.*

Illus. 109.—*Dorchester.   South walk.*

Illus. 108.—*Rheims.   View of formal part of Gardens marked B on
plan, Illus.* 107.
By courtesy of L'Association des Cités-Jardins de France.*

definition of the old wall. Even the wall itself may find some *Illus.* 110.
modern counterpart; where the ground is sloping and the district
adjoins a park or belt of open space, the retaining wall may be a
charming boundary, its monotony broken by garden houses and
gates instead of the old turrets and bastions. The *ha-ha* or sunk
fence, too, gives a good defining line. But the line of limitation
may take many forms. Where woods exist and cannot be entirely
preserved, a narrow belt of woodland, just enough to serve as a
screen, may be secured, and through it may be taken a path or drive.
An avenue of trees requires some years to mature, but a wide grass
glade with such an avenue would be in time a most successful *Illus.* 109
feature; and while the larger trees were growing it might be *and* 267.

Illus. 110.—*Hampstead Garden Suburb Boundary Wall.*
Being built by The Garden Suburb Development Company (Hampstead), Limited.

rendered delightful if planted with fruit-trees or other blossoming
trees or shrubs. In large towns or areas it would be desirable to
secure wide belts of park land, playing fields, or even agricultural
land. In any case, we should secure some orderly line up to which
the country and town may each extend and stop definitely, so
avoiding the irregular margin of rubbish-heaps and derelict building land which spoils the approach to almost all our towns to-day.
These belts might well define our parishes or our wards, and by so
doing might help to foster a feeling of local unity in the area. As
breathing spaces, they would be invaluable; as haunts for birds and
flowers, and as affording pleasant walks about the towns, free from
the noise and worry of modern street traffic, they would give
endless pleasure and would in a very true and right way bring into

the town some of the charms of the country. It is not an easy
matter to combine the charm of town and country ; the attempt
has often led rather to the destruction of the beauty of both. A
certain concentration and grouping of buildings is necessary to
produce the special beauties of the town, and this is inconsistent
with the scattering of buildings which results from each one being
isolated in its own patch of garden ; but it is not inconsistent with
the grouping of buildings in certain places and the provision of
large parks or gardens in other places. If we are to produce really
satisfactory town effects combined with the degree of open space

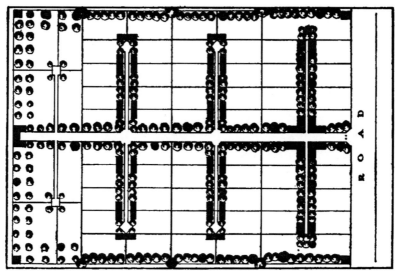

Illus. 111.—*Design for group of allotments, showing orderly arrangement of sheds, &c.*

now thought advisable, we must work on the principle of grouping
our buildings and combining our open spaces, having areas fairly
closely built upon, surrounded by others of open space, rather than
that of scattering and indefinitely mixing our buildings and our spaces.
It must be admitted that small holdings and allotment gardens
which are so apt to occupy the agricultural belt immediately adjacent
to a town are generally a somewhat depressing sight. This, however, I am convinced is an accidental feature of small culture as
often practised in this country. The ground is laid out in a haphazard way ; shanties composed of old orange boxes and ragged

Illus. **112.**—*Rothenburg, Standpoint VII. on Fold Plan III. Town Gateway—the Roderthor.*

Illus. **113.**—*Rothenburg. Standpoint VIII. Fold Plan III. Town Gateway—Robolzellerthor.*

Illus. 114.—Porte de Chinon at Richelieu which was laid out by the great Cardinal about 1635. See description in " The Mistress Art," by Mr. Reginald Blomfield, A.R.A.

Illus. 114a.—Karlsruhe, Ludwig Platz. See Illus. 198a.

Illus. 115.—Avenue leading into Dorchester.

169

felt, with greenhouses of all shapes and sizes, are dotted about without any order, and no thought whatever is devoted to the appearance of the area, either by those responsible for the whole or by the individual cultivators. These allotments and small holdings have but replaced the old cottage garden and the small peasant's homestead, both of which we know to be capable of being beautiful enough to satisfy the most fastidious. The tenants of allotments are in the main seeking to do with scant means and implements, without shelter or suitable buildings, what a richer man does in his walled or hedged garden, and one could not wish for anything more beautiful than some of these fruit and vegetable gardens, decorated as they often are with so many flowers and blossoming fruit-trees that the plainer beds of vegetables form, as it were, a fitting background. In the town of Nottingham, too, which has for many years been noted for its allotments, one sees how the area may be redeemed merely by well-grown hedges which screen some of the untidiness of the miscellaneous shanties. Given a moderate use only of glass-houses and the provision of suitable barns or buildings, arranged in an orderly manner and of some simple harmonious design, it is easy to imagine a group of allotments laid out so as to become as *Illus.* 111. charming as the glorified kitchen garden we find within the walled enclosure attached to many a mansion in England.

Having found suggestions in the ancient wall, we must not forget the gateway and the importance of marking in some way the entrances of our towns, our suburbs, and our districts. The character of treatment will be quite different from that of the *Illus.* 112, ancient gateway, which was designed too much for excluding 113, *and* 114. the unwelcome guest to be suitable to modern conditions; but in many ways it would be fitting to mark the points where main roads cross our boundaries and enter towns, or new districts within the towns. For example, some little forecourt of green surrounded by buildings and led up to by an avenue of trees would strike at once the necessary note; and many other simple devices will occur to *Illus.* 109, the designer for giving the required emphasis and dignity to these 115, 116, 245, points of entrance. In the modern towns, however, the roadways 272, 273, 274. as channels of entrance and departure are less important than the railways, and it is in the treatment of our railway stations that the suggestion of the entrance gate may be utilised. The great arch-way at King's Cross Station has about it such suggestion; and if an open space in front of it could have replaced the low mean buildings and the narrow entrance lane, where the cabs and omnibuses jostle one another and threaten destruction to the arriving and departing

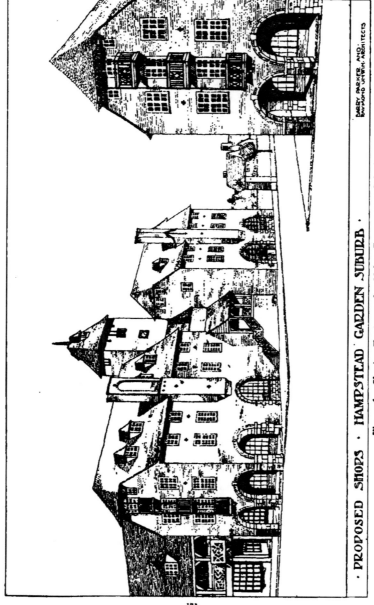

· PROPOSED SHOPS · HAMPSTEAD · GARDEN SUBURB ·

BARRY PARKER AND;
RAYMOND UNWIN. ARCHITECTS

Illus. 116.—Showing Treatment of a Modern Entrance to a Suburb.

172

passenger, some little dignity could have been given to this one of London's modern gateways. Too often, as at Paddington, the station is entirely obscured by the hotel building in front, and the actual entrance and exit is nothing but a mean gangway on each side of, or through, the hotel building ; but one can imagine other treatments of railway stations with ample space in front for traffic, and with the hotels flanking the entrance, leaving the opening of the station with some genuine suggestion of gateway as the central feature. Euston Station, indeed, was laid out somewhat on this *Illus.* 117. plan, although the size of the station has now outgrown the original

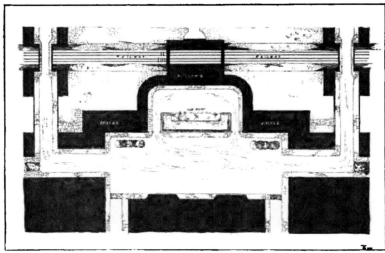

Illus. 117.—*Suggestion for a Station* Place.

design, and much of the entrance and departure has to be arranged at other than the main gateway.

Something of the gateway idea attaches also to bridges, for when they do not form the actual entrance into a town they at least form the entrance or exit point from one part of the town to another, and in the treatment of bridges and their approaches something of this idea should be expressed. In some cases it may be possible to roof in the footways of bridges in an exposed position to protect the passenger from storm or from the steam and smuts of the locomo- *Illus.* 118. tives when the bridge passes over a railway ; while the abutments of the bridge or the piers on which the ends of the girders rest in a girder bridge may well be emphasised by small and somewhat tower-shaped buildings, which would not only add much to the effect of the bridge, but could be made serviceable for many purposes—offices for professional men, lodges for public servants, small shops

Illus. 118.—Suggested Railway Bridge for Letchworth, Garden City.

and stores, &c., &c. The railway bridge over the Rhine at Mainz may be mentioned as an example of a girder bridge which acquires dignity from the bold and somewhat gate-like treatment of the piers on which the girders rest.

VI.—OF CENTRES AND ENCLOSED PLACES

IT is not easy for us to-day to realise the great part which the centre played in the life of an ancient town. So much more of that life was carried on in the open air, so much more of the intercourse and exchange of ideas was effected by speech in the market-place, in the days when printing and the newspaper were unknown, that it is very difficult for us who gather the news of all the world at our breakfast table, and transact the main part of our business by letter or by telephone, to realise, for instance, the importance of the agora in the life of a Greek city or of the forum in that of a Roman town. We find some parallel to this in the market-place of *Illus.* 119, the English country town, which in many places is still on market *120, and* 3a, days a very real centre of the communal life of the district. We *p. 7.* have seen in a former chapter how the city wall, though unsuitable *Illus.* 110. to modern times, may nevertheless offer useful suggestions to the designer of our towns to-day. Here again, although the change in the lives and habits of the people has rendered the re-creation of a Greek agora or a Roman forum hardly possible, nevertheless the examination of plans of Greek, Roman, and other ancient towns can hardly fail to impress upon us the great value of having a centre to our plan. The Greek city is marked alike by the unpretentious character of its private dwelling-houses and the splendour of its public buildings and meeting-places. The great central feature of the town was the agora. There is a good account of these agoræ in " The Architecture of Greece and Rome," already referred to. They seem to have been of two kinds : (1) a great meeting-place where the people assembled for public functions, and (2) other meeting-places, usually smaller, where they met for traffic and trade. These two open spaces were surrounded with peristyles or colonnades, often of two storeys in height, forming shady walks and meeting-places ; sometimes the centre was filled by an artificial lake, as at *Illus.* 121. Ephesus. Around this grand central space were grouped the council *Illus.* 122, chamber, or senate house ; the theatre, often partly cut in the hill- *18, and* 19. side ; the hall of music ; the gymnasium, where the adults practised physical exercises ; and the pallestra, or physical training school for boys ; and the race-course ; and in close proximity would usually be found the second agora, or market-place proper, where goods were bought and sold and business was transacted.

This group of *places* and buildings would usually be further adorned by temples dedicated to various gods and goddesses, though in some cities these do not seem to have been grouped immediately round the agora.

What a different picture of life from our own is brought to our mind by these public buildings ! We cannot but be astonished at the predominance of the arts, music and the drama, and physical culture, as evidenced by the gymnasia and race-courses, over what we are apt to regard as the more serious purposes of life.

From the excavated remains of ancient Greek cities it is evident what a splendid group of buildings formed their centre. No doubt the arrangement of these varied much in different places and in *Illus.* 12, 13, different periods. It was a marked characteristic of the Greeks to 14, *and* 15. seize upon any natural condition offered by their site to form a *Illus.* 16, 121, fitting centre, and the Acropolis at Athens is an example of the *and* 122. formation of a central group of buildings on a commanding hill, around which the town was grouped. In many medieval towns the great church or cathedral seems to have been the important centre. *Illus.* 123 Certainly, as at Amiens and Chartres, the magnificent pile towering *and* 124. up is fitted alike in position, scale, and dignity to form the central feature of the town. The plans of many other cities are also marked *Illus.* 25 by this large central feature. The forum of Pompeii, the arcaded *and* 26. market-place at Monpazier, and the splendid group of *places* and *Illus.* 36 *and* buildings forming the centre of Ragusa are instances in point ; while 37. in Paris the Louvre, with its surrounding *places* and buildings, forms *Illus.* 39. a central group of such magnificent scale as to dominate even the *Illus.* 163E immense extent of the city. Indeed, the very elements of design demand that we should give due importance to the suggestion of central features which we gather from most old cities. We need to establish a relation and proportion between the different parts of our design. We need to emphasise some parts and subordinate others, and the best way to do this in town design is to have definite centres. The effect of our public buildings is lost if they are scattered indiscriminately about the town ; they are imperfectly seen in ordinary streets, and no totality of effect is produced such as may *Illus.* 125. be obtained by grouping them in central *places*, or squares, or along river banks. If grouped in this way the buildings help one another, the violent contrast of size and scale between them and the surrounding buildings is to some extent avoided, and if the buildings are well arranged the total result obtained may be of a character to impress the imagination and of an extent to form a genuine central feature in the design of the town.

The main centre would naturally be occupied by Government or municipal buildings and others necessarily related to these. But many subsidiary centres are desirable also. An educational centre suggests itself, where schools might be grouped in conjunction with art schools, gymnasia, technical colleges, playing fields, and other

Illus. 119.—*Beverley Market-place.*

Illus. 120.—*Wells Market-place. See Illus.* 295.

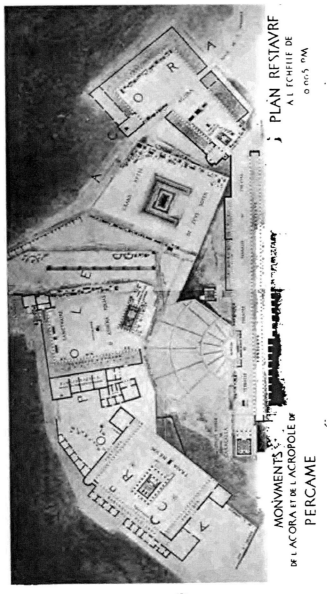

Illus. 121.—*Reproduced by kind permission of M. Maxime Collignon.*

Illus. 122.—*Conjectural re-creation of Pergame by M. Collignon.*
Reproduced by his kind permission.

181

Illus. 123.—*Chartres and its Cathedral.*

Illus. 124.—*Amiens and its Cathedral.*

183

Illus. 125.—Vienna, Kaernterring.

accessories, which by their proximity would add to the efficiency one of another.

But even in districts, suburbs, parishes, and wards it is desirable that there should be some centre. There should be some place where the minor public buildings of the district may be grouped and where a definite central effect on a minor scale may be produced. The importance of this central point can hardly be exaggerated. It will be wise, therefore, at a very early stage in our planning to select suitable sites for the main and subsidiary centres, and as these are to serve, not only as sites for the public buildings, but also to focus the common life of the community, both these points of view must influence our selection. To secure that they shall be genuine centres where people will be likely to congregate, they must either be themselves the focal points of the main traffic lines, or must lie very near to these points, the latter in many ways being preferable. We have seen that one focal point of traffic is likely to be at or near the railway station, and that in the modern town the railway station at which the majority of people will arrive and from which they will depart seems to demand much the same emphasis that was given to the ancient town gateways. . Considerations of fitness and convenience, then, alike suggest that in front of the station there should be an open space or *place* to give dignity to this main entrance to the town and to afford space for the bustling traffic which must congregate there, and in the planning of this *place* the pedestrian should receive consideration. He should not, the moment he emerges from the station, be in danger, whichever way he turns, of being run over by road traffic. We see stations planned so that *Illus.* 126, *G,* the front opens on to a busy street and other busy streets form the *H, and J.* flanks, so that whichever way the stranger turns on emerging, before he has time to realise the direction which he ought to take, or to get any grasp of the general lie of the town, he must rush across *Illus.* 117. some crowded thoroughfare. Far better that the station should be recessed in a *place* with no roads flanking it.

It is worth remembering when planning sites for stations, town halls, or other buildings where people are likely to need to wait for trains or appointments, that it would be a great boon if some open-air waiting-room were provided, some sheltered garden where the waiting time could be passed in quietness amid pleasant surroundings, instead of in the noise of the railway station or the bustle of the busy business centre.

The station *place* should not usually be the central square of the town, even where the railway station comes sufficiently near the

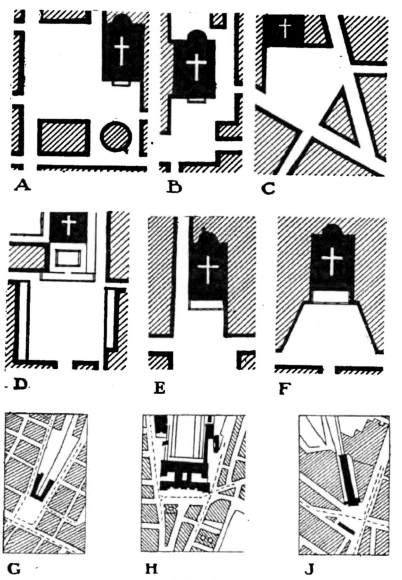

Illus. 126.

A. *Piazza del Duomo, Pistoja.*
B. *Domplatz, Regensburg.*
C. *S. Maria Novella, Florence.*
D. *S. Annunziata, Florence.*

E. *S. Pietro in Vincoli, Rome.*
F. *S. Bartolomeo all'Isola, Rome.*
G. *Brussels, Gare du Nord.*
H. *Munich, Central Station.*
J. *St. Petersburg, St. Nicholas Station.*

188

actual centre of the town area, though in this case probably the
central square should not be very far removed from the station, and
may be connected with it by broad and important thoroughfares or
avenues.   The noise of the railway and the necessary bustle of
traffic would render the station *place* itself unsuitable to be
the main square or assembly-ground of the town ; and quieter surroundings would also be better for the public buildings and Government offices.   In many cases the station will lie outside the town,
though it is probable that this will be less true of new towns than
of the old, the prejudice against railways which led to their being
kept outside so many towns having to a large extent died out ; and
the probable reduction in the future of both the noise and the smoke
arising from railways will tend still further to remove this prejudice.
Where, however, the station does lie outside the town, probably the
best arrangement will be to have again some main avenue leading
from the station direct to the central *place*.   It is certainly desirable
that some view of the central buildings of the town or district
should be obtainable by the stranger, and that the main framework
of the plan should be revealed to him as quickly as possible when he
leaves the station, wherever it may be placed, so that he may easily
grasp the general lie of the town, and be able to find his way about
in it.   The possibilities in this direction will, of course, depend very
much upon individual circumstances and on the size of the town or
district to be dealt with.   In a large town there may be several
existing stations, and, therefore, several such focal points to be considered ; often there will be a probability of new stations being
required, and if so, suitable positions should be provided for them.
It should be within the power of the town to secure that any future
railway falls in with such provision, and carries out its work in such
a way as to complete the arrangement intended.

In choosing, then, a suitable site for the main centre of our town or
district, in addition to its relation to the main entrance and traffic
lines we must consider that it is desirable that its buildings should
be well placed and as widely seen as possible.   This would suggest
the choice of some hill-top, and undoubtedly it is often desirable to
choose the summit of some rising ground ; but neither the height nor
the steepness of the access must be too great, as in either case the
line of traffic will tend to be too much diverted from the central
position.   A small rising ground in the centre of a valley is a position
well seen from the whole of the valley or basin.   Sometimes the most
prominent position will be found part way up one of the slopes of
the valley.   Where there exists a river front, harbour, or sea shore,

*Fold Map
VII.*

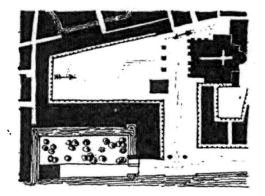

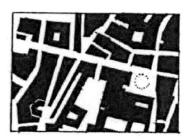

A

B

C

D

E

F

Illus. 127.

A. *Piazza S. Marco, Venice.*
B. *Piazza del Duomo, Verona.*
C. *Piazza Erbe, Verona.*

D. *Piazza Signoria, Florence.*
E. *Karolinen Platz, München.*
F. *Max Joseph Platz, München.*

Illus. 128.—*Astbury, Church and Village.*

Illus. 128a.—*Wallingford.*

the attractiveness of this would suggest the advisability of putting *Illus.* 127*a*,
the central *place* near or overlooking it.   163*e*.

But the idea of the centre should not be confined even to centres of
districts, parishes, or wards. Each area should have its special
central feature or point of interest round which its plan should be
grouped, and up to which it should lead. At the point where
several roads converge there should always be something of an open
space arranged, to give freedom for circulation of traffic, and architectural effect to the various road-junctions. These points may
have to be considered mainly with respect to the added convenience

Illus. 129.—*A small Country Market-place.*

of traffic, and only secondarily as offering special sites for buildings.
In other cases settlements or groups of buildings having, for one
reason or another, some form of common life will suggest supple-
mentary centres—such groups, for example, as those formed by the
various co-operative building societies and the co-partnership tenants'
societies, or the settlements erected for the convenience of the
employees of particular factories or workshops. Various markets
and exchanges also suggest central spaces in connection with them ;
and harbours, docks, or landing-stages, in places where they are
available, require open spaces which the charm of water will generally
make specially attractive. These *places* or central points may take

Illus. 126,
127, 162, 163.

Illus. 128.

Illus. 294,
295.

Illus. 129,
130, *and* 131.
many different forms according to the purpose to be served. We find in old towns a wealth of suggestion : successful instances may be seen of *places* of almost every conceivable shape, regular and irregular ; ·while the open greens of our English villages, the quad-rangles of colleges, and the closes of cathedral towns will offer many varied suggestions for the treatment of centres suitable to the different requirements, as will also the charming little *places* which afford shady standing ground for the country women's stalls in so many of the French towns and villages.

It must not be thought that any open space is a true *place*, or that because successful *places* are found of all kinds of irregular shapes that therefore any shape will do. This is very far from being the case.

Under the influence of Baron Haussmann and the engineer town planners, although the word *place* was retained to designate the spaces formed at the junctions of the many diagonal or radiating roads used by them, the true idea of a *place* was quite lost in Paris. It was not until Camillo Sitte drew attention to the artistic side of town planning in his book " Der Städtebau " that the true meaning and importance of the *place* was realised. If we examine German plans made before the spread of his influence, we shall find them

Illus. 72.
Illus. 80.
Illus. 82A.
carrying on mainly the Haussmann tradition, and shall usually look in vain for the true *place*.

Camillo Sitte devoted a large part of his volume to the examination of *places*, and to elucidating the principles of their design. He holds, as does generally the modern school of town planners in Germany, that the irregular *places* of the Middle Ages were definitely designed on sound, artistic lines to produce the definite effects aimed at, and were by no means the result of accidental growth. It is likely that this theory is being pushed farther than the evidence will support. There is, however, no doubt that in the Middle Ages there was such a strong and widely prevalent tradition of the right and wrong in building at any period, that the builders seem at least to have been generally capable of seizing upon accidental irregularities, and making something definitely fitting and beautiful out of them ; so that unconscious growth and conscious design seem to have been working towards much the same end, and probably it is not possible to distinguish between them, nor is it necessary for our purpose. It is enough if we can discover to what is due the pleasing effect produced.

The *place* is the more modern form of the Greek agora and the Roman forum. We have no English word exactly equivalent.

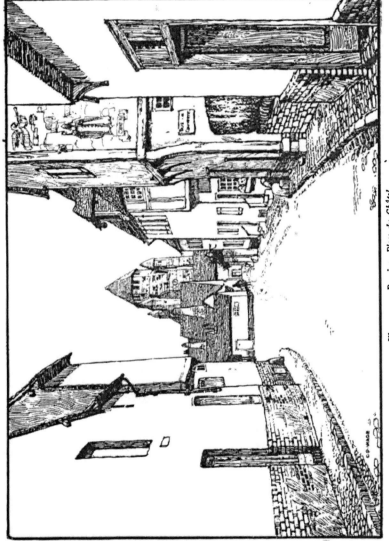

Illus. 130.—*Provins, Place du Châtel.*

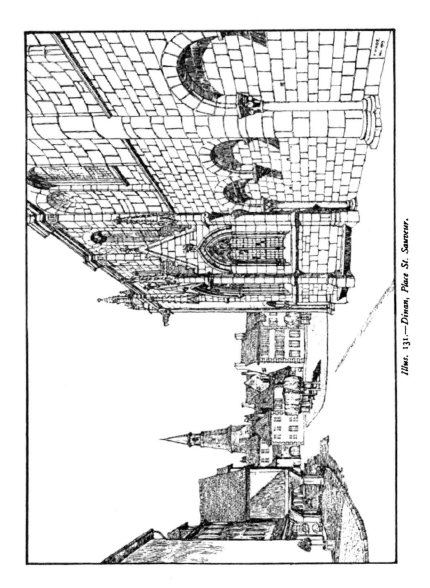

Illus. 131.—*Dinan, Place St. Sauveur.*

The English market-place was often a true *place*, but not always. The English word "square," besides limiting the shape to a regular form, denotes something often quite different. We must, therefore, be content with the simple French word *place ;* it has the advantage of being essentially the same word as the Italian *piazza* and the German *platz ;* and if at present it does not convey a sufficiently definite idea, perhaps it may be possible for us to pack more meaning into it. *Illus.* 119, 120, 135, 59.

A *place*, then, in the sense in which we wish to use the word, should be an enclosed space. The sense of enclosure is essential to the idea ; not the complete enclosure of a continuous ring of buildings, like a quadrangle, for example ; but a general sense of enclosure resulting from a fairly continuous frame of buildings, the breaks in which are small in relative extent and not too obvious. If we examine a series of ancient *places*, we shall see that, whether from accident or design, the entrances into them are usually so arranged *Illus.* 131. that they break the frame of buildings very little, if at all.

Plans of many such *places* are given, and if these are examined it will be seen in how very few cases can any one entering a *place* by one of the streets get any extended view out of it along another *Illus.* 140-street. If this has been entirely the result of design, great ingenuity 143, 127 A–D. has been displayed in some cases in contriving to mask the entrance of the streets from many points.

If we compare the photographs of some of these *places* with the plans, this will be more evident. A photograph of the Piazza *Illus.* 132. Erbe at Verona reveals no break in the line of surrounding build-ings, and yet if we examine the plan we shall find that no less than *Illus.* 127C. eight different streets enter this *place*. In the north-west corner is shown an instance of a not uncommon plan by which two roads enter a *place* at the corner, in such a way that when looking across the *place* no direct view down either street is open, but the buildings at the corner—in this case the tower—block the view and complete the frame.

In the Marien Platz at Munich also is shown an instance of several *Illus.* 133 roads entering near the end of the *place* without breaking the line *and* 172A. of the buildings. In this case the result is attained by diverting the course of the road immediately after its leaving the *place*. A similar example may be seen in the old market-place at Dresden, where the *Illus.* 134 church tower, filling the angle of two streets entering at the corner *and* 142. of the *place*, completes the ring of buildings.

Even in the market-place at Nuremberg the same result is attained, *Illus.* 136 although in plan the enclosure of the *place* appears at first sight very *and Fold Map I.*

Illus. 137
and 127E.
incomplete.   If we contrast with this the modern Karolinen Platz at Munich, we shall see how entirely this sense of enclosure is lost by the arrangement of large radiating streets, converging in such a way that from almost all points the frame of the buildings is completely broken, and the eye is led out of the *place* along the street vistas of the different roads.

Illus. 138
and 127F.
In the Max Josef Platz in Munich, in the position from which the photograph is taken we see again the frame of the buildings entirely broken by the long, straight road at the side of the Royal National Theatre.   It will be seen from the plan that the other angle of this *place* is entirely closed.   If this view is contrasted with the view of

Illus. 139.
the market at Bad Kissengen, in which the Town Hall building occupies a somewhat similar position, it will at once be noticed how the course of the street brings into view the other buildings along it, thus closing the vista.

This enclosure of a *place* is not only important because it gives a sense of completeness and repose to the *place* itself, but also because of the importance of providing a proper frame and background to the public buildings ; and if we examine the various *places*, plans of which are given, we shall find that in nearly all cases the public

Illus. 128.
buildings are not in the centre but on one side ; very often they are actually attached to their surrounding buildings or are separated

*Illus.*126 A-F,
127 A *and* B,
140–143, 146.
from them by such narrow openings that when viewed across the *place* the gap between them is not evident.   Camillo Sitte quotes the almost universal custom of the ancients to prove that buildings are not seen to the best advantage when seen in isolation.   Where it is desired that several sides of a building shall be visible from a distance, instead of placing it in the centre of a *place*, *places* may be arranged on its different faces with other buildings approaching or connected at the corners, in such a way that they will form a sort of frame for each view, and from no point will the building be completely detached and isolated in the pictures obtained of it.   A good

Illus. 140.
Illus. 141.
Illus. 143.
instance of this arrangement may be seen at Ravenna, where *places* exist on the north and west sides of the cathedral ; at Salzburg, where there are *places* on three sides of the cathedral ; and at Pisa, where there are three irregular-shaped *places* on three sides of San Stefano.   In these instances it will be seen that although sufficient space is afforded for a good view of the building to be obtained on several sides, yet in no case is it seen isolated in the middle of an open space or detached from its fitting framework.

It has become too much the custom to build our churches and other public buildings in isolated positions on comparatively large sites.

Illus. 132.—*Piazza Erbe, Verona. For Plan see Illus.* 127C.

Illus. 133.—*Marienplatz at Munich. See Illus.* 172a.

Illus. 134.—*Old Market-place at Dresden, showing how the church closes the opening at the corner of the square, where two roads enter. For plan see Illus.* 142.

Illus. 135.—*Cornhill, Bridgewater, from Fore Street. See Illus.* 59.
By kind permission of Mr. Alfred Whitby.

Illus. 136.—*Nuremberg Market-place. See Fold Map I.*

Illus. 137.—*Karolinen Platz, Munich. For plan see Illus.* 127E.

203

Illus. 138.—*Max Joseph Platz, Munich. For plan see Illus.* 127F.

Illus. 139.—*Bad Kissengen Market-place.*

This is not the way to produce satisfactory pictures or to show the buildings to the best advantage. In a picture so very much depends on relation, surroundings, on the contrast of one part with another, and it is the same with street views. For one thing, size is not in itself appreciated. It is only apprehended by its relation to some known standard, by a comparison, or by contrast. It is not when we are close to Chartres or Amiens or Beauvais that we realise their *Illus.* 123 *and* 124.

Illus. 140.—*Ravenna.*

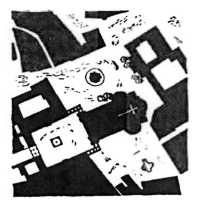

Illus. 141.—*Salzburg.*

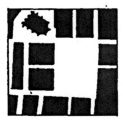

Illus. 142.—*Dresden, Market-place.*

Illus. 143.—*Pisa.*

impressiveness; but it is when we obtain some view which shows these cathedrals towering up above the surrounding houses, and when we are enabled in some degree to measure them by their relation to and contrast with these houses, that we realise the full splendour of their dimensions.

In the pictures given of Augsburg and Regensburg it will be seen how the smaller buildings give scale to the towers and churches *Illus.* 144 *and Frontis-piece.*

Illus. 146.
Illus. 147.
Illus. 140, 141.

with which they are grouped. If we contrast these photos with the one given of the cleared church at Ghent which now shows a building treated in the modern manner, the correctness of this view will, I think, be apparent.

Undoubtedly the sense of enclosure in *places* was much more easily attained in the old towns, particularly old Gothic towns, where the streets were so narrow that a very slight divergence from a straight line was sufficient to close the view. In the picture of the old market-place at Stuttgart one has only to imagine two modern 50-feet streets replacing the two narrow ones leading out from the end of the square, to realise how entirely they would break the frame of buildings and destroy the sense of enclosure. But still, much may be done even with modern streets ; and it is to be hoped that the absurd restrictions which require all streets to be of a certain minimum width, whatever their purpose, will be modified, and that it will become possible again to make reasonable use of narrower streets and passages for pedestrians which may enable us to form our *places* with fewer large openings, while providing, by means of smaller openings and archways, for ample convenience to foot passengers.

It will be apparent from the examples given, many of which are admittedly of great beauty, that definite rules for the size and proportion of *places* cannot be laid down. They should bear some relation to the size of the buildings likely to surround them. An over-large *place* will tend to dwarf buildings. Sitte points out also that tall buildings, narrow in proportion to their height, such as the west ends of cathedrals, seem to require *places* deep in the dimension at right angles to their front ; while wide buildings of lesser height, such as are many town halls, picture-galleries, and the north and south fronts of cathedrals, seem, on the other hand, to show best on *places* wide in the direction parallel to the building, and shallow in the direction at right angles to it. He also recommends that *places* should not usually be square but rather oblong, the length and the width bearing some definite proportion one to the other. Usually the length should not be greater than three times the width. Such rules, however, can at best only indicate one method likely to prove successful. Proportion in town planning, as in architecture, is a matter that cannot be reduced to figures, but must be judged of in each case according to the circumstances, one of the difficulties of the town planner being that he must lay out his streets and *places* often with very imperfect knowledge of what will be the character and height of the buildings surrounding them.

Illus. 144.—*Augsburg. St. Ulrich's Church from Maximilian Strasse.*

For Illus. 145 *see Frontispiece.*

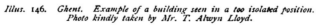

Illus. 146.   *Ghent.   Example of a building seen in a too isolated position.
Photo kindly taken by Mr. T. Alwyn Lloyd.*

Illus. 147.—*Stuttgart, Market-place.*

Illus. 148.—*Piazza S. Marco, Venice. See Illus.* 127A.

211

Illus. 149.—*Piazza S. Marco, Venice. See Illus.* 127A.

Illus. 149a.—*Paris. Place Vendôme. For plan see Illus.* 163B.

213

For this reason probably it will be wise to follow fairly simple straightforward lines in cases where he will have no means of controlling the buildings ; for though many of the finest effects have resulted from departure from the simplicity of regular lines, there is undoubtedly a danger, if the town planner aims at effects depending on a too special treatment of certain sites and buildings, that he may not only lose the effect he aimed at, but lose also the sense of orderly design which it was within his power to reach.   In considering the question of regular and irregular treatment the style of architecture must also be considered, and there can be no doubt that as irregularity is a most marked characteristic of Gothic times and towns, so Gothic architecture is the more adapted to give successful groups on sites of irregular shapes.   The truth of this may almost be illustrated by the two ends of the Piazza San Marco   *Illus.* 148. in Venice.   Looking towards the cathedral, few would notice, and   *Illus.* 149. none would be troubled by, the splayed side of the square, which gives a wider and more picturesque view of the church itself ; but, on the other hand, looking from the cathedral, the strongly marked horizontal lines and formal treatment of the square seem to emphasise the irregularity of its plan, which, if not a serious disadvantage, cannot at least be felt to be any advantage to the buildings.

Before we pass on to consider the planning of modern *places*, let us linger over the plan of the beautiful little town of Buttstedt, and   *Illus.* 150. seek to glean for ourselves from it and from the views given some of the secrets of that beauty which led Camillo Sitte to believe that the whole was carefully planned with a view to producing the picturesque effects we see.   The centre of the town consists of a large, apparently shapeless, open space, in which stand the Church and the Rathaus.   From this space the streets lead off in various directions, and are linked together by a sort of Ringstrasse, probably following the lines of some old town wall.   The town was at one time the centre of an important cattle market, while a wide portion of the Ringstrasse appears from its name to have been the site of a pot market.   The emphasis in the design of the central area of the town, and the way the whole leads up to this, is very marked.   This central open space stands on the top of a hill, the ground falling away sharply on the west, gradually in other directions.   If we examine this central space more carefully, we shall find that it is divided by the buildings into what forms practically a group of three *places*, irregularly shaped it is true, but, for the purpose of the picturesque views of the buildings, well proportioned. The tall and narrow east end of the church, with the tower rising above it, is viewed from what Sitte would have described as a deep narrow *place*, marked I. on the plan ; while the north-east end of this forms a *place* of different proportion, more suited to the broad end elevation of the Rathaus. The space marked II. serves as a wide, shallow *place*, in the sense used by Sitte, for the long side elevations of both the Rathaus and the church ; while the space marked III. on the plan affords a somewhat similar *place*, from which is viewed advantageously the south elevation of the church. At first sight these buildings appear to have been dropped casually into the

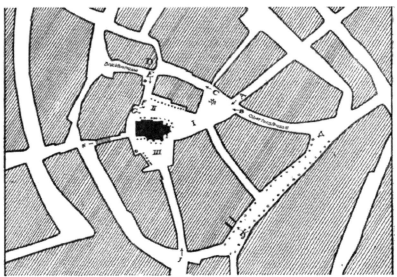

Illus. 150.—*Plan of part of the town of Buttstedt. This plan and the following eight sketches are made from illustrations in " Der Städtebau," by kind permission of Editor and Publisher.*

open space, but if we look more closely we shall see that, although a way is clear all round, they do not in fact stand isolated in the centre of the *place*, but approach so nearly to the buildings at two or three of their corners that from whichever direction they are viewed the frame of buildings around them is unbroken. Except for the Neuestrasse, a modern straight road from the railway station, all the roads leading out of the square, in some cases along slightly curved lines and in others opening out from points entirely screened by the buildings, are so contrived that from no

point in the open space is the frame of the buildings broken or the
sense of enclosure disturbed. View A shows the church from the *Illus.* 151.
end of *place* No. 1, and though seen in its most detached position,
it has nevertheless a complete background and frame of buildings
in which no gap is evident. View B shows the east front of the *Illus.* 152.
Rathaus, with the fountain and its few acacia-trees in front, and
illustrates with View C how admirably a break in the direction of a *Illus.* 153.
street may prevent the isolation of a building. Instead of the
Brücktorstrasse being a continuation of the Obertorstrasse, there is a
definite break of line ; the opening into the Brücktorstrasse is
hidden by the Rathaus building and the end of the view is closed,

Illus. 151.—*Buttstedt. View from
Standpoint A on plan.*   *Illus.* 152.—*Buttstedt. View from
Standpoint B on plan.*

and the frame is completed by the buildings at the point D on the
plan. The small road leading to the north is at such an angle that
its opening is not seen until actually reached, and from it another
view of the corner of the Rathaus would be obtained. From the
Sammelgasse also a perspective view of the Rathaus, with the church
tower beyond, forms a group again closing the view. If the centre
is approached from the Brucktorstrasse, the west end of the Rathaus
fills the view, while a small enlargement at this point has the effect
of a small *place* facing this end of the building. From this point,
E, a very beautiful view of the northern side of the church is *Illus.* 154.
shown, framed in by the corner of the Rathaus and the buildings

Illus. 155 *and* 156.

opposite, with the widening for the tiny *place* appearing in the foreground. From the points F and G are obtained views of the *place* II., showing the interesting southern side of the Rathaus, with

Illus. 153.—*Buttstedt. View from Standpoint C on plan.*

Illus. 154.—*Buttstedt. View from Standpoint E on plan.*

a row of small acacia-trees marking the line of the building and the north side of the church, while the buildings beyond close the view out of this long *place*. Approaching from the south-west, a charming flight of steps gives access to the central *place*, the buildings

Illus. 155.—*Buttstedt. View from Standpoint F on plan.*

Illus. 156.—*Buttstedt. View from Standpoint G on plan.*

Illus. 157.

clinging to this hillside, with the west end of the church and its tower rising on the crest, are particularly pleasing. See view H. From the Kirchgasse the tower of the church rises as the central

feature of the street picture, while the whole of its south elevation
opens out as *place* No. III. is approached.   See view J.   Both   *Illus.* 158.
along Marktstrasse and the Obertorstrasse the street views end in
the Rathaus, while at various points along what we have called the

Illus. 157.—*Buttstedt, View from Standpoint H on plan.*

Ringstrasse, glimpses of the church tower are seen through
openings in the buildings, as in view K.   *Illus.* 159.
Whether this arrangement has been the result of conscious design
or the product of a more or less unconscious instinct, we must
admit the beauty of the effects produced and the success of the
whole.   Here we have a little town consisting of the simplest and

9

plainest buildings in the main, and yet, owing to the splendid placing of its two public buildings and to the arrangement of its streets and *places*, the whole presents a degree of beauty and impressiveness quite astonishing; and we may well ponder over the details of this and many another such plan, and the features springing from them, and try to glean for ourselves the harvest of suggestion and guidance which they afford in the art of town planning, which though so old is in reality to us a new art to-day, the principles of which we have to re-learn for ourselves from the work of other times and other lands.

For a fuller account of this little town, with further illustrations, the

Illus. 158.—*Buttstedt, View from Standpoint J on plan.*

Illus. 159.—*Buttstedt, View from Standpoint K on plan.*

reader is referred to the December, 1908, number of that admirable periodical *Der Städtebau*, which well sustains the distinction of being, I believe, the only periodical in the world devoted entirely to town planning. To the kindness of the editor and publisher I am indebted for this and much other information, as well as for many illustrations used in this book.

The effect of enclosure in a *place* is so important that many methods have been suggested for obtaining some considerable degree of enclosure, even with the modern wide streets. In some *Illus.* 126F, cases the *place* may be formed entirely on one or both sides of a 160E, 163B. main thoroughfare having no outlets in the recessed portion of the *place* other than those of quite minor size, such as footways; and where there exists anything of a market in the old-fashioned sense, or where public buildings, such as the town hall, which numerous people must frequent, can be so situated as to keep the *place* well used, such a plan would be in many ways a good one; if the stream of traffic does not pass through it, there is always a danger that some other point will become the natural centre and the *place* itself become deserted and deteriorate in character.

Furthermore there are ways of securing a sufficient background for the buildings and a sense of enclosure in a fairly large *place* if the roads are so arranged that from the main points where people would stand to view groups of public buildings, they do not afford direct vistas. The roads may pass out of the square at right angles to the line of vision, or if along the line of vision, their direction may be diverted sufficiently early for the vista to be closed with other groups of buildings. In this way it may be possible to make a *place* in the traffic centre where it will be most constantly used, without sacrificing the frame and background required for the public buildings. Also it may be arranged that these same public buildings form terminal features along some of the main roads converging towards the centre of the town.

Enclosure, however, is not the only desirable effect to be produced. Professor Lethaby has pointed out in one of his lectures how carefully the view of the sea has been guarded in Constantinople. The views out of a town into the country beyond have always a special charm, and it may be well worth while to secure these distant views of sea and mountain, and even to bring into the heart of the town glimpses of sunset glory, where openings to the west can be secured.

One finds very charming little pictures at times at the ends of such long vistas. There is one from the Square at Lisieux. Indeed, these long vistas seem to have a special charm for the French people as they are commonly to be found in French towns. They are none the less pleasing to the eye because their effect cannot be conveyed in a photograph, where, as a rule, the distant vista fades away into vagueness. In like manner the return view along these open roads may be so arranged as to give those approaching the town a distant glimpse of its public buildings.

One simple form of *place* may be made at the junction of four streets by breaking the line of direction, the result being that the

Illus. 160C. view down each street is closed and a figure resembling a turbine is produced ; or the roads may be brought in at the corners of the *place* in such a way that, while giving plenty of space for the turning of traffic, the buildings will close the view.

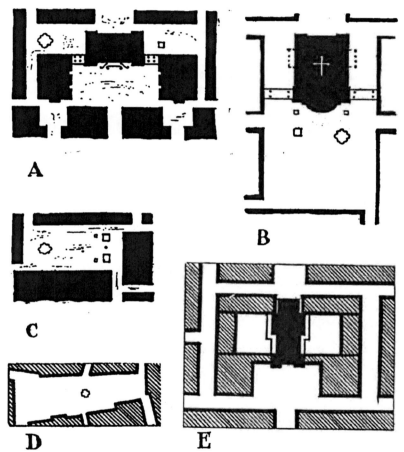

Illus. 160.—*Places and groups of places adapted to modern conditions, as recommended by Camillo Sitte. D is the Neuemarkt, Vienna.*

Illus. 160D. The new market at Vienna affords an example of the way in which the streets can be brought into a modern *place* without unduly breaking the frame of the buildings ; while illustrations 160A,

160B, and 160E, taken from Camillo Sitte's book, show how these principles may be applied to regularly shaped *places* and groups of *places*.   In each of these examples it will be noticed how *places*

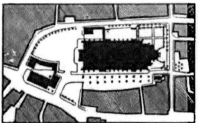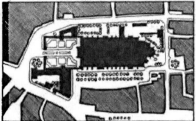

Illus. 161.—*Two alternative proposals for treating the Münster Platz at Ulm.*

are formed to afford views of the different sides of the chief buildings and how the picture is made to develop itself in the

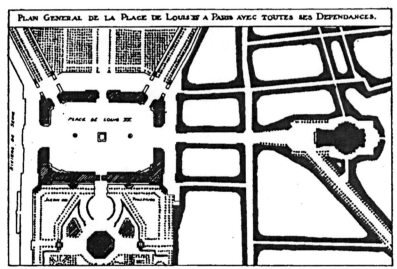

Illus. 162.—*Original design for the Place de la Concorde and the Place de la Madeleine, made by the architect Gabriel about the year* 1753.

main on concave lines.   It is an important point to remember that, owing to the nature of vision, a group of buildings taking generally a concave line is likely to be more pleasing than one taking the

o

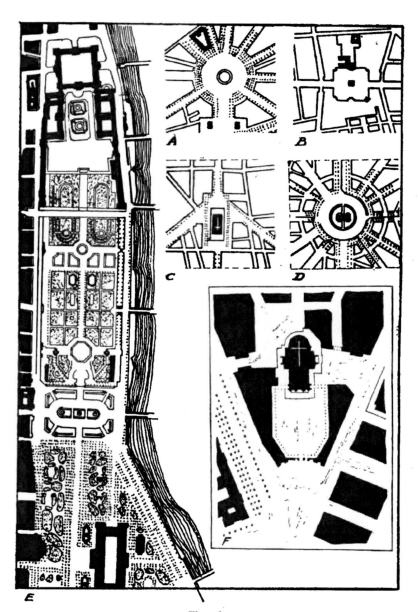

Illus. 163.

A. Place de la Nation, Paris.
B. Place Vendôme, Paris.
C. Place de la Madeleine.
D. Place de l'Etoile.
E. Louvre and Place de la Concorde, Paris.
F. Votivkirche Platz, Vienna.

convex line ; and that where, as in illustration 160B, the building
must for some reason stand detached, projecting forward into the
main *place*, it is a matter of great importance to link it up by
means of arcades, or in some other way, so as to give it a frame
and connection with the other buildings.

There is another type of *place* which is more of the nature of
a forecourt to a building. The Piazza in front of St. Peter's
in Rome is a well-known example ; and in the laying out of
Vienna, a *place* on somewhat similar lines was arranged in front *Illus.* 163*F.*
of one of the churches, an illustration of which is given.

There is a fine group of regular *places* at Nancy, some views of which *Illus.* 41–45.
are given. In some parts a general sense of enclosure is secured, in
others it is somewhat markedly wanting, although the elaborate iron
gates and arcades which fill some of the open sides and corners go
some way towards completing the picture, and are helped by the
background of foliage.

Camillo Sitte was very emphatic in his opinion that the centres
of *places* should be kept free from statues and monuments, and
that these should be placed at the sides or in the corners, as in
the Roman Forum or in the Forum of Pompeii. Many charming *Illus.* 26 *and*
pictures of old street fountains and drinking troughs might 27.
be given showing how these will fall into the picture when not *Illus.* 32,
too much isolated. When statues are in the middle of busy 114*a*, 105*a.*
roads they cannot be seen with comfort or safety and their effect
is lost in the traffic.

Here, again, no definite rule can be laid down ; there occur central
points which one feels instinctively need to be marked and *Illus.* 149*a*
emphasised, and there occur other spaces where it seems of equal *and* 163*A,*
B, and D.
importance to avoid anything that would break up the simplicity *Illus.* 164.
of the space itself.

The plan of the town square at Letchworth may perhaps serve *Illus.* 165
to illustrate some of these points, though it was planned before *and Fold*
Map VII.
the writer had the good fortune to come across Camillo Sitte's
book. Here it will be seen that the square is the centre into
which many roads converge from different parts of the town ; and
along several of these roads, particularly those to the east and
west, views of the distant country will permanently remain open.
A wide main avenue leads from the station to the Town Square
and commands directly a view of the façade of the Municipal
Buildings, these being the most important buildings dominating the
square. It is intended that the roads on each side of them shall be
partially closed by an arcade, while in any case they extend but

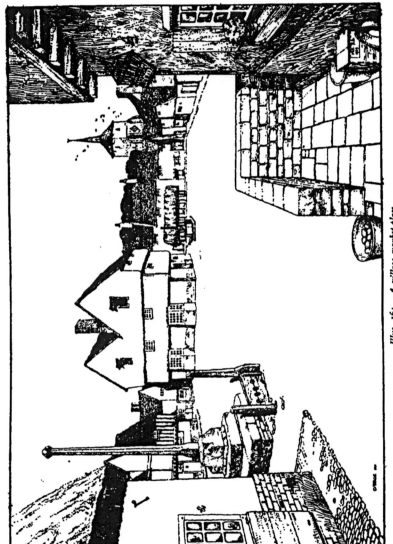

Illus. 164.—A village market-place.

a short distance before they diverge, and groups of buildings
will close the vista and form a background for the Municipal
Buildings themselves. The façades of the buildings on each side
will also be in full view, up to the point where we see instead
the ends of the square, so that a fair sense of enclosure in these two
corners will be obtained. The roads branching off east and west
from the front of the Municipal Buildings are placed at such
an angle that a perspective view of the buildings will be obtained
along them. The curves of Eastcheap and Westcheap will have
somewhat the same effect in giving background and frame to

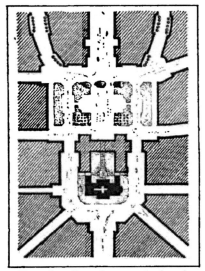

Illus. 165.—*Town Square at Letchworth.*

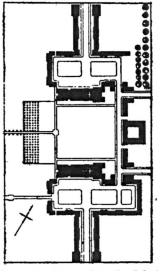

Illus. 166.—*Hampstead Garden Suburb.*
Central Place. See Illus. 167.

the buildings on the north side of the square. On the south side
of the Municipal Buildings it was intended to place the central
church of the town, and views of this building were secured from
east, west, and south, also from south-west and south-east, the
south façade of the church being intended to be the main one :
while the church itself was intended to form the south side of
a smaller quadrangle of which the Municipal Buildings would form
the other three sides.

With roads 40 or 50 feet wide, or even wider, as main roads
in a modern town must usually be, unless the *place* is of considerable

extent, it is very difficult to secure much sense of enclosure, particularly when, as in the instance just referred to, it is to be made in any sense a centre to the framework of roads, and all that will be possible in some cases will be to secure closed and completed street pictures from each of the roads leading into the *place*, or to secure definite sense of enclosure at one end or in certain corners.

Illus. 166.
Illus. 167.
Fold Map VI.

The treatment of the central *place* in the Hampstead Garden Suburb may perhaps be taken as affording a contrast to that at Letchworth just described. Here the arrangement is on four-square lines, to suit Mr. Lutyens's fine Renaissance design for the whole of the buildings round this group of *places*. The two main approaches from the south and from the north lead up to enclosed *places*, the view being terminated by the north and south sides, respectively, of the church and the chapel. Between these two *places* is laid out a large open space or green, the western side being kept quite open, and the slope in the foreground planted as an orchard ; while on the east a row of buildings with an institute in the centre overlooks this green. It is proposed to attach the vicarage, halls, and Sunday schools to the church and chapel to complete to some extent the enclosure on three sides of this larger *place*. The whole is situated on the flat top of rising ground, and the treatment has been adopted in order to combine a sense of enclosure in the *places* with a sense of space and openness in the green ; and while securing background and frame to the main views of the chief buildings, to secure something of the wide outlook over the surrounding country which the rising ground affords. Particularly has the view of Hampstead Heath been kept open, and the view from it up into the central square. The roads entering from the east side lead up to the east end of the church, which will form the terminal feature of the street picture here also.

Illus. 168.

A subsidiary centre in the Hampstead Suburb has been formed by means of an irregularly shaped green, round which some of the smaller public buildings will be grouped.

Illus. 169.
Illus. 170.

Other examples of small subsidiary centres are afforded by the plans of the Ealing Tenants' Estate and that of the Anchor Tenants at Leicester. In the former case a wide avenue is made to serve as the central feature ; one or two public buildings are arranged at points where the cross roads lead into this, and the avenue is laid out in such a way as to afford space for seats and wide, shady promenades.

In the latter case a small square is arranged as the centre, and

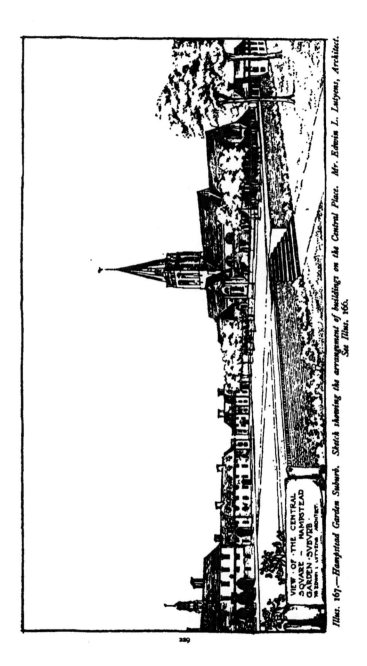

VIEW · OF · THE · CENTRAL
SQVARE – HAMPSTEAD
GARDEN · SVBVRB ·
Mr EDWIN L·LVTYENS · ARCHITECT ·

Illust. 167.—Hampstead Garden Suburb. Sketch shewing the arrangement of buildings on the Central Place. Mr. Edwin L. Lutyens, Architect.
See Illus. 166.

here it is intended to build the institute, school, place of worship, and co-operative store, which are likely to be required by the community. In this scheme the necessity, for drainage purposes, of arranging one of the roads to follow pretty closely the contour lines of the undulating surface has been taken advantage of to bring two of the roads into the square diagonally, so that the

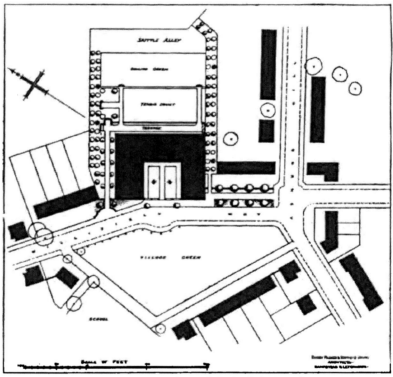

Illus. 168.—*Hampstead Garden Suburb. Subsidiary Centre.*

views along them may be closed by the side of the square opposite them.

171.   In the plan of Earswick, near York, a green, large enough to serve as a playing field and recreation ground, was taken as the most fit central feature for the village, and where the main road runs alongside of this green it is intended to arrange for a few shops, and for the grouping of the public buildings.

Illus. 169.—*Plan of the Ealing Tenants' Estate.*

The making of Brentham Way, leading from the Estate to Mount Avenue, was not permitted, because its length exceeded 600 feet, until land was acquired enabling the cross-road A, B to be planned.

It is by no means easy to secure the proper development of centres; where an estate or district develops slowly there will always be some tendency for those interested in the various semi-public buildings, such as places of worship, shops, &c., to

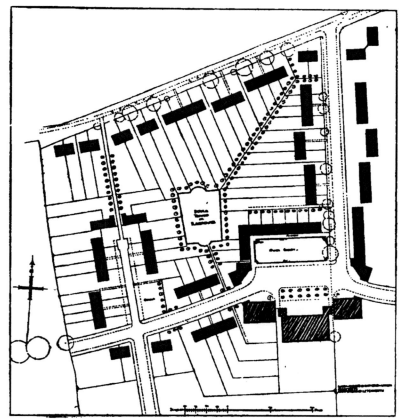

Illus. 170.—Leicester Anchor Tenants' Estate. Plan shewing part of the estate with the village centre.

take short-sighted views of the future development, and to insist on placing these buildings on sites adjacent to the first groups of houses built, so that it may easily happen that only to a limited extent can the centre be developed in the way originally intended. Nevertheless, it is well that the centre should be fixed

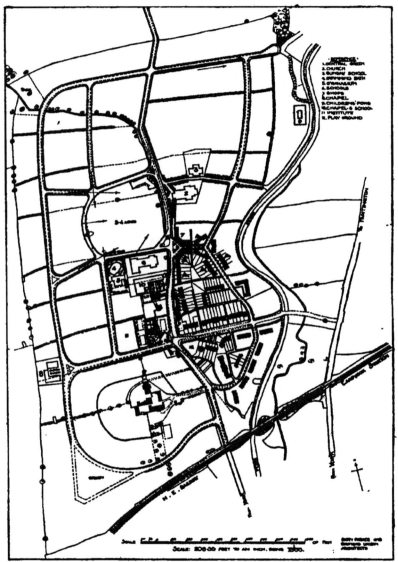

Illus. 171.—*Plan of Earswick, near York, being built by The Joseph Rowntree Village Trust.*

and form the main feature of the plan. It is probable that in the full development of the scheme other public buildings whose requirement was not foreseen may help to fill up the centre, and as the public become somewhat accustomed to the use of foresight in the laying out of towns and suburbs, they will the more readily come to acquiesce in the placing of their public buildings on these pre-arranged central spaces.

VII.—OF THE ARRANGEMENT OF MAIN ROADS, THEIR TREATMENT AND PLANTING

ROADS are primarily highways for traffic. They serve also a secondary purpose in affording sites for buildings. They should therefore be considered in relation to both these functions, and in the order of their relative importance. For the roads in a town to satisfy properly their primary function of highways, they must be so designed as to provide generally for easy access from any point in the town to any other. But they should provide, in addition, special facilities for the ebb and flow of particular tides of traffic, such as that from the outskirts to the centre and back again which daily takes place in most large cities, or that across the town from a residential district to a quarter occupied by works, factories, or other places of employment, or to important railway stations, harbours, and other centres of industry.

A general scheme of roads may be based on various theoretical figures; the most common is that representing a trellis, in which streets run in two directions only, crossing one another at right angles, and dividing the town into building lots, square or oblong in shape. This arrangement, while it is convenient and economical for the building blocks, is open to serious objections; it does not provide convenient roads for passing to and from the centre, and, except when going in two directions, all traffic must travel along two sides of a triangle to get from point to point. In addition to this, the arrangement produces a monotonous effect; the street pictures are not closed, and the vistas wander off in an indefinite, vanishing perspective, often devoid of interest or variety. *Illus. 37 and 63.*

In many of the more modern systems the objection to the trellis arrangement of the roads is to some extent being met by introducing diagonal streets to accommodate the traffic to and from the centre of the town; the result produced, however, is not entirely happy. The shapes of the plots, spaces, and road junctions which are created by these radiating streets crossing the square network of roads, are not such as to produce satisfactory buildings, or beautiful open spaces. *Illus. 68 and 10.*

If we examine the plans of old towns which have grown up more naturally, we find that to a very large extent they consist of main arteries branching out from the nucleus of the town in different directions—forming, in fact, an irregular radiating system; we find, further, that there has been a general tendency for cross roads to grow out from these main roads, approximately *Illus. 8.*

at right angles, and that these have in many cases been diverted or curved round to meet others; and that in the end a very irregular network of streets has grown up, the outline of which would be more nearly represented by a spider's web than by any other figure. This resemblance is distinctly traceable in the plan of Moscow; and in many other town plans, although the theoretical figure of the web is less noticeable, it will be found that the more rectangular arrangement, which may have been characteristic of the original nucleus, has been departed from in such a way as to give much the same convenience for traffic that the spider-web form would have given; for complete convenience, however, there are needed, in addition

Illus. 172.
Illus. 8.

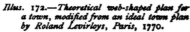

Illus. 172.—Theoretical web-shaped plan for a town, modified from an ideal town plan by Roland Levirloys, Paris, 1770.

Illus. 172a. — Munich, Marienplatz. See Illus. 133.

to the roads following the spider-web lines, others crossing the town and linking up points between which there is likely to be considerable traffic.

Illus. 47.
See Lange Strasse.

In the designing of a new area, while such theoretical considerations will be helpful, it will, nevertheless, be necessary to lay down the main lines of traffic with special regard to the existing circumstances of each case; particularly will this be so when dealing with the extension of an existing town; and it will only be in the rare instances in which new towns have to be laid out on ground the nature of which leaves fairly free choice to the designer that anything like a close approximation to a theoretic figure will be likely to be attained.

In laying down a main framework for our network of roads, while the nature of the ground will usually introduce much irregularity of form, I cannot but think that some sufficiently simple and largely conceived design of main roads and central *places*, to give the plan a character of its own is desirable. This framework must be of such a size as adequately to introduce a sense of scale and of the due proportioning and relation of the parts, and to make of the whole something of a true design.

Such framework once designed, the exact symmetry or regularity of it is a matter of secondary importance, often of no importance at all; for while the regularity and symmetry of certain points may be vital to the production of the desired effect, the eye can never see more than a small portion of the area at once, and cannot judge either distances or angles over a large area, so that considerable departures from the regular figure may be made without their being apparent except on the paper plan.

Except in cases where it is desirable to keep open distant views, straight roads indefinitely prolonged without change of direction or deviation of line are not only monotonous and destructive of satisfactory street pictures, but when running parallel to the direction in which high winds are liable to blow, are objectionable as developing their force to the utmost and creating a maximum of dust. Along these main roads a change of direction or a break in line must be managed in such a manner as not seriously to impede traffic. The electric tram, street railway, and motor-car all require that abrupt changes of direction or sharp curves should be avoided. In very large towns where the traffic in the streets is considerable and the marshalling of it becomes a problem, the necessity arises for small *places* at the junctions of roads, purely for the purpose of giving ample space for its circulation. The traffic problem is a complicated one, and there is a rather marked difference of opinion between the German and French schools as to the best way of dealing with it. Camillo Sitte, who may be taken to represent the German school, shows by diagrams the *Illus.* 173. possible collision points in different forms of road junctions, and how these increase in number to a remarkable degree with every additional street joining in at the point; from which he argues that to bring each street singly into another produces the minimum number of collision points, and is, therefore, the best for traffic, and that the junction of more than four streets at one point must necessarily be very dangerous and undesirable.

Herr Stübben shows, however, that some of the diagrams, which have been used to prove the relatively small number of collision points with two single road junctions as opposed to one junction where four roads meet at right angles, are incorrect, owing to the fact that at each single junction the vehicles entering from the side street into the one running at right angles are alone taken account of, whereas there should be a second line of figures to represent those which purpose to cross from one side street into

Illus. 173.

the other.   A reference to the illustrations will make this clear.

Illus. 174.

German town planners now constantly break the direction of their cross roads as shown in Illus. 174*b* partly in order to secure this

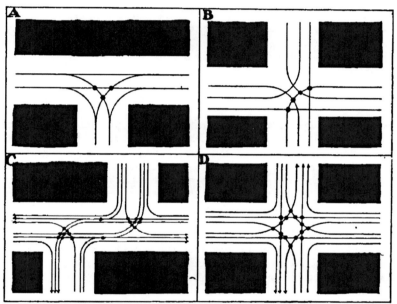

Illus. 173.—*Relative number of collision points at different road junctions.   A and B diagrams as given by Camillo Sitte; C and D as given by Dr. Stübben.*

imagined immunity from collision, but also to secure the closing of the street vistas.   In Illus. 174*a* the view up the two cross streets is indefinitely prolonged, while in Illus. 174*b* the view is in each case definitely closed by the buildings opposite ; moreover (Illus. 174*c*), the arrangement affords an opportunity for creating a small *place* with one of its angles closed, and the view into it from two of the streets, a closed view.   There is, however, much to be said in favour of the theory upon which the French school of town planners have acted, that it is in every way advantageous for traffic that a number of streets should meet at one point, and that ample provision should here be made for its circulation. Where the traffic is sufficiently dense to be necessarily controlled by a police officer it would seem wise to reduce the number of points requiring this control, and wherever the traffic is sufficiently dense for Camillo Sitte's collision points to represent even approximately the truth, it will also be dense enough to require police regulation. On the other hand, in cases where the traffic is comparatively sparse, the chances of collision would be but slightly greater at a point where many roads meet than at the point where one road joins another. Danger arises, and delay is caused to traffic, by every change of

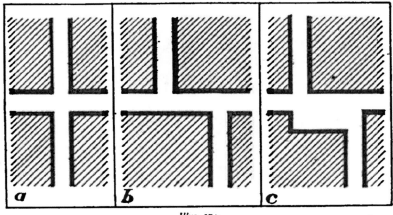

Illus. 174.

direction of the vehicle, and it is obviously simpler, and less likely to cause confusion, to drive straight across a main street, when the condition of the traffic will allow it, than to drive into the street, take a turn, go along the street some distance, take another turn and go out of it ; particularly is this the case with such vehicles as motor-cars and electric trams, any turn of which, especially at right angles, always causes difficulty and danger.

The great fallacy of diagrams in such a case as this arises, however, from the fact that the human element is not represented by them. They may show theoretically the number of collision points for machines moving at regular paces, with some approach to accuracy ; but it is impossible to compare diagrammatically the danger arising

at one multiple road junction, where the risk is sufficient to cause
every driver to move cautiously, with that at several single road
junctions, at each of which, though there is an element of risk, it
will not be sufficient to suggest the necessity for special caution.

I am inclined to think, therefore, that from considerations of traffic,
the German system, if we may call it so, as put by Camillo Sitte, can
by no means be accepted as the whole truth.   It perhaps most

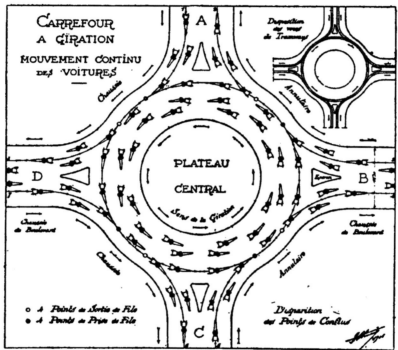

Illus. 175.—*Road junction for the circulation of traffic as suggested by M. Eugène Hénard
and published by his kind permission.*

nearly approaches to the truth when chiefly horse traffic is concerned, and when that traffic reaches the greatest degree of density
which can be left to regulate itself without police supervision.
Where traffic is sparse, to be constantly pulled up and made to turn
sharply at right angles must be an inconvenience ; and to be able
to drive without interruption to a main point, from which roads can
be taken in many directions, must help the rapid distribution of

carriages. Monsieur Eugène Hénard, in "Études sur les Transformations de Paris," suggests that for really busy centres, where many roads converge, the most convenient arrangement is to have a round space with the traffic circulating in one direction. Vehicles coming from any one road can fall in with the line of traffic, circulate with it, and fall out again when they reach whichever of the other roads they wish to pass down. With a view to assisting pedestrians to cross such a circulating space, M. Hénard suggests that *Illus.* 175. subways should be provided from all the footpaths leading to a space in the centre where the passengers in like manner could sort themselves and depart along the subway to whichever of the streets they might wish to reach. This would not, of course, prevent their crossing above ground when the condition of road traffic would allow. The Place de l'Étoile, in Paris, may serve as a good instance of this *Illus.* 163A arrangement, and here the Arc de Triomphe forms a central feature. *and* 163D. Probably such central feature, to be entirely satisfactory, should be in the form of an obelisk or circular building, so that it might look *Illus.* 179. its best from whatever point of view it might be seen, and so that it would form a fitting terminal feature to all the streets leading up to the open space. Of course no sense of enclosure can be secured in a *place* of this character, and some care is required to produce anything like a satisfactory effect in the buildings themselves, so that one would regard it as an undesirable form of *place* except in cases *Illus.* 137 where traffic considerations must be the all-important ones. *and* 188.

It is very needful that at all street junctions there shall be such a degree of openness, as will enable the traffic in one street to be early perceived by the drivers of vehicles coming along another. This may be secured by setting back the corner buildings and by the formation of small *places* at these points. We had, however, better leave the consideration of this until we come to deal with the second function of roads.

For our most important and busiest highways we may well take a hint from the main railway lines, where central tracks are provided for the through expresses, and outside tracks for the slow stopping trains. This system has been largely adopted in continental cities, where on the main roads and boulevards multiple tracks have been provided. Through traffic in such a system is not impeded by vehicles stopping, turning, entering, or leaving the track, only by those which have to pass right across it ; and the number of points at which these crossings can take place may be restricted. In many of these roads special tracks are provided for tramways, for riding, *Illus.* 176 and for cycling, in addition to those for the ordinary fast and slow *and* 176a.

traffic of vehicles.   With such an arrangement a great improvement is possible in the position of the tram lines; these can be so planned that the trams pass along the side of the footway, so that people boarding or leaving the cars do so in safety.   It is our English custom to run our trams in the centre of a wide roadway, and the poor pedestrian has to make a dash, at the risk of his life, through all the traffic of the street before he can reach the car.

In the case of cars driven by electricity or motor power it has been found possible, both in America and on the Continent, to run the trams along a belt of grass, with a footway on each side, and thus the tramway becomes a street decoration, introducing a wide grass margin.   These wide streets or boulevards are further decorated

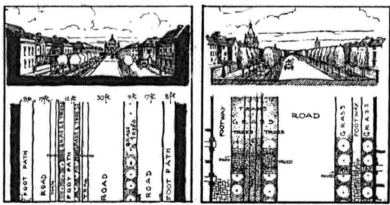

Illus. 176.—Designs for Broadway, Garden City, Letchworth.

with avenues of trees, and are favourite promenading grounds in the evening, when the amount of traffic is reduced.   Such roads, however, are costly, both in the amount of land required for them and in the construction and maintenance of the numerous tracks, and, while roads of this form are desirable and their expense justified for main thoroughfares in large towns, they must not be recklessly adopted.   Continental cities are undoubtedly, in many cases, suffering severely from needless extravagance in the laying out of roads of much greater width than the requirements justified.   This has had the effect of increasing greatly the return necessary to be obtained from the land, and has consequently intensified a tendency, already sufficiently strong, to crowd too many buildings upon the land, and to carry these buildings too high.

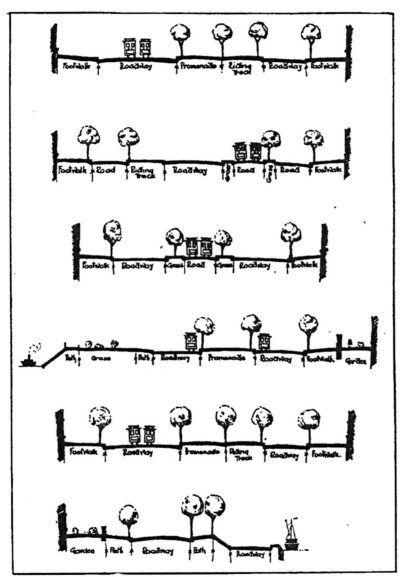

Illus. 176a.—Some examples of German multiple track roads.

Much greater variation in the width and character of roads is desirable than it has been usual to provide for in England; in fact, it is only in comparatively few English town bye-laws that provision is made for the municipality to be able to secure any variation at all in the widths of the streets; usually a minimum width is fixed which applies in all cases.

The question of building roads will be referred to later, but even for roads for which traffic considerations may be regarded as the most important, very great variation in widths should be provided for, and roads of different types and characters arranged. It will

Illus. 177.—*Sections showing the great variety of widths of roads used in Germany. The figures give the dimensions in metres.*

Illus. 177. be seen from the illustrations given what great varieties of width are used in German towns.

Roads, however, in addition to being avenues for traffic, serve the only less important function of providing sites and frontages for buildings, and it does not always follow that the form of road and road junction which would be the most convenient for traffic would necessarily afford the best sites for buildings, or provide the most beautiful grouping of these when erected; it will therefore be necessary in some cases to concede something from one point of view or another, in one case sacrificing the beauty of the buildings for the greater convenience of the traffic and in another sacrificing a little of the directness of the traffic lines for the purpose of securing the more beautiful grouping of the buildings.

Much of the picturesqueness of old Gothic towns springs from the narrowness of the streets. Not only does this narrowness give the sense of completeness and enclosure to the pictures in the streets themselves, but it is much easier with such narrow streets to produce the effect of enclosure in a *place* into which they may lead. Where roads are wide and bounded by small buildings, the definite street effect is apt to be lost altogether, the relation between the two sides is not sufficiently grasped, and on such roads some quite

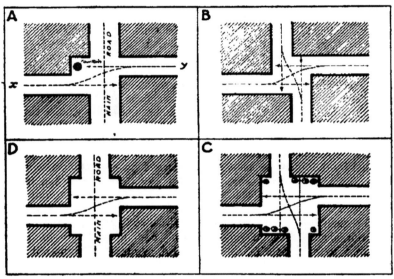

Illus. 178.

different effects may need to be worked out, if they are to be successful. There seems to be no reason why a certain number of narrower streets and passages could not be usefully provided, even in modern towns, to give access to buildings of a character for which it is not necessary to secure a large amount of open space.

We have seen in speaking of *places* and squares how important to the effect is a sense of enclosure, the completion of the frame of buildings; and much the same applies to street pictures.

When considering the buildings therefore, in order to secure a fairly frequent completion of the street picture, we shall desire to

close from time to time the vista along the street; this result is
secured by a break in the line of the street; or by a change of
direction, or curve, either of which has the effect of bringing
into view at the end of the street some of the buildings on the
concave side.

It is upon the treatment of street junctions that much of the effect
of the town will depend.   Having once secured sufficiently easy
lines for the traffic, and an adequate degree of openness of view
about the junction, we may turn our attention mainly to producing
a satisfactory grouping of the buildings.   Where streets cross at
right angles, and it is desired to close the vistas along one of
Illus. 178.   the streets, a simple arrangement is that shown in Illus. 178A,
where the small open *place* allows the traffic on the cross street
x, *y* to take an easy sweep.   Where it is desirable to close
the view along all four of the roads the plan shown in Illus. 178B
may be adopted.   In this case the picture seen from each of the
four streets is terminated by the building opposite the end of it;
not only so, but from the buildings on four sites an open view
straight down one of the roads is obtained, and they would therefore be specially attractive for residential purposes, and also for
business purposes where prominent position is desirable.   A modification of this arrangement is shown in Illus. 178C, where the *place*
formed by the junction is slightly enlarged so that an earlier view
is obtained of vehicles entering from any direction, and a more
complete frame is secured for the view down each street from the
place itself.   The same modification can, of course, be applied to the
arrangement shown in Illus. 178A (see Illus. 178D).   Roads, however,
will not always meet at right angles.   Sometimes three roads are
required to meet at a point.   A useful, symmetrical junction can
be arranged in this case, treated in several ways, so as to secure a
terminal to the street picture, while the obtuse angle affords easy
lines for the traffic in all directions (see Illus. 181A and 181B).
Illus. 182.   Where two roads join at an acute angle it may be possible to
Illus. 183.   create a quite effective, irregularly-shaped *place* giving enclosed
street pictures in many directions, while affording sufficiently easy
lines for traffic (see Illus. 181C and 181D).
Illus. 184.   Where streets cross at an acute angle, a long enclosed *place* may be
formed by bringing two of the streets with a curve into the *place*, as
shown in Illus. 184; or the crossing may be treated symmetrically;
if it is not important to close the street pictures, this may be done as
Illus. 185.   shown in Illus. 185.   If, however, terminals are needed to the street
Illus. 186.   views, their lines may be made to converge on the buildings as

Illus. 179.—*Market Cross and cross roads, Chichester, showing closing of the views.*

Illus. 180.—*La Rue Soufflot, Paris.*

247

shown in Illus. 186. Indeed, when once attention is given to the
subject, there are very many ways in which street junctions can be
treated, either to secure open vistas or closed-in pictures, as may in
each case be most desirable. Some examples, showing how buildings have been treated at the corners formed by the junction of *Illus. 16a,*
roads meeting at various angles will be found in the illustra- *28a, 85, 103b,*
tions. Many small, irregular *places* and street junctions, from *116, 137, 180,*
which most picturesque results have sprung, will be found on *188, 190, 195,*
examining the plans given of old Gothic towns. *198a.*
Fold Maps
I. and III.

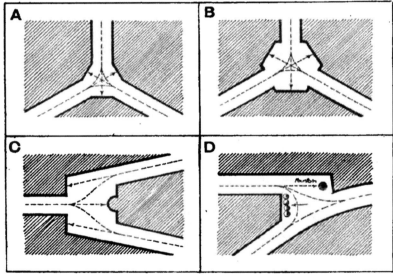

Illus. 181.

It may be interesting to compare some irregular street junctions,
such as are being very widely used in modern German town plans,
with more regular plans so arranged as to secure a similar sense of *Illus. 187.*
enclosure. At first sight some of these irregular shapes seem to
have no purpose or meaning, but a closer examination of them will
show that they are cunningly devised to give enclosed views and to
render possible the erection of irregularly picturesque groups of
buildings. See Illus. 187, where the regular plans are placed under
the irregular ones.
Sitte and some of the German town planners, in advocating the use
of curved streets, have perhaps not done quite justice to the advan-

Illus. 182.—*Sketch of a road junction similar to* 181 *D.*

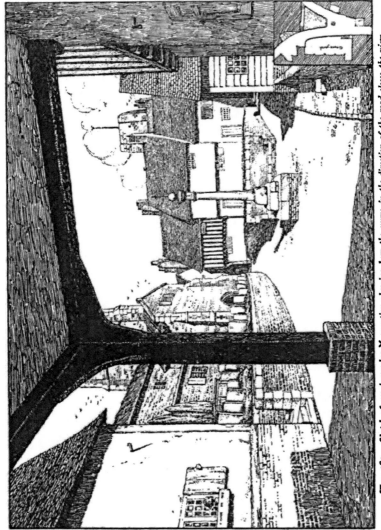

Illus. 183.—Sketch of an irregular Y junction showing how the curve in the direction of the road closes the view.

tages which attach to the straight street. These advantages shortly
stated are : directness of access from point to point ; convenience
and economy in the arrangement and laying of tram lines, &c. ;
Illus. 180. the symmetry and simplicity of the character of the street picture
produced ; the convenience of rectangular buildings and building
Illus. 188. sites ; the production of long vistas, which, where they can be ter-

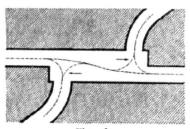

Illus. 184.

minated by a suitable building or view, have great charm ; or where
trees are planted, the avenue effect is in itself a delightful one.

The chief disadvantage of the straight street, on the other hand, is a
tendency to monotony, due to the fact that the street picture remains
much the same for its whole length ; and that, except in the immediate
Illus. 189. foreground or in the terminal feature, the acute perspective at which

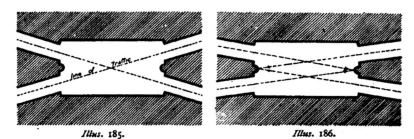

Illus. 185. *Illus.* 186.

the buildings are seen tends to destroy any interest which they
might have ; this disadvantage may to some extent be met by a
judicious breaking of the building line.   It will be seen by referring
to photographs of any straight street, such as the Rue Soufflot in
Paris, given in Illus. 180, that the cross streets, which form breaks
in the line of buildings, have the effect of bringing into the picture,
in exchange for the portion of the vanishing perspective which is

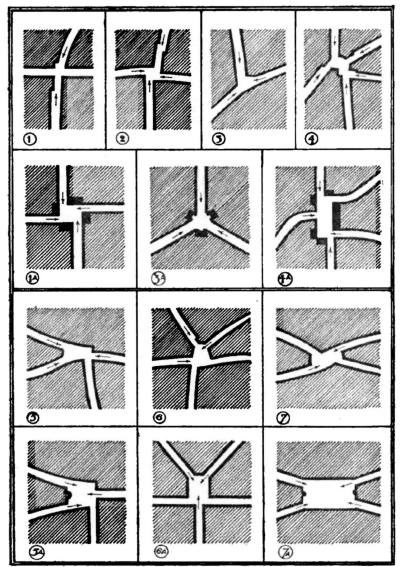

Illus. 187.—*Sketches of various road junctions. Nos.* 1 *to* 7 *show irregular junctions as found on many modern German town plans. Nos.* 1A *to* 7A *show more regular types of road junction securing much the same result in the way of closed street views.*

displaced by the street, part of the side elevation of the building, which is nearly square with the line of vision, and adds interest to the view. Where the purpose of the buildings will allow of such treatment, it is possible, by judicious variation of the building line, *Illus.* 190. to build up a street picture in a straight street, in which a long vanishing perspective is very largely replaced by portions of the *Illus.* 191. sides of buildings seen in front elevation, and in this way quite picturesque street effects may be arrived at.

The setting back of some of the individual buildings in a street not only has the effect of breaking up the monotonous row, but affords an opportunity for the creation of forecourts to some of the build- ings, which, when suitably treated, are very charming in themselves, *Illus.* 193 and are a means of introducing foliage and flowers into the picture. *and* 202. Where in a straight street there is no interesting terminal feature to lead up to, it is especially desirable in this way to introduce interest and variety into the foreground. Where the street picture is closed by some terminal feature of special beauty and interest, a more simple and monotonous treatment may be permitted, and will even serve to enhance the effect by contrast with the more ornate centre. *Illus.* 180. The breaking of the building line and the creation of forecourts must be done with much restraint and judgment, if the result is to be successful. The quiet monotony of the straight front may easily be replaced by a restless monotony of alternate buildings and gaps; or the street line may go to pieces and a sense of mere disorder be produced, if suitable proportion is not maintained between the parts built up to the street line and the parts set back.

M. Hénard, in "Études sur les Transformations de Paris," already referred to, gives some ingenious and suggestive designs for breaking up the street lines, giving greater frontage to the buildings and more extended outlook from the windows. But, as shown in his diagrams, the frequent repetition of equal buildings and spaces would hardly lessen the monotony and might destroy that sense of dignity and repose which often redeems a straight, uninteresting street from meanness.

Illus. 193 It is as an occasional contrast to the street lines that breaks or fore- *and* 202. courts are so welcome. The fine old tree breaking out into the otherwise treeless street view produces a very different effect from that which would result from a regular alternation of trees and buildings.

Straight streets, as used in Paris, not only form fitting frames for the views of monumental buildings, but they extend the effect of such buildings over a far wider area than would otherwise be in-

Illus. 188.—Champs Elysées, view towards the Tuileries, Paris.

Illus. 189.—*Rue de Rivoli, Paris.*

Illus. 190.—*Werntnerstrasse, Vienna, showing the improved street picture owing to variation in the building line.*

fluenced by them, so that the streets of whole districts seem to *Illus.* 149a,
acquire dignity from the monument which is seen at the end of 188, *and* 189.
them.   A straight street leading up to a terminal feature, if a
simple and obvious arrangement, nevertheless often produces a very
pleasing effect.   It is somewhat stiff and formal in character, no
doubt, but it is at least safe.   It is generally possible in planning
such a street to secure with some certainty the placing of a reason-
ably symmetrical building at the end of it ; whereas if a more
irregular, picturesque effect is aimed at, it may be entirely frustrated,
should the buildings not be carried out in a suitable manner.   The *Illus.* 194.
buildings closing a street picture may take many irregular forms and

Illus. 191.—*Plan and sketch of street showing on one side the uninteresting vanishing perspective of the unbroken building line, and on the other the more picturesque result
of breaks.*

yet look quite satisfactory, as will be gathered from the illustrations ; *Illus.* 195.
but there is distinct risk if, owing to a curve in a street, the end of
the picture is crossed by the lines of a row of buildings having little *Illus.* 196.
grouping in their design or little distinction in their character. *Illus.* 198.
I am inclined to think, therefore, in spite of the general absence of *Illus.* 197.
straight streets in medieval towns, and in spite of their tendency to
formality, stiffness, and monotony, that they have both use and
beauty of their own, and that they may with advantage be freely
used by the modern town planner.   After all, when one wishes to
go from one point to another, the obvious course is to take a

straight line, where the contour of the ground or other cause does not suggest doing otherwise.

But one must equally admit the special usefulness of curved roads ; the great advantage to traffic of changing direction by means of curves instead of abrupt angles, the ease with which curved roads can be adapted to the contours of the ground, made to link up existing tracks, or to avoid obstacles or features of interest, which it may be desirable to preserve. Furthermore, the curved road affords to those passing along it an ever-changing picture, a new grouping of the buildings coming into view at every point. It is only necessary to glance at the series of views of the Oxford High Street to realise this, and to see what very beautiful street pictures may result from the way in which, in a curved street, the spires of buildings along it keep rising into view over the shoulders, as it were, of the lower buildings.

Illus. 199–205.

Many of these beautiful pictures seem to have grown up accidentally, and the town planner must be on his guard against the supposition that it is easy to design accidents. While, therefore, he must recognise the beauty of curved roads, he must resist the temptation to produce aimlessly wandering lines, in the hope that happy accidents may result therefrom.

Illus. 206.
Illus. 207.

Curves may, of course, be as formal as straight lines ; we have scarcely yet begun to realise the great variety of combinations of straight lines and curves which are possible within the limitations of orderly design ; probably these are enough to give full play to the beauties which spring from both curved and straight streets.

Illus. 192.

Moreover, rarely will it happen that the site will be so level, and so devoid of existing roads, rivers, valleys, woods, or other features, as not to provide ample reason for the introduction of many irregular lines ; and these irregularities, produced in response to natural conditions, following accurately the contours or avoiding obstacles, will be likely, being justified by the requirements and natural lines of the site, to be justified also in appearance. In many English suburban areas the vague idea that a curve is always more beautiful than a straight line seems to have taken possession of the mind of the surveyor, and a series of meandering lines, without scheme or relation, has been the result.

In the central portion of towns or districts, where a certain stateliness of effect is desirable, and where sites will be required for large public buildings, probably straight streets, combined with some simple and regular curved lines, will be the most successful.

The general tendency of modern architecture suggests square and

Illus. 192.—Warwick, showing picturesque, irregular street line.

Illus. 193.—A straight street with break showing foliage and inadequate terminal feature.

Illus. 194.—*Ulm, showing an irregular street terminal.*

Illus. 195.—*Rothenburg, Klingasse, Standpoint IX. on Fold Plan No. III.*

Illus. 196.—*Tewkesbury High Street, showing the want of sufficient feature in the distance.*

Illus. 197.—*Augsburg, Karolinen Strasse, showing successful street treatment.*

Illus. 198.—*Holborn, showing an unsuccessful grouping of buildings along a street.*

Illus. 198a. —*Karlsruhe, showing successful treatment of acute-angled corner on the Ludwig Platz. See Fold Map IV. and Illus.* 114a.

regular sites for public buildings, and it is probably wise for the town planner to consider such tendency, even if his own sympathies lead him to prefer a freer or more picturesque treatment, such as characterised the Gothic period ; for he must not forget that, though he may provide the sites, he cannot dictate the kind of buildings that will be erected. On a regular site it is not difficult to erect an irregular, picturesque building, if such be desired ; but for an irregular site it may be very difficult to design a successful building in a style which depends largely on symmetry, balance of mass, and simplicity of line for its effect. In the suburbs of towns and in villages, where anything of a stately effect may not be attainable or even desirable, a much freer arrangement may be adopted. One may

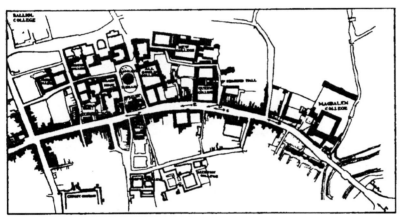

Illus. 199.—Plan of the High Street, Oxford, showing view points. Traced from the Ordnance Survey Map, with the sanction of the Controller of H.M. Stationery Office.

say generally that a much greater degree of adaptation of the site to the plan will be justified in important central positions, than would be desirable in other parts of the town, where the right course would seem to be to adapt the lines of the roads much more completely to the site.

Many German writers point to the varying width of streets in old *Illus.* 208. Gothic towns as being the cause of much of the beauty of the street pictures found in them. Camillo Sitte particularly instances the *Illus.* 209. Rue des Pierres in Bruges, a plan and sketch of which, taken from *Illus.* 210. his book, are given to illustrate this point. Much of this variation in width has probably been due to accidental reasons, and, like other accidental effects, can only with considerable risk be consciously imitated.

Probably also the main beauty of the sketch he shows arises, first, from the change of direction of the road, which brings the cathedral tower into the street picture ; secondly, from the sudden narrowing of the road after passing the Place Stevin, which closes the street picture with the corner buildings of that *place*. These two points may certainly be attained by careful and orderly arrangement, and it is clearly the province of the designer to create such pictures, by changing the directions of his roads or by reducing their width, which may often be a sensible and proper thing to do, where much of the traffic of a main road becomes diverted by a cross or diagonal road.

Illus. 169. Short lengths of road of increased width, to allow for a double avenue of trees and to enable the footpath to be carried up between such avenues, or to allow space for a few seats at the side of the footpath, may add to the variety and charm of a suburban road. The gradual widening out of a roadway for some distance where
See S. Giles, Oxford, Illus. 83. two main roads converge, or where the increase of traffic seems to require it is a legitimate variation ; but in spite of the undoubtedly beautiful and picturesque effect obtained in Gothic towns by irregular street lines and irregularly varying widths of streets, I cannot but feel that in newly designed work such variations need definite justification, and that anything in the way of departure from regularity, merely for the purpose of producing variety in an indefinite sort of way, had better be avoided.

Trees and grass form the natural decoration for streets and *places* in towns, wherever the condition of the atmosphere will allow them to grow. The free use of greenery is certainly one of the pleasing characteristics which first strikes the Englishman when visiting continental cities. Like every other form of decoration, however, this needs to be used with considerable judgment and restraint. Breadth and simplicity of treatment seem to be essential to good result. Many fine streets and *places* in continental towns are spoiled for lack of restraint in the character of the gardening and planting adopted. Broad stretches of grass and simple masses or avenues of foliage are generally successful, if well placed. But spaces cut up into numerous beds, and these again worked into patterns with variegated leaves and flowers, too often tend to destroy the sense of quiet, which is necessary for good town
Illus. 211 and 212. decoration with foliage. A reference to the two views given of the fine Schloss Platz at Stuttgart will, I think, illustrate this. In

Illus. 200.—Oxford High Street. Standpoint A on Illus. 199.
Photo by H. W. Taunt.

Illus. 201.—Oxford High Street. Standpoint B on Illus. 199.
Photo by H. W. Taunt.

Illus. 202.—Oxford High Street. Standpoint C on Illus. 199.
Photo by H. W. Taunt.

Illus. 203.—Oxford High Street. Standpoint D on Illus. 199.
Photo by H. W. Taunt.

Illus. 204.—Oxford High Street. Standpoint E on Illus. 199.
Photo by H. W. Taunt.

Illus. 205.—Oxford High Street. Standpoint F on Illust. 199.
Photo by H. W. Taunt.

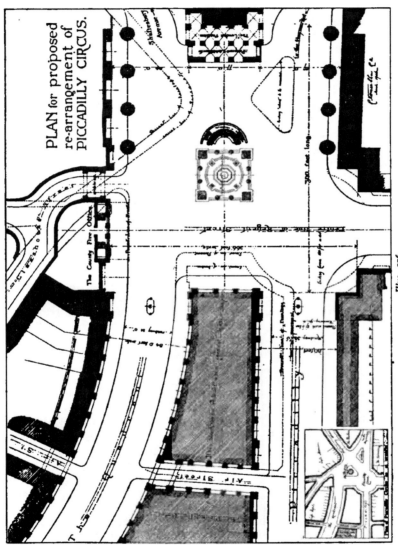

PLAN for proposed re-arrangement of PICCADILLY CIRCUS.

Illus. 206.

Reproduced by kind permission of Mr. R. Norman Shaw, R.A.

277

Illus. 213.
Illus. 214.

Illus. 36a
and 94a.

Illus. 215.
Illus. 216.

Illus. 109,
188.

one case the fussy lay-out of the garden space has been cut out of the picture and nothing left but the masses of foliage, which add immensely to the effectiveness of the view. In the other the garden is shown in full, with all its elaboration of footpaths, fountains, flower-beds, and band-stands. Far better would have looked a plain stretch of greensward, cut perhaps by one or two broad paved footways necessary for general convenience. In the fine Popplesdorfer Allée at Bonn may also be seen the contrast of one portion of its wide road treated with plain grass and trees, and another portion with some elaborate pattern worked in beds of flowers, and again I think it will be admitted that success lies with the simpler treatment. The avenue effect, as the French have instinctively felt, is one of the finest to aim at in decorating streets with trees, and very great variety may be attained without destroying the essential avenue feeling. It is necessary to maintain a unity of effect by planting a fair length at a time with one particular tree. The variety which is attained by mixing or alternating the types of tree on any street, is one which loses its interest after about half a dozen trees are passed, and its total effect when carried out over a large area, is only to spread monotony farther than is necessary ; but by treating each road differently, planting each with one particular kind of tree and the adjacent roads with a different tree, it is possible to stamp each with some individuality of its own and produce very considerable variety in a district. Particularly can this be done in the suburbs, where the atmosphere will generally allow a large variety of trees to flourish. Our allies the Japanese celebrate some of their greatest holidays and festivals at the blossoming of the cherry or the plum, and turn out into the places set apart specially for the particular tree to enjoy their holiday by revelling in its blossom. If we can give to our streets some individuality, may we not find that our people, going to and from their work, will change their route, taking the almond-planted street in the early spring, the plum, the crab, and the hawthorn streets later ; and later still the streets planted with acacia and catalpa, or with the trees whose early foliage is their glory, such as the sycamore. In the autumn those planted with trees most noted for the colour of their berries and fading leaves—the rowan, the hawthorn, the beech, and many others—will be preferred.

Then, of course, there are the larger trees where space will allow—the horse chestnut, the elm, the plane, and the lime—the latter pleasing by the delicate green of its foliage and charming for the fragrance of its flowers. But not alone by varying the kind of tree can we

Illus. 207.—*The Quadrant, Regent Street, showing a portion of Mr. Norman Shaw's design.*

Illus. 208.—*Dorchester, West Street.*

vary the decoration. In some streets we may have continuous
avenues, in others be content with here and there introducing a *Illus.* 235,
mass of foliage in a recessed forecourt ; in others, again, where the 272, *and* 291.
building lines of the houses vary, we may emphasise still further
those portions by planting avenues where our houses are set back
farther from the road and the trees have more room to grow,

Illus. 209 *and* 210.—*Plan and sketch of the Rue des Pierres, Bruges.*

and omitting them where the houses are set up to the building line.
In places, also, we may introduce a double avenue, planting one row
of trees between the footpath and the roadway and another row
either in a second grass margin between the footpath and the
front gardens of the houses, or in the hedge or within the gardens
themselves; thus securing not only to the main roadway, but to each
footpath, the effect of passing through an avenue of trees.

Illus. 180. At junctions of roads spaces may be found where the planting of a few trees will introduce colour and the form of foliage into the picture. Where it is desired to have in *places* or streets the decoration of flowers in addition to that of grass and foliage, as far as possible the beds should be arranged with some background, and the lines should be simple and not needlessly broken. Where, for example, some long, bare, factory building or high wall runs along by the street, a strip in front of this might well be planted with flowering shrubs or with flowers. A long herbaceous border, or one of hardy perennials, would look well in such a position, and dignified approaches to towns, public *places*, or buildings might well be arranged on these lines. Above all, in the treatment of garden spaces in streets we should avoid frittering away our ground and wriggling our lines, which can only result in the destruction of the simplicity and repose of the effect, without adding anything whatever to the variety.

In deciding upon the treatment of any piece of open ground which can be devoted to a green or garden, it should first of all be clearly in the mind of the designer what the piece of ground will be available for. If it can be used only as decoration, then it should be planted from this point of view, and treated so that it must help the total effect of the scene of which it will form part. Where a large area is available it should be decided whether it is to be used as a place of repose or as a promenade, or whether, in the case of a fairly large open space, part of it may be laid out for promenading purposes, and part for rest and quiet. For promenades some openness of outlook, contrasting with occasional enclosures and portions passing through copses or shrubberies, will be attractive, while long borders planted and decorated with flowers and shrubs will add variety and interest to the walk; but in this, as in all else, the details must not be too minutely varied; the masses of each kind of treatment should be large enough and bold enough to produce a strong individual effect. The beds of each kind of flower should be generous in quantity and extent, like those of rhododendron, azalea, and iris, and the wide glades of bluebells in Kew Gardens. Compare the pleasure and interest, the total beauty and impressiveness, in passing from one to another of these groups, with that derived from ordinary park beds, in which we find the azalea and rhododendron alternating singly with one another and many other shrubs, with here and there a small clump of iris or a root of hyacinth, all mingled together in a manner destructive at once of unity of effect, and producing the maximum of monotony when spread over a large area.

Illus. 211.—Stuttgart, Schloss Platz, Standpoint I. on plan.

Illus. 212.—Stuttgart, Schloss Platz, Standpoint II. on Illus. 211.

Illus. 213.—*Burghof, Vienna, showing broad, simple use of grass and trees to decorate an open space.*

Illus. 214.—*Vienna Schlossgarten, showing broad, simple treatment in the garden lay out.*

For places devoted to repose, some sense of enclosure should be secured. Here good use may be made of the tall, trim hedge, the plain, well-kept lawn, the formal tank, the lily pond or fountain, *Illus. 96a.* the surrounding flower border restfully arranged with a corner sheltered from wind or shielded from sun, beauty not only to attract but arranged to rest rather than excite the beholder.

The children, too, should not be forgotten in the open spaces. The *kinderbank*, or low seat to suit their short legs, should always be provided, and where possible spaces of turf supplied with swings or see-saws, with ponds for sailing boats, and with sand pits where these can be kept sufficiently clean. These spaces should be either definitely enclosed so that the wear and tear of the turf may not destroy the appearance outside the enclosure, or better still, should be in the centre of stretches of grass sufficiently large for such wear and tear

Illus. 215.—Popplesdorfer Allée, Bonn.
Showing portion with simple grass.

Illus. 216.—Popplesdorfer Allée, Bonn.
Showing portion with variegated flower bed.

not to be of serious moment. But, if spaces are small, they must be devoted to one or other of these purposes, and must be designed accordingly. If they are large, variety will spring from the careful adaptation of the different parts to the different uses. The great value of water in such a scheme, as introducing life, light, and colour, should be remembered ; and where, as was arranged in one of the open spaces in the Hampstead Garden Suburb, the pond can be so placed that the rosy hues of the sunset will be reflected in the water, and be seen from different streets or groups of houses as the sun changes its setting point with the changing seasons, a natural decoration of the greatest beauty will be provided.

Where the space available already contains the natural beauty of running water, rocky ravine, heights and hollows, woods or heath, probably the designer's art will be exercised to preserve these, and to contrive ways by which the public may be taken to enjoy them

with the minimum damage to the existing beauty, rather than
to substitute some artificial scheme of his own.   Where the
space at his disposal lacks these natural attractions, then he must
create his own features of interest and beauty, and probably he will
do this best by working along some orderly and formal lines to
adapt the space for some particular purpose, or to produce upon it
some particular effect.

Where some degree of co-operation can be stimulated among the
individual owners or occupiers of groups of houses, some little consistent treatment of the garden spaces may very greatly enhance the
decorative effect of these upon the street.   Where room has not
been allowed in the road itself for trees to be planted, they might
quite well be placed immediately inside the forecourt gardens,
and by arrangement with the tenants a consistent scheme of spacing
the trees could be carried out.   On rows or groups of houses also if
each tenant would plant a vine or wistaria or some other such creeper,
and train it along the upper portion of the houses, a beautiful frieze
of decoration would result, which would at once produce an effect of
unity, and add dignity to the whole group of buildings.   The
gardener, like the architect, has fixed his eye too exclusively on the
individual plot ;. he has thought too much of the bulbs in his own
individual beds.   We need to think of the street, the district, the
town as larger wholes, and find a glorious function and a worthy
guidance for the decorative treatment of each plot and each
house in so designing them that they shall contribute to some
total effect.   For is it not a finer thing to be a part of a great whole
than to be merely a showy unit among a multitude of other units ?

VIII.—OF SITE PLANNING AND RESIDENTIAL ROADS

BETWEEN site planning and town planning there is no line of demarcation, and the main principles which govern the one would also apply to the other; but there is none the less a considerable difference between the two, and it is convenient to treat them separately, because in site planning the first consideration will be the arrangement of the buildings and the development of the site to the best advantage, whereas in town planning the first consideration must be the general convenience of the town, and the arrangement of the main roads. When the main roads have been laid down and the main traffic requirements have been provided for, the spaces left between these through roads can be developed more from the point of view of making the best of the sites for the buildings, and less from the point of view of public convenience. This, therefore, forms a real difference; and, moreover, where town planning is undertaken by municipalities it will certainly be well to leave a good deal of freedom in the matter of site planning, particularly in cases where the land is held in largish parcels, to the owners or societies who may be developing the land.

Site planning cannot be carried out successfully in too wholesale a manner, without monotony resulting. It requires a degree of thought for the individual buildings, for the aspects and minor characteristics of the site, which it is almost impossible to obtain if the land is treated in a wholesale manner.

It is only necessary to look at some of the German town plans, where the design has been carried to the extent of showing the whole of the subsidiary building roads and *places*, to see how the stock of ideas of a particular town planner, which may be very good in themselves, is hardly adequate to give variety and individual treatment to the many streets, *places*, and buildings that are required for a large town. No doubt site plans must be subject to a certain amount of guidance and approval on behalf of the town planning authority. There will at times be minor traffic roads for linking up the more important ones, even on smallish sites, and the community is clearly entitled to see that the sites are well planned on healthy and sanitary lines; but no one more readily than the town planner himself will admit that it is impossible when dealing with a plan of a very large area to take full advantage of each individual site, or to give sufficient time and play of fancy and imagination, to produce the best result. It may, indeed, be helpful when engaged in town planning, to work out tentative site plans for different areas. It may, for example, be necessary to do this to see whether the larger parcels of land, which are left between two main roads, are of such shape and size that they will cut up economically for building purposes; but such tentative schemes if prepared should be left open for revision by the site planner when he comes to deal with them. My experience has been that when the town planner himself becomes the site planner, and concentrates the whole of his thought on one portion of the site, arranging buildings and open spaces upon it, he can generally improve considerably in detail on the preliminary scheme sketched out in connection with his town plan.

In site planning a thorough study of the site and a survey of its levels, its trees, the prospects which it affords, and any features of interest it contains are as essential to success as in the case of town planning. It has been too common for site planners to work out their plans on paper only, and to save themselves trouble by clearing away trees and hedgerows, wherever these happen to come in the way of the plan. No system can be more foolish, for a new building estate, at best, looks raw and poor, the gardens empty or filled only with small struggling shrubs and plants; and nothing so helps the early appearance of a building site as the preservation of

Illus. 217, 217a, *and* 227.

existing trees, and even sometimes of existing hedgerows. Where, for example, a road can be made to run alongside a well-grown old hedgerow a beautiful decoration and a special characteristic is at once secured for that road, and a sense of privacy for the gardens, which it would take perhaps many years to secure by new growth.

In planning out a site, whether large or small, one of the first considerations should be to determine the centre point of the design. In any but very small sites there are likely to be required some buildings of a larger or more public character than the dwelling-houses—such, for example, as churches, chapels, public halls, institutes, libraries, baths, wash-houses, shops, inns or hotels, elementary and other schools; and it would probably be well, having decided which, if any, of these are likely to be required, to group them in some convenient situation, and of them to form a centre for the scheme. Churches and chapels require to be near to the population that they are to serve; they should be on fairly prominent sites, and they should not be placed sufficiently near to one another, or to other halls likely to be used on Sundays, for the singing in one to interfere with the service in another.

In the case of shops and refreshment-houses, the requirements are rather different, the essential thing being that they should front to the roadway which has, or is likely to have, the greatest amount of traffic passing to and fro. Shops, moreover, generally succeed best

Illus. 217.—Station Road, Earswick.

when in groups of a sufficient number to form what is known
among the shopkeepers as a "market"; odd shops scattered about
are not liked.   Sometimes it would be best not to attempt anything
in the way of a centre beyond a portion of wide roadway, which might *Illus.* 221,
contain shops and a few public buildings, on the lines of the main 222.
village street with which every one is familiar.   In other cases it
may be possible, while keeping the shops on the main streets, to *Illus.* 171.
develop opposite them a green or square around which some of the
other buildings may be grouped; but whatever be the form, there
can be no doubt of the importance, even on small sites, of having
some central feature up to which the design may lead.

In considering the planning of sites for residential purposes,
it will very often not be possible to aim at enclosed architectural
effects such as would be desirable in the town; the planner must
be very careful not to sacrifice to some particular effect which he
wishes to secure the convenience and pleasure of those who are to
occupy the buildings; otherwise his scheme will probably fail to be
carried out.   Beauty of surroundings forms undoubtedly one of the
main pleasures and attractions of the residential district, and it will
probably be economical to devote much thought, money, and land
to the laying out of such a site in an attractive manner, but types of
beauty must be sought which do not clash with strong prejudices or
desires on the part of future householders.   This will often lead to
a greater degree of openness in the spacing of the houses than from
a purely architectural point of view might be desirable.   But here *Illus.* 241
again it may be possible, by grouping buildings, for them all to *and* 242.
command a wider outlook and have a more general sense of space
than could be obtained by scattering them; and it may easily be
possible to reconcile those whose first idea would be to secure a
detached house in the middle of its own plot of ground, to taking
a house forming one of a group, if the grouping is so arranged that
there is obviously a considerable gain in the matter of outlook.

In site planning we at once meet with the question of formal and *Illus.* 60a,
informal treatment discussed in connection with town planning, and 51–55, 86,
much the same principles must apply here.   It is probable that the *and* 223.
variety of arrangements that may be made, on orderly lines, of
buildings and building roads is vastly greater than at first sight
one would expect.   Sufficient reasons will generally be found on
the site itself to cause or suggest irregular buildings and interesting
accidental features.   These one may welcome, and on the skilful
handling of these rest the success and beauty of the plan when
carried out; but in site planning, as in architecture, the seeking after

features for their own sake is very liable to lead to fussiness. It is far safer, whether one's plan leans to the formal or informal, to do nothing for which one has not good reasons. We may well remember the value of little open spaces, spots where folk may repair from the bustle of the street to stop and rest awhile; very small spaces may serve such purposes. Playing places for children may often be secured in the centres of building areas, which without the making of an additional and costly road would be of little value for building purposes; points too where fine views are obtained, and where the sunset can be seen, can often be preserved by the devotion of a very small area of ground and would add much to the pleasure to be obtained in the district.

Illus. 219 *and* 232.

Both in town and site planning it is important to prevent the complete separation of different classes of people which is such a feature of the English modern town. Mrs. Barnett in her writings has laid special emphasis on this point and has referred to the many evils which result from large areas being inhabited entirely by people of one limited class. Indeed, it was one of her special aims in promoting the Hampstead Garden Suburb Trust to show to how much greater extent the intermingling of the different classes might be brought about. It is not within the power of the town planner to alter the prejudices of people, or to prevent entirely the growing up of the East End and West End in a town; but a good deal may be done in this direction by care and forethought; certainly within limits, more or less wide, there is no difficulty in mingling houses of different sizes. There is nothing whatever in the prejudices of people to justify the covering of large areas with houses of exactly the same size and type. The growing up of suburbs occupied solely by any individual class is bad, socially, economically, and æsthetically. It is due to the wholesale and thoughtless character of town development, and is quite foreign to the traditions of our country; it results very often in bad municipal government and unfair distribution of the burdens of local taxation, misunderstanding and want of trust between different classes of people, and in the development and exaggeration of differences of habit and thought; it leads, too, to a dreary monotony of effect, which is almost as depressing as it is ugly. In the English village we find all classes of houses mingled along the village street or around the green, from the smallest labourer's cottage to the large house of the wealthy farmer, doctor, or local manufacturer, and even at times there is included the mansion of the lord of the manor. How much this adds to the charm of the village street may be gathered

Illus. 218.—*Hampstead Garden Suburb, Temple Fortune Hill.*

Illus. 219.—*Playing ground at Earswick.*

Illus. 220.—*Ashbourne, Derbyshire. Photo kindly taken by Mr. J. B. Pettigrew.*

Illus. 321.—Village Street, Dunster, Somersetshire, looking up.

12

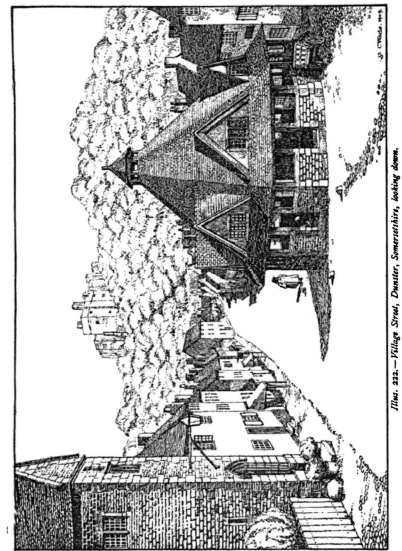

Illus. 222.—Village Street, Dunster, Somersetshire, looking down.

from the illustrations given.   If, then, the site that is being planned *Illus. 86, 221, and 222.*
is one which we expect mainly to have a working-class population,
we should still try to arrange some attractive corner in which a few *Illus. 223.*
rather larger houses may be built ; we should induce the doctor to
live among his patients by affording him a suitable site, and give an
opportunity for those who have been successful in life, and may have a
little leisure to devote to the public work of the district, to live in
suitable homes among others not so fortunate. And whether or not
we shall succeed will depend very much upon the arrangement.
We shall not, for example, expect to let plots for larger houses if
the approach is arranged along a street of the smallest type of
cottages.

In arranging our site plan we must keep in mind economy in the
length and gradient of the roads, facility for drainage, and such
practical matters.   Where a road can be made to run at the bottom
of a hollow, the arrangement will be found economical and satisfactory in many ways ; the houses on each side being on ground slightly
above the road, a minimum depth of drain will be required ; while any
surplus material arising from the excavation can usually be spread
upon the road without raising it above the level of the houses.
Roads following the lines of natural drainage are, therefore, from
these practical points of view desirable, and difficulties of dealing
with surface water will likely be avoided ; where, on the other hand,
roads run across hollows, they are likely to need filling and cutting,
excessive depth of drain, excessive depth of foundations for the
buildings where they face the banked portions of the road, and considerable expense for retaining walls and steps where the buildings
face the cuttings.   Where roads run along the hillside, it is usual
to cut one side and fill the other, and this is probably the most
economical arrangement from the point of view of the road itself ;
but it is wise to do more cutting than filling, and even more
economical on roads intended for residences, particularly if the
removal of the surplus material is easily manageable.   In roads on
the side of a hill the sewer must be laid deep enough to drain the
houses on the low side ; this adds considerably to the expense, while
the plots on the low side are of less value because either the house
will stand below the level of the road, which is not usually thought *Illus. 224.*
desirable ; or it must be raised at considerable expense of extra
foundation ; it would therefore be wise to err on the side of
cutting such roads to greater depth than would be done if the first
cost of the road were alone considered.

The sites which stand above the road gain in attractiveness,

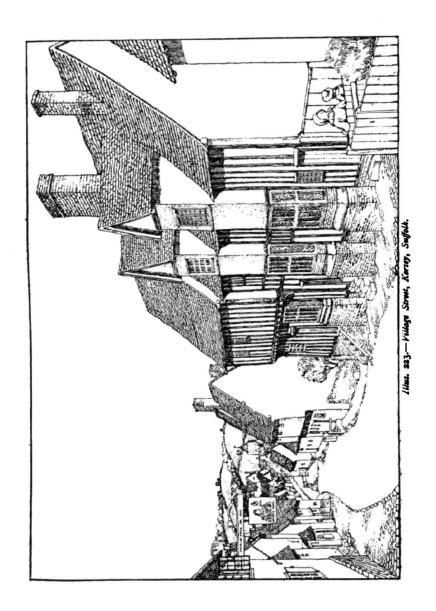

Illus. 223.—*Village Street, Kersey, Suffolk.*

except in the cases of large houses where a carriage drive is
required, so that the cost of a retaining wall is not resented
by the plot-holder in the same way that he is apt to resent
the cost of extra foundations.

The question of the character of building roads in this country
certainly requires much re-consideration.   There are two circumstances which have complicated the situation.   First, the width
of roads has been used, under our form of building bye-laws, to
determine the distance between the houses, and as a means of
securing a greater degree of open space than would otherwise
be obtained.   The result is that the widths of roads under the
bye-laws commonly in force in the English towns, are not regulated

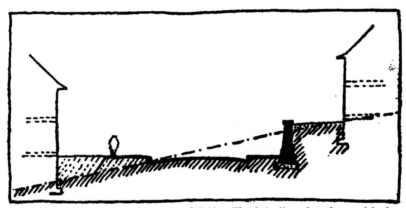

Illus. 224.—Cross-section of a road on hillside. The chain lines show the actual level
of the ground.

with regard to requirements of traffic, a minimum width for
streets is arbitrarily fixed, 40 to 50 feet being usual, and all
roads are required to be laid out at least this width ; usually there
is no power for the local authority to require greater width,
although 40 to 50 feet is as utterly inadequate for the main
roads of a town as it is excessive for the purpose of giving access
to a few cottages.   As a consequence, roads have to be widened
at vast expense to allow for trams and for traffic, while cottages
are built fronting to dreary wastes of asphalte and macadam, one
half of which could with great advantage be added to their gardens
or laid out as grass margin.

The second condition which greatly influences the character of our roads is that the cost of their construction is borne by the owners or lessees of the land and frontages, while the cost of maintenance, after they have become public roads, is borne by the local authority.   The result of this is that in order to reduce as much as possible the liability of the public for maintenance, all roads are required to be finished in the most expensive and durable manner, irrespective of whether the traffic on them is likely to require or justify such expense.   It is, of course, right and proper that roads should be sufficiently substantially made to carry their probable traffic, with a reasonable cost for upkeep; but the fact that the capital outlay is stipulated for by the party that pays for the upkeep and does not pay the first cost, has resulted in a very great waste of capital on roads where such outlay is neither justified by the requirements nor necessary to bring the upkeep within reasonable limits.   A large residential hotel, a mansion such as Chatsworth or Blenheim, will be adequately served by a simple carriage drive from 13 to 20 feet wide.   The population of such a building will be larger than that of a row or group of cottages and the amount of wheel traffic to and from it many times as great; yet for the cottage road asphalte or concrete paved footpaths, granite kerbs and channel, and granite macadamised surface, the whole from 40 to 50 ft. wide, and costing, with the sewers, &c., from £5 to £8 a lineal yard, are required by the local authority, under our existing bye-laws.   It will be seen at once how this excessive cost tends to limit the frontage of the houses.   Where an attempt is being made to build cottages under £200 in cost, the charge of £3 per yard for the half-share of the road becomes a serious matter, and the houses must suffer, both in size and frontage, to quite an unnecessary extent.   Where traffic is likely to be heavy, and where the building roads will serve also to link up main roads or be likely in the future to develop into main roads, suitable provision must, of course, be made.   But where, as frequently happens, it is virtually certain that the road will only be used for the daily visits of the milkman's cart and the daily rounds of the coal merchant's van or the doctor's gig, it is clear that a well-made track, more of the nature of a gentleman's carriage drive, with a grass margin on each side, and in some cases a simple gravel or paved footway of narrow width, for use in wet weather, is all that need be demanded; and that with the small amount of traffic coming down such a road, the maintenance against wear and tear would be no

Illus. 217.

Illus. 225 *and* 226.

Illus. 227.

Illus. 225.—*Poplar Grove, Earswick. Published by courtesy of Mr. F. W. Sutcliffe, Whitby.*

Illus. 226.—*Poplar Grove, Earswick, showing a simple and economical treatment of road.*
Published by courtesy of Mr. F. W. Sutcliffe, Whitby.

Illus. 227.—*Asmuns Place, Hampstead Garden Suburb. A carriage drive used in place of an expensive road. Photo by Mr. J. P. Steele, Stoke-upon-Trent.*

Illus. 227a.—*Hampstead Way, showing entrance to Asmuns Place. Photo taken by* **Mr. J. P. Steele, Stoke-upon-Trent.**

greater than in the case of the vastly more costly road usually required.

The cost of roads varies very much, according to the price of material and labour in the district, and according to the requirements of the local authorities. In some cases a separate system of drainage is provided for surface water, which of course adds heavily to the cost, though it is probably a most desirable arrangement from the point of view of sewage treatment. The authorities in some districts permit the sewers to be laid in the roads at depths as shallow as will allow for the reasonable drainage of the houses to be built. In other districts greater minimum depths are required to provide against future contingencies, and to protect the pipes from possible injuries, owing to the passage of traction engines and other heavy traffic. In some districts drains are allowed to be laid in the ground without concrete ; in others a bed of concrete under the drains is required, while in some places drains need to be entirely surrounded by concrete. These and many other such details affect the cost of roads so that it is not possible to give any estimate. Further, it must always be remembered that the cost of a road may mean one of two things—either the construction of the road in accordance with the bye-laws for the purposes of building, or this, plus the cost of making up the road to suit the standard of perfection which will be expected when the road is taken over by the local authorities. The owners or lessees of the plots fronting to the road are legally liable for this latter expense. It is usual for the land-owner who lets out the site to bear the first cost, but custom varies considerably as to how much of the work is included in the first cost and how much in the second. Sometimes the road is so thoroughly made up to begin with that the subsequent cost is reduced to a minimum. At other times the preliminary making up of the road is only carried to such an extent as will give an effective cartage road for building operations ; and the kerb and channel are laid, and any paving and asphalting to the footpaths carried out after the road is built up, and when it is about to be taken over by the local authorities. Where building operations are being carried out on an extensive scale by the same person or body who is responsible for the making of the roads, probably it is better to be content with the simple building road in the first instance, and to make up the road properly once and for all when the buildings are completed, and it is about to be taken over ; it is often found when a road has been pretty thoroughly made in

the first instance and some time elapses before it is taken over, that
it is so damaged by the building operations—kerbs and channels
chipped and displaced, and the surface so deeply scored with ruts—
that the local authorities practically re-make the surface, re-lay
kerbs and channels, &c., before they will accept the road, which
entails a very heavy cost.   In some districts, however, building
operations are not allowed to be commenced until the road is made
and the kerb and channel laid, and in these cases there appears to be
no option to the builder in the matter.   The whole question of the
apportionment of the costs of construction and maintenance of
roads and their character seems to need thorough investigation,

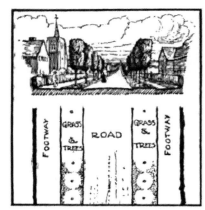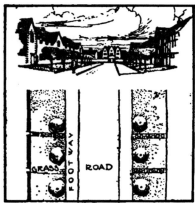

*Illus. 228.—Examples of lighter building roads and drives as used at Earswick, Letchworth,
and Hampstead.*

and it is to be hoped that the interest in such matters roused
by the town planning movement will result in this being done.
To meet this difficulty to some extent the Hampstead Garden
Suburb Trust obtained an Act of Parliament (the main clauses of
which are given in "Practical Housing" by J. S. Nettlefold), under
which the width of road to be constructed according to bye-laws
was limited to 40 feet, and the Trust were allowed if they made
their roads of greater width than 40 feet, to devote the extra
space to grass margins in which trees could be planted.   At the
time the Act was passed the local bye-laws fixed 40 feet as the
minimum width for all roads, but new bye-laws were being prepared
in which 50 feet was fixed as the minimum.   Another clause
allowed the Trust to construct roads not exceeding 500 feet in

length of a width of 20 feet, provided that the houses on each side of such roads should not be nearer to one another than 50 feet. By the same Act, on the other hand, the Trust agreed to limit the number of houses to the acre, on the average over the whole of the estate, to 8. This Act suggests that the local authorities might offer an inducement to landowners, and others developing estates, to limit the number of houses to the acre by offering concessions in the matter of road construction. Reference to the Hampstead Suburb plan will show that these *Illus. 228a* short roads have been extensively used and have led to the formation of many groups of houses around greens, tennis-courts, and *Fold Map* squares which could not practically have been arranged without *VI.*

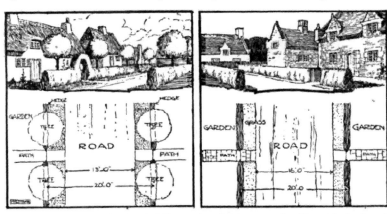

Illus. 228a.—Examples of lighter building roads and drives as used at Earswick, Letchworth, and Hampstead.

the powers given under this Act. It will be seen from the Act that it is not intended that these roads should be taken over by the local authorities, and although 20 feet is dedicated for the purpose of the road, in many cases a carriage drive of 13 or 14 feet is all that it is intended to construct. Many of the main roads in the suburb will exceed the minimum of 40 feet, some being 50 feet and some 60 feet, and in these cases usually grass margins planted with trees will be provided. Special concessions have also been made with regard to the character of the roads on the estate of the Harborne tenants in Birmingham. In other cases—as, for example, in the village of Earswick, near York, and at the Garden City at Letchworth—no bye-laws as to the character of roads and streets

Illus. 228,
228a, *b, and*
c.

have been in force, and it has there been possible to experiment
with roads of various characters and widths, illustrations of many
of which are given.

The direction of the building roads must be considered from every
point of view, besides that of drainage and convenience of construction. The question of the aspect of the buildings is an
important one, and here the site planner is often in the difficulty
of being obliged to lay out the roads without knowing, or having
any control over, the character of the buildings which will be placed
upon them. In such cases there is no doubt that roads having their
direction mainly north and south have a very great advantage in

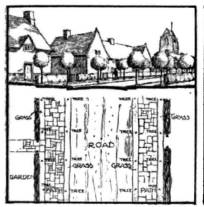
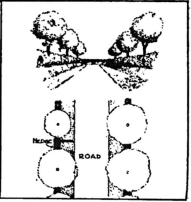

Illus. 228*b*.   *Illus.* 228*c*.
Examples of lighter building roads and drives as used at Earswick, Letchworth, and Hampstead.

that the houses will have a fair amount of sunshine on both their
open·sides. Where roads run east and west the houses will get
more sun on the south side, but, on the other hand, the north sides
will get but little in the summer and none in the winter. Many
people desire a south front to their house, and roads having a
general direction east and west are desirable from this point of
view, if the buildings can be arranged and planned accordingly.
Houses with a south aspect need a greater frontage, as all the
best rooms should be on the south side, and in the case of houses
on the south side of the road which have a north aspect, there is,
especially with small houses and cottages, the difficulty that the
front of the house should be to the garden. Without very
careful planning this is liable to result in untidy backs to the

road, but with care may result in a most attractive type of
house, having its best rooms overlooking the garden and away
from the dust and noise of the street. It is probably best,
on the whole, that the roads should not be cut quite due east
and west, so that either in the early morning or in the late afternoon during the greater part of the year the sun may shine on the
more northerly side of the buildings. The relative advantages
of a southern outlook and of an east and west outlook will vary

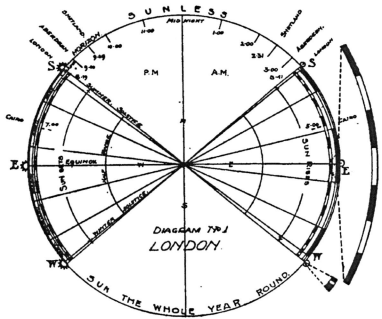

Illus. 229.—*Diagram I., contrasting the sunrise and sunset amplitudes through the seasons
at London and other places, with details enlarged 20 times, comparing the daily
sections at the equinox and solstices. The above diagram is taken from the Rational
Almanac, by Mr. M. B. Cotsworth, and is published with his kind permission.*

according to the latitude of the house. Taking the latitude of
London, it will be seen from the diagrams given that for the few *Illus.* 229.
winter months the advantage of the south front is very great, but *Diagrams I,*
that for the remainder of the year an east and west aspect secures a *II, III.*
very large amount of sunshine on both sides of the house, and has
the advantage of giving sunny and shady rooms for both morning
and afternoon, and avoiding the excessive heat of the midday sun.

A reference to Illustration 229, Diagram III., will show that on Midsummer Day the sun, when unclouded, from 4 a.m. to 10 a.m. would be shining well into an east window, while from 2 p.m. to 8 p.m. it would be shining into a west window; so that for six hours in the morning and six hours in the evening a house facing east and west would have the sun shining into it. On the other hand, a house facing due south would receive little sun before 9 a.m. and little after 3 p.m. Also, owing to the height of the sun above the horizon during these hours, it would penetrate less into the rooms. One would expect that there would be no difference between the amount of sunshine in the morning and in the afternoon, but from the following table it appears that there is rather more sunshine

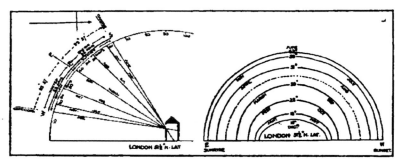

Illus. 229 —*Diagram II., showing relative elevation and approximate path of the sun above the horizon in the different months of the year in the latitude of London, and the meridian section showing the relative elevation of the sun at mid-day. The above diagram is taken from the Rational Almanac, by Mr. M. B. Cotsworth, and is published by his kind permission.*

recorded after noon than before noon in this country. Taking into account also that the sunshine before 8 a.m. is little enjoyed. while that from 4 p.m. to 8 p.m. is perhaps the most enjoyed, it would seem that some preference might well be given to a west over an east aspect. While, therefore, taking the whole year round, there can be no doubt that an aspect south or slightly west of south may be considered the most desirable for dwelling rooms, it will be found that where dwelling rooms must be placed on both sides of the house, ample sunshine would be secured with an east and west aspect through the greater part of the year, and that during the summer months a considerable amount of sunshine would penetrate windows facing somewhat north of east or west.

Table showing relative Duration in Hours per Annum of actual Sunshine before and after Noon recorded at four Stations, the Average for fifteen Years being taken.

	Valencia.	Aberdeen.	Falmouth.	Kew.
Before noon	700·46	655·88	840·87	700·23
After noon	758·55	682·66	895·02	760·64

In France, where a road runs north and south and it is desired

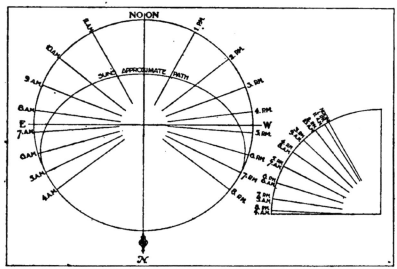

Illus. 229.—Diagram III., showing the approximate path of the sun and its position at each hour of the day on Midsummer Day, with a vertical section giving the altitude at different hours.

to give the houses a southern frontage, one often sees little rows of houses placed with their ends to the road, access being obtained by a simple pathway. It would seem desirable to modify the usual *Illus.* 230. form of building bye-laws to allow of this arrangement, under certain restrictions as to the number of houses and as to the *Illus.* 220. distance apart of the rows. We shall refer to the matter of aspect again in dealing with the setting out of the building plots; meantime another consideration must be borne in mind, namely, that of the wind. It is certainly not desirable to have too many roads following unbroken for any considerable distance the line

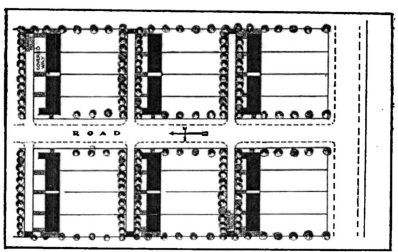

Illus. 230.—*Diagram showing arrangement of groups of houses at right angles to a road to secure a southern aspect.*

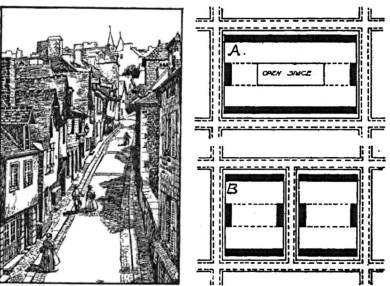

Illus. 231.—*Sketch showing picturesque treatment of steep street at Dinan.*

Illus. 232.—*A shows area with cross road omitted. B shows extra cross road not justified by frontage gained.*

Illus. 233 — Verona. Castello S. Pietro.

Illus. 234.—Bad modern treatment of steep street.

Illus. 234a.—Hampstead Garden Suburb. Street terminal and built-up corner. See Illus. 235 and 254.

of the prevailing winds, or of those winds which are likely to be violent or to produce excessive dust.   Here, again, local conditions must be borne in mind, though, speaking generally for this country, south-west is probably the prevailing direction of the wind.   A diagram is given showing the extent and average intensity of the different winds in four districts.   *Illus.* 101.

In undulating or hilly countries the question of the gradients of the roads will very largely influence their direction.   On a main traffic road a gradient greater than 1 in 30 may be regarded as a disadvantage, though for short distances steeper gradients may not be a serious drawback, and building roads with steeper gradients may be used where sufficient reason exists.   In some districts the special charm of the site may be its elevation, and it may be desirable to emphasise this by carrying certain roads and ways straight up the hillside, with little or no regard to the steepness of the gradient. Undoubtedly one finds in old towns many beautiful examples of such steep streets, as at Clovelly in our own country, and at Dinan in France.   *Illus.* 231.

The steep street, however, adds very greatly to the difficulties of   *Illus.* 233. building, and although the clever handling of problems due to these difficulties may lead to very beautiful and picturesque results, there is no doubt that the common methods of dealing with buildings on steep sites by means of a number of repeated steps or jumps in the roof, or still worse by means of the sloping line of roof which is carried   *Illus.* 234. parallel to the road instead of being kept square with the floor line, are so unsatisfactory that it would be prudent to avoid aiming at the special effects to be derived from steepness, unless one is fairly sure that the designing of the buildings will fall into capable hands. In places where small subsidiary roads can be used—and one must hope that all places may soon be included in this category—it may even be wise where a main road runs through a building estate to arrange the houses so that most of them front on to such subsidiary drives, only a few having a frontage direct to the main road.   The character of modern traffic, particularly the present character of motor traffic, has rendered frontage to the main   *Illus.* 275 road anything but desirable for residence ; the dust, the noise, the   *and* 276. smell are all objectionable features ; and though at first sight it may seem extravagant not to make use of the main frontage, it would not be found so in practice, the subsidiary roads costing comparatively little.   Moreover, it is not possible to utilise the whole of the frontage both on the main and the cross roads to the utmost extent, and if the frontage on the smaller side roads is more desirable, little will be lost by sacrificing a portion of the main road frontage.

With reference to the desirability of straight or curved roads little need be added to what has already been said with regard to the main roads of the town, except that in the planning of sites for residential purposes greater freedom of treatment may well be adopted, the stateliness which may be desirable for the treatment of the central portions of the town not being appropriate very often to the residential district. The width apart of the buildings on residential sites will tend to give greater freedom in the treatment of the street pictures; and where the streets are planted with trees and the houses set back considerably from the road, a good deal of freedom may be taken in the treatment of the two sides; but whatever the character of the street, it is of the utmost importance to avoid mere aimless wiggles.

IX.—OF PLOTS AND THE SPACING AND PLACING OF BUILDINGS AND FENCES

IN dealing with the laying out of building roads, we have incidentally referred to the size of the plots required as a determining factor, but for convenience did not in that chapter consider the matter in detail. It is necessary first to decide upon the approximate number of houses which are to be built to the acre.

Under the modern urban bye-laws as adopted in most English towns the number of houses to the acre is only limited by the regulations which fix, first, the minimum width of streets ; secondly, *Illus.* 2. the minimum space allowed to be left at the back of buildings.

The first bye-law provides in effect for an open space varying in different districts from 36 feet to 50 feet in front of the building, not exclusively belonging to it ; this space is usually occupied by road and footways. The second bye-law usually requires at least 150 square feet at the rear of the building, and in addition requires that the open space shall extend to the full width of the building, and shall be not less in any case than 10 feet in depth where the building does not exceed 10 feet in height. The depth of the open space increases in proportion to the height of the building, reaching a maximum under the old bye-laws of 25 feet for a building 25 feet high, in some of the newer bye-laws going up to 40 feet for a building exceeding 35 feet in height. It will be seen that for cottages, which usually do not exceed 25 feet in height, the maximum depth of open space at the rear usually secured by the modern bye-laws is 25 feet. With the narrow frontages usually adopted for small cottages, it is possible under these bye-laws to crowd as many as 50 houses to the acre or even more. There can be no doubt that this number is altogether excessive for reasonable health and comfort ; it provides for no garden ground, only a small back yard attached to each cottage.

It is not possible to fix any absolute limit for the number of houses to the acre which can be regarded as a maximum compatible with health and comfort. Very much depends upon the size of the houses and their arrangement. It is not easy yet to weigh the disadvantages that might arise from enlarging our towns to such an extent as would give a much lower number of houses to the acre all through, but one may safely say that, according to circumstances, the desirable number would be between 10 and 20 houses to the acre, and in this case I refer to the net measurement of the building land, excluding roads. There will necessarily be areas in the centre of towns where buildings will be crowded to a greater extent than this

13

figure would suggest ; but in any district where cottages are likely to be built it should not be necessary to exceed the maximum number of 20, and wherever possible the number should be reduced to 10 or 12. Twelve houses to the net acre of building land, excluding all roads, has been proved to be about the right number to give gardens of sufficient size to be of commercial value to the tenants—large enough, that is, to be worth cultivating seriously for the sake of the profits, and not too large to be worked by an ordinary labourer and his family.   There will, of course, be men who can work more, and men who can only work much less, but in the laying out of the land there are sure to occur great varieties in the size of the individual gardens which will allow for these differences, and it is only the average number of houses to the acre that needs to be very carefully considered from the point of view of health, the exact size of each garden being a matter of comparative indifference.   This figure of 1·2 houses to the acre has now been fairly well tested, having been adopted in the main at Bournville (although here there are some larger gardens), at Earswick, at the Garden City at Letchworth, at Hampstead, and at many other places.   That a greater number of houses to the acre than 12 may be planned, and yet produce a healthy suburb is proved on

Illus. 169.   the estate of the Ealing Tenants and many others.   On some parts of the estate at Ealing the houses approach 20 to the acre, excluding roads and larger open spaces reserved for recreation grounds.   A

Illus. 235.   comparison of the plan with that of the industrial quarter of the Hampstead Garden Suburb, for example, will at once show the difference produced in the size of the gardens and the degree of openness by the extra number of houses.   One of the difficulties of the usual open space bye-law is that it takes no account whatever of the size of the building ; the large hotel or boarding-house, covering perhaps a quarter of an acre in extent, cannot usually be compelled by the local authorities to reserve any greater space around it than a strip of 25 feet at the back.   In fixing from 10 to 20 houses to the acre as something like the right number, cottages only were considered.

In order to meet this difficulty, when framing the Garden City Building Regulations which are at present enforced under the terms of the lease and are not bye-laws in the ordinary sense, additional provisions were made by which the number to the acre varied in accordance with the value and presumably the size of the houses.   A further regulation provided that as a general rule in the case of dwelling-houses not more than one-sixth of any site should be covered by the buildings, some exception being allowed in shop and corner sites, and in a few other

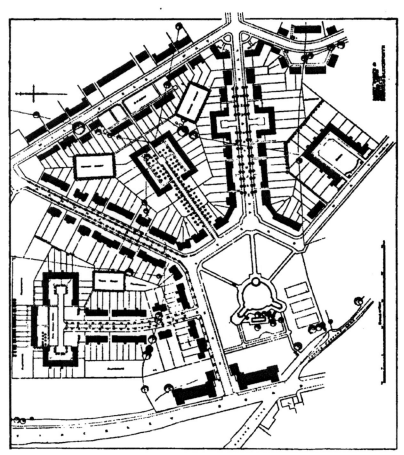

Illus. 235.—Part of Hampstead Garden Suburb developed by the Hampstead Tenants, Limited, and laid out for cottages.

cases. Taking this rule of one-sixth of the site being covered by buildings, it will be seen from the following table the building area which is permissible on sites of the following sizes :—

Schedule showing Area of Plots with Building Area for each.

Size of plot in fraction of acre	1	1/2	1/3	1/4	1/5	1/6	1/7	1/8	1/10	1/12	1/15	1/20
Area of plot in yards	4,840	2,420	1,613	1,210	968	807	691	605	484	403	323	242
Building area in yards at ⅙ of plot	807	403	269	202	161	134	115	101	81	67	54	40

For one-twelfth of an acre this would give a square measuring about 24 feet each way, which is larger than is usually occupied by small cottages.

Illus. 236.—Provins, showing the advantage of a framed view and a pleasant curved street line.

Having determined generally the class of house to be built and the number to the acre, the next point to determine is the most suitable shape for the plots, bearing in mind that economy in road-making would suggest narrow plots and great depth, but that the apparent economy of this arrangement is greater than the actual economy, owing to the fact that the cross roads become longer, and that with this arrangement they have little value for building purposes. The frontage required must, of course, depend on the size of the house and on its arrangement. There can be no doubt that the usual

Illus. 237.   *Illus. 238.*
Typical projecting Backs, showing extent of projections and narrow width between them.

Illus. 239.—Hampstead Garden Suburb. View of the Backs of some of the Hampstead Tenants' Cottages. Contrast Illus. 237 and 238.

frontages allowed in suburban districts are too small, and this fact, *Illus. 2.*
taken in conjunction with the particular form of the space bye-law *Illus. 237.*
adopted in this country, has resulted in a very objectionable type *Illus. 238.*
of house with long projections running out behind. To avoid these *Illus. 239.*
projections greater frontage is required. In the case of cottages this *Illus. 240.*
should rarely, if ever, be less than 15 feet, which will allow a cottage
having a living room, kitchen, and two bedrooms to be fairly com-
fortably planned. Where three bedrooms are required a frontage
of from 18 to 20 feet is desirable. For the type of cottage having
a living room, parlour, and scullery, with three bedrooms over,
frontages should be from 20 to 23 feet, if the aspect of the house
is east and west or thereabouts, and from 25 to 28 feet if it is
north and south. For where the aspect of the cottage is east
and west one of the living rooms may face each way with advantage, but where it is nearly due north and south both the living
rooms at any rate should be on the sunny side of the house. For
this a frontage of 25 feet suffices where the entrance is on the
north side of the house, or where, as in the case of semi-detached
houses, it can be at the side; but it will only serve where the
entrance must be on the south side by using one of the living
rooms as a passage room. Unless the houses are to be built
in long, continuous rows, allowance must be made in addition for
spaces between the groups of houses and for a certain loss of
frontage which must always take place at the corners of roads. By
reference to the table which is appended, giving the frontages of *See page* 327.
rectangular plots, with varying depths and a varying number of
houses to the acre, it will be seen that with plots 150 feet deep and
12 houses to the acre an average frontage of 24 feet is obtained.
If the cross roads are planned in such a way that some advantage
can be taken of their frontage also to make up rather more than is
lost at the corners, and if the types of house can be mixed, giving
some of shorter frontage and some of longer, I have found that
this is a very good general depth to aim at for cottages, where from
10 to 12 to the acre are required. The depth is also a good one
for rather larger houses where not more than 8 or 10 to the acre
are to be built; so that where building roads are running nearly
parallel for any considerable distance a space of 300 feet or 100
yards between the roads will be found very often a convenient one
to leave. If the space is increased much beyond this, the houses are
apt to be short of frontage for comfortable planning, unless the
number to the acre is greatly reduced. On the other hand, if the
space is much reduced, any variation in the grouping of the houses

o

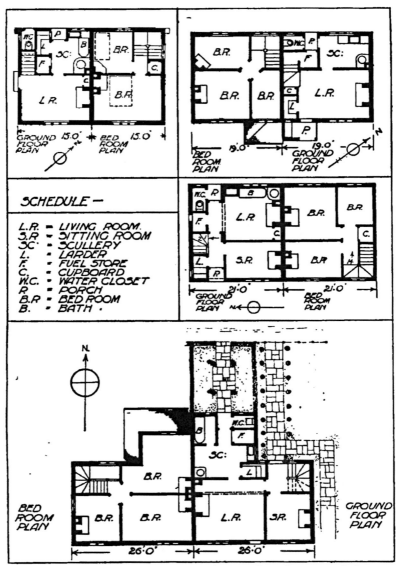

SCHEDULE —

L.R. = LIVING ROOM.
S.R. = SITTING ROOM
SC· = SCULLERY
L. = LARDER
F. = FUEL STORE
C. = CUPBOARD
W.C. = WATER CLOSET
R. = PORCH
B.R. = BED ROOM
B. = BATH·

Illus. 240.—Examples of cottage plans showing different frontages required.

is apt to bring them too near together at the back. Very often, however, the spaces enclosed by roads will be uneven in shape.

TABLE B.

Frontages of rectangular Plots of different Depths.

Depth of Plot in feet.	100	120	125	130	135	140	145	150
Size of Plot in feet.								
1 Acre	435·6	363	348·4	335	322	311	300	290·4
½ ,,	217·8	181·5	174·16	167·5	161	155·5	150	145·2
⅓ ,,	145·2	121	116·16	111·6	107·3	103·6	100	98·8
¼ ,,	108·9	90·75	87·12	83·75	80·5	77·75	75	72·6
⅕ ,,	87·12	72·6	69·7	67	64·4	62·2	60	58·08
⅙ ,,	72·6	60·5	58·08	55·83	53·3	51·83	50	48·4
⅐ ,,	62·23	51·86	49·78	45	46	44·428	42·8	41·49
⅛ ,,	54·43	45·37	43·56	41·875	40·25	38·875	37·5	36·3
1/10 ,,	43·56	36·3	34·84	33·5	32·2	31·1	30	29·04
1/12 ,,	36·3	30·25	29·04	27·91	26·83	25·91	25	24·2
1/15 ,,	29·04	24·2	23·23	22·3	21·46	20·73	20	19·36
1/20 ,,	21·78	18·15	17·42	16·65	16·1	15·55	15	14·52

It is quite a mistake to suppose that it is always economical to put the maximum number of houses which can be contrived on any space. This will be seen from the diagrams here given. Cases *Illus.* 232. may frequently occur where the loss of ground to provide an additional cross road to open up the centre of some area of land, and the cost of the road itself, when taken together are not compensated for by the increased value of the central area of land thus developed, and it may often be wiser to reduce slightly the number of houses to the acre rather than to cut up the land with too many roads. In the example given, a parcel of land measuring 600 feet by 400 feet is taken; and assuming that a suitable depth for the plots would be 150 feet, it will be seen that there is in the centre of this parcel of land an area 300 feet by 100 feet undeveloped by the road frontages already provided. If an additional cross road is made of the width of 45 feet, we first lose on each of the main roads a frontage of at least this extent and possibly of a greater, if the houses are required to be set back on cross roads to a building line behind the frontage. We shall, secondly, lose land amounting to ·45 of an acre which, at £300 per acre, would represent £135. We should have to make 400 feet of new road, which would cost, let us say, 30s. per foot, or £600, making a total money cost of £735. It will be seen from the above that unless we can increase the value of our land by more than £735 we shall gain nothing whatever by making the road, and might just as well have left the open space in the centre to be used as a recreation or allotment ground, from which at any rate some revenue could have been obtained.

Of course where inexpensive, subsidiary roads such as have been used in the Hampstead Garden Suburb estate are allowed, it would be possible to utilise this area of land to form a green in front of the houses on the main road, thus producing an attractive feature in the road, and at the same time securing an additional number of houses by the increased frontage provided around the green.

The necessity for greater frontage on plots where the houses will face nearly due north or south, applies to larger villas just as it does to cottages, and for much the same reasons. On roads where the houses must face north or south it may be a great advantage to frequently break the building line, setting it backward or forward so that for many houses there may be an additional open side provided on the east or west. Where this can be done sufficient sunshine to keep the less important rooms of the house healthy may often be admitted from the east or west, enabling the north side of the house to be effectively utilised. It will already be apparent how very important it is when laying out building plots to consider the plans of the houses likely to be erected upon them ; and important as this is in the case of large plots for large houses, it becomes even more important in the case of smaller plots for cottages, where the possibilities of the site are so much reduced, and there is so much less probability of any individual treatment being given. So much, indeed, is site planning bound up with the planning of the buildings, that to secure the best result possible from any site the architect who plans it should be in close co-operation with the designer of the buildings, or should himself design them. Where this can be arranged the laying out of the land may be done with some degree of certainty that the aims of the site planner will be realised. Many things may then be attempted and successfully carried through which it would not be wise to attempt in cases where the site planner's work ends with the laying out of the plots, and the buildings have to be left in the hands of individual builders or architects who may have little knowledge of or respect for the particular aims of the man who planned the site. But

Illus. 277.

Illus. 272.

whoever the site is planned by, and however necessary it may be to sacrifice possibilities in the placing of buildings in favour of more customary methods which will be more likely to be carried out by the local builder, it is the buildings which must be the primary consideration in laying out the site; so much so that the designer, if he is wise, will lay out his buildings roughly, not only before he considers the division of his plots, but before he fixes the exact lines of his roads. If he is content with merely cutting up his spaces into what he will call "lettable" plots, there is little likelihood of any beautiful result or satisfactory grouping of the buildings which will be placed on them. Having laid down approximately the position of the roads, the right placing of the buildings must then command his attention; he must decide on the main building lines and masses, placing any important features in his design, such as the terminal feature at the end of a road, or any buildings required to limit the size and give a sense of frame to the street picture which he is dealing with. *Illus.* 236, Having placed his buildings roughly and decided on the general 256, 257. picture which he is desirous of obtaining, it will be time enough then to consider the plotting of the land, working from these important and fixed points. It is usually easy to adapt the boundary lines of the plots to suit the buildings, much easier than to adapt the arrangement of the buildings to any preconceived plot lines. The planner, having considered the placing of his buildings with a view to the street pictures and the frontage lines, must not forget the spaces behind the buildings. Nothing more thoroughly expresses the shoddy character of our modern town development and the meanness of the motives which have inspired it than the treatment of the spaces at the backs of buildings. It seems to be forgotten that from all the houses around such a space the outlook of the inhabitants must be on to the backs of their neighbours' houses opposite, but just because these are not seen from the public street outside all attempt to make them even passably decent according to the excessively low standard which governs the fronts of such buildings has been neglected. The removal of the excessive back projections will of itself be a great improvement, but a little care in the arrangement of the houses and in their design may very often make the spaces at the backs as beautiful as or even more beautiful than the fronts. For one *Illus.* 239. thing, there is generally a sense of enclosure already secured in the backs of the houses which lends itself to producing satisfactory architectural effects with very simple treatment.

In residential districts the site planner must not only give much thought to the buildings themselves, but must try to secure an attractive outlook from them, which can be done to some extent by beautifying the streets and the spaces between the houses. But few who can afford to obtain a house with some distant outlook from its windows choose to live in one the outlook from which is limited by the houses on the other side of the street; and it is for the site planner who is engaged in laying out sites for smaller houses,

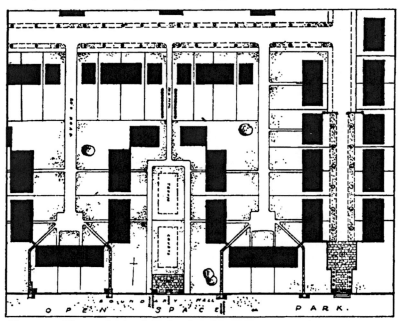

Illus. 241.—*Diagram showing how the view of an open space may be secured to a large number of houses, also how the land may be developed by roads at the back of the houses.*

where each cannot stand in large grounds of its own, to secure for as many as possible of these houses some extent of outlook by arranging breaks in the street line, by setting the houses back round greens, by planning his roads so that they may command some distant view or may lead on to some open space; and wherever a specially fine view is obtainable, by grouping as many of the houses as possible so that they may enjoy it. Definite breaks may also be left between buildings, and in fact, if only this

matter is kept well in the mind of the planner when he is laying
out his sites, there are numerous ways in which some extent of
outlook may be secured, and the architect who is impressed
with the importance, architecturally, of securing close grouping
of his buildings and a sense of enclosure for his street picture must
not let himself be carried away by these ideas, but must remember
that some sacrifice of the sense of enclosure may well be justified
if thereby a pleasanter outlook may be obtained from the windows
of the houses.   It is, however, by a combination of the two
principles that the most successful results may be obtained.   By

Illus. 242.—*Hampstead Garden Suburb.   Sketch showing group of houses round a green.*
See Illus. 241 *and Fold Map VI.*
Being built by The Garden Suburb Development Company (Hampstead), Limited.

combining the houses into groups at certain points and producing
satisfactory effects, it will be found possible to leave a greater degree
of openness at other points where enclosure may not be required.
For example, there may exist some large open space, and instead
of building semi-detached villas facing this, thus confining the
enjoyment of it to one row of houses, which by their detachment
would produce little architectural effect, an alternative arrangement
may be adopted by which spaces may be left in the frontage line
of buildings varying from 50 feet to 150 feet in width, and
groups of houses may be laid out around drives or roads at right   *Illus.* 241
angles to the open space, and in this way the view of it may be   *and* 242.
extended to a greatly increased number of houses, while at the
same time some definite grouping of the buildings may be obtained
as seen from the open space itself.

The plan of the Hampstead Garden Suburb shows various ways in which the view of the Hampstead Heath Extension has been secured to a great number of houses not built on the plots immediately fronting on to the space itself. Most of these arrangements have been rendered possible by the special powers obtained by the Hampstead Garden Suburb, allowing them under certain conditions to use carriage-drives to give access to groups of houses, in the place of ordinary roads as required under the bye-laws. Other examples will be seen on this plan of breaks arranged in

Fold Map VI.

Illus. 277 and 280.

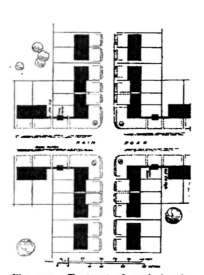

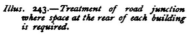

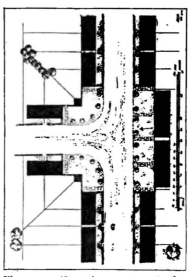

Illus. 243.—Treatment of road junction where space at the rear of each building is required.

Illus. 244.—Alternative arrangement where greens are left at the corners.

the road lines by means of greens or small cross roads, by which there is secured for a great number of houses a much more extended outlook than if it were limited by the distance to the houses immediately across the street. Many groups of houses have also been arranged to command the view down roads, at the same time using the buildings as terminal features in the street pictures; an arrangement which adds to the beauty of the roads themselves, while making the houses more attractive on account of their more extended views. Both on account of the houses themselves and in order to produce a satisfactory effect in the streets, special attention must be given to

Illus. 261, 262, 264.

the planning of the buildings at street junctions and the bends of
the roads. The usual modern bye-laws as to open space, requiring
as they do that this space shall be at the rear of the building, and
making little or no provision for corner sites, has resulted in the
production of the most unsatisfactory treatment of street corners;
and their ugliness has been exaggerated by the want of care in the
treatment of the ends of the buildings at the corners of side streets. *Illus. 260*
Some liberty should be allowed in the treatment of corner-sites. As *and 260a.*
the building has usually two open sides, a very small amount of air-
space at the rear is all that is necessary to secure through ventilation.

Illus. 245.—Sketch showing effect of junction planned as Illus. 244.

Where modifications in the bye-laws are not obtainable, the old
methods of treating street corners must for a while continue; but at
least some decent arrangement of the buildings may be made, so
that the junction of the road is developed and emphasised as a
feature of interest, and is taken advantage of to give extended
outlook from the windows. For this purpose special treatment
of the corner buildings is required, with all the open sides designed *Illus. 243.*
as front elevations, and windows arranged to command the *Illus. 244,*
different views opened up by the cross roads. *245, and 293*
In some districts the space at the rear of buildings is allowed

Illus. 246.

to be taken as an average measurement, in which case the corner treatment shown in Illustration 246 may be adopted. Even under the more rigid existing bye-laws the ends of the buildings should be considered as front elevations, and the erection of a high wall, with arched openings through to the rear, might serve to link the houses together and help the architectural effect. Where only one street branches off from the main road, and where it is not desired to keep open any special view opposite this street, the junction may be emphasised by breaking the building line

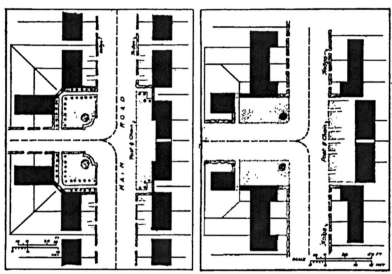

Illus. 246.—Road junction where average measurement for open spaces at the rear is allowed.

Illus. 247.—Road junction where space at the side of the building on a corner site may be substituted for space at the rear.

Illus. 244 *and* 247.

opposite, and so producing something in the nature of a small square ; this would balance the break which occurs owing to the street junction, so that looking down the main street from either direction a frame for the street picture and some extent of front elevation of buildings on each side of the road would be secured. On corner sites where the area at the side of a building is allowed to count in the place of that usually required at the rear, many other

Illus. 247.

arrangements become possible, such as that shown on Illustration 247. Other plans for treating the junctions of roads by means of houses

Illus. 250–252.

placed across the corner are shown in Illustrations 250–252.

In the latter case a continuous line for the buildings may be obtained, *Illus.* 252.
which is often very important for producing a satisfactory effect. *Illus.* 248.
The restlessness of many arrangements of street corners and junctions *Illus.* 249.
is due to breaks in the roof lines, and it is only to a limited degree *Illus.* 258.
that the use of high hedges or walls may help to tie the buildings *Illus.* 259.
together and to emphasise the grouping. Often roads cannot be
planned to cross one another at right angles, and many special
arrangements will be required in these cases. Very often it will be
wise to neglect the road line to some extent and secure some

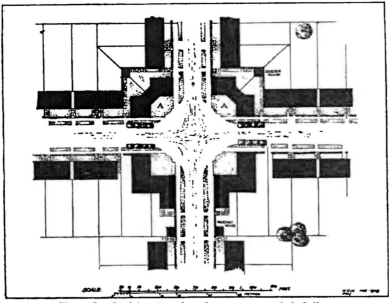

Illus. 248.—*Road junction where the corners are entirely built up.*

building line that will in itself be satisfactory; in other cases it
may be possible to secure that the roads shall meet, forming three *Illus.* 234a
equal angles in one central point. When this can be arranged, *and* 258a.
various symmetrical plans for treating the corner become possible, *Illus.* 253.
such as those shown on Illustrations 253–257. *Illus.* 254.
In the case of Illustration 253 the houses forming the terminal *Illus.* 255.
features to the roads are set forward, and their angles form a frame *Illus.* 256.
to the terminal feature opposite, down whichever of the roads the
view is taken. In the case of Illustration 255 the picture is limited *Illus.* 257.

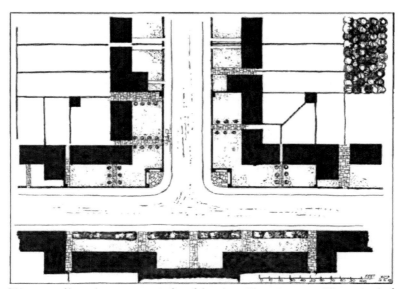

Illus. 249.—Alternative arrangement of road junction with continuous roof line maintained.

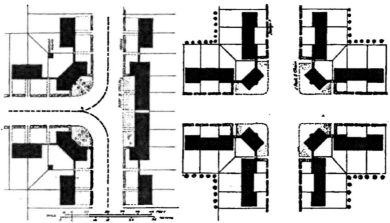

Illus. 250.—Road junction with specially designed building, finishing square with both roads.

Illus. 251.—Road junction with four buildings set diagonally.

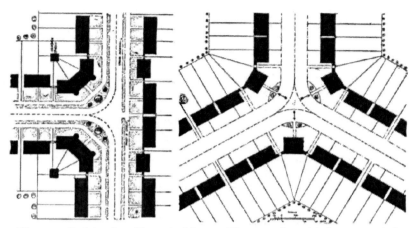

Illus. 252.—Road junction with group of three cottages designed to turn the corners.

Illus. 253.—Symmetrical arrangement for the junction of three roads, with detached projecting buildings forming street terminals. See Illus. 257.

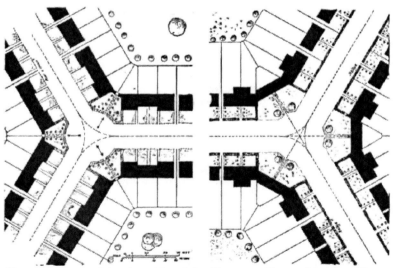

Illus. 254.—Three-road junction with arched opening as terminal feature of each road.

Illus. 255.—Three-road junction with continuous roof line maintained. See Illus. 258a.

by the buildings which are square with the road, and the terminal feature consists of a long, narrow house planned to carry line with the houses on each side, somewhat as shown in Illustration 252, or recessed a little as shown in Illustration 255. Illustration 254 shows an alternative arrangement where an opening between the buildings, which may be of greater or less extent according to the desirability of giving greater or less outlook at the end of the street, forms the central terminal feature. Where desirable, this opening may be partly closed by a wall or an archway as indicated on the plan.

Where roads are meeting at an irregular angle, sometimes the buildings may take a general hexagonal form as shown in Illustration

Illus. 257.
Illus. 258a.

Illus. 234a.

Illus. 261.

Illus. 256.—Sketch showing effect of treatment planned as Illus. 255.

Illus. 261. 261. Illustrations 262 and 262a show a rather interesting example of the way in which the town planner's preliminary ideas of a road junction were modified by the architect to whom was entrusted the design of the buildings around it, the essentials of the scheme being *Illus.* 262. maintained. Illustration 262 shows the buildings arranged for detached or almost detached houses round a junction where four *Illus.* 262a. roads meet. Illustration 262a gives the block plan of the buildings as designed by the architect.

Illus. 257.—*Hampstead Garden Suburb. Photo showing road junction treated as plan Illus. 253. Photo taken by Mr. J. P. Steel, Stoke-upon-Trent.*

Illus. 258.—*Photo of built-up corner as shown at A on plan 248.*

Illus. 258a.—*Hampstead Garden Suburb. Photo of built-up corner. See Illus. 255.*

Illus. 259.—*Arundel, showing completely built up corner.*

Illus. 260 *and* 260a.—*Typical Modern Street Corners as seen from main road and from side road.*

341

Sometimes the angles at which roads meet, or the character of their
curves and bends, do not lend themselves to the placing of terminal

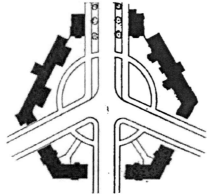

*Illus. 261.—Irregular road junction where the buildings are planned to finish square with
each road in groups, forming an hexagonal figure.*

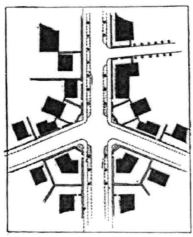
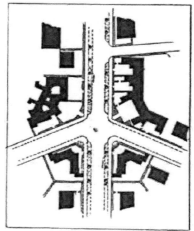

*Illus. 262.—Irregular road junction planned
for detached buildings affording terminals
to two of the road pictures, and frames
for the remainder.*

*Illus. 262a.—Plan of buildings for the
same junction as Illus. 262, designed
in groups by Mr. M. H. Baillie
Scott.*

features square with the line of vision, nor should we desire to
repeat such treatment monotonously.   An alternative plan is to
arrange something of a cluster of buildings showing some grouping

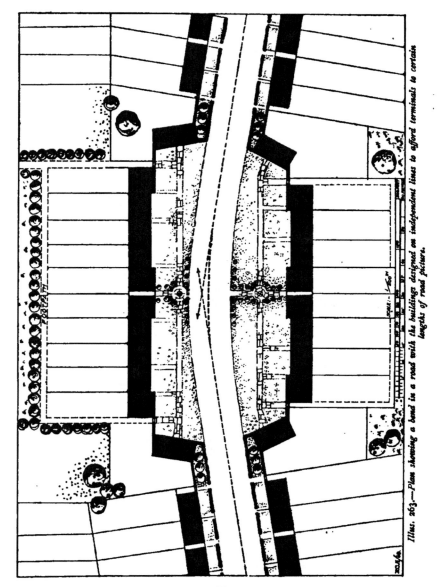

Illus. 263.—Plan showing a bend in a road with the buildings designed on independent lines to afford terminals to certain lengths of road picture.

in the roof lines which, when seen in perspective, may form a *Illus.* 221, satisfactory finish to our street 'view.   153, 156, 97.

In planning buildings round a green where any specially interesting view exists, it may often be desirable to splay the sides somewhat. This would very greatly add to the extent of view obtainable from the houses, particularly those on each side.

On curved roads it will very often produce a satisfactory street picture to allow the houses to follow pretty much the line of the road, generally keeping the face of the buildings square with a line touching the curve opposite the centre of the group of

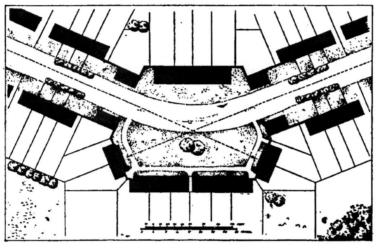

Illus. 264.—*Similar arrangement to that shown on Illus.* 263 *for bend of smaller angle, and with terminals and buildings designed to frame and define the street pictures.*

buildings. This arrangement is apt sometimes to produce an awkward line cutting diagonally across the centre of the street picture, owing to the vanishing perspective of the roof lines on the one side of the street which alone fill up the centre of the view; in such a case it may be desirable to so group the buildings that terminal features square with certain lengths of road will come into the picture. Where houses are built fairly closely together, in rows or groups of three or four, it may be desirable *Illus.* 263– to make such arrangements to avoid breaking up uncomfortably 266. an otherwise orderly series of roof lines. Several examples of this treatment are shown in Illustrations 263–66.

o

The question of roof lines is one of considerable importance to
the total effect of the site when planned.   It is true that a mass

Illus. 285.
of irregular roof lines may be exceedingly picturesque ; but where
a considerable number of these lines are arranged in a regular
and orderly manner, if it becomes necessary to break this orderly
arrangement, it must be done with some care, otherwise a jarring
note of disorder may be introduced.   Many sites seem to require,

Illus. 267.
and certainly lend themselves to, irregular planning ; such an one
is the Bird's Hill Estate of the Garden City Tenants at Letchworth,
where an irregularly shaped piece of land on the hillside,

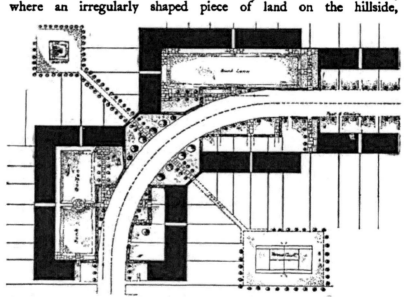

Illus. 265.—Groups of buildings designed to maintain square roof lines on a curving road.

commanding considerable views to the south and west, and having
a depth too great to be developed entirely from the road frontage,
and too small to require a second road, had to be dealt with.
Here definite breaks in the line of the buildings were arranged
to keep open the views from some of the cottages which, owing
to the aspect, were made to face into the interior spaces ; and
partly in order to open up more of the western view of the cottages
surrounding the short drive, and partly to avoid an awkward angle
with Group 4, Group 5 was splayed in relation to the drive.

Illus. 268.
On the adjacent piece of land known as Pixmore Hill, also

Illus. 266.—Imaginary sketch of village scene where the buildings are square with each other on a road curving as shown on Illus. 265.

developed by the Garden City Tenants, the general shape of the plot being square, the development was carried out on more regular lines, and except that a few of the groups were set across the north-eastern corner to preserve the existing copse at that corner, nearly all the groups of cottages on this site were placed square with one another. Such departures from the regular plan as may arise from the attempt to take some advantage of the features

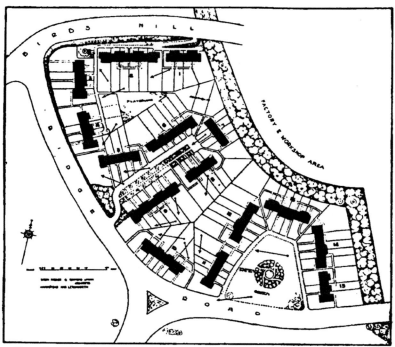

Illus. 267.—Garden City Tenants. Bird's Hill Estate, Letchworth. Irregular lay-out to suit site, with plantation defining the area.

of the site the designer should feel free to adopt, at the same time adopting them in a straightforward and orderly manner. It is the mere aimless arrangement, such as one finds springing from an ill-considered reaction against formal design, that offends against one's sense of order without satisfying any definite requirement of the case.

In considering the shape of plots, apart from the question of

the expense of the road frontage, it is by no means clear which
is the best to adopt. There is strong prejudice on the part of the
public in favour of detached or semi-detached houses. This has
probably arisen to some extent from the very poor party-walls
generally built between houses, and the consequent annoyance
arising from the noise of one house being so clearly heard in
the next. There are, of course, conveniences in the planning,

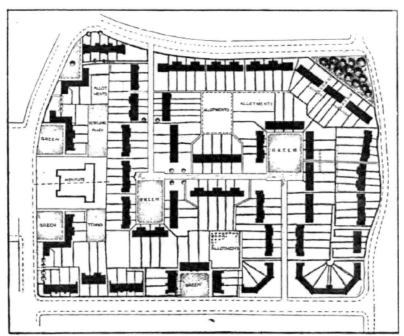

*Illus. 268.—Garden City Tenants' Cottages, Pixmore Hill, Letchworth. More regular
lay-out, with carriage drive developing central area.*

lighting, and ventilating of detached houses, in that windows
can be obtained on all four sides, and to a less degree in semi-
detached, where they can be obtained on three sides; but even
where houses are built in groups of from three to six, if the central
ones are given ample frontage in proportion to their areas, it
is easy to plan them so that thorough lighting and ventilation
are obtained; greater length of garden can be arranged and
greater distance between the backs of the houses is thus secured.

Illus. 269.
Illus. 270.
If the two diagrams shown are compared with one another, the advantages and disadvantages of the two arrangements will at once be seen. With the square plot and the detached house in the centre of it, the garden is necessarily cut up into several pieces at the front and sides which are of little practical value, while the main garden at the back has no single dimension large enough to produce any sense of size or to develop any vista. In the long, narrow garden, however, the reverse is the case. All the ground is in the most valuable position; and having one long dimension, good vistas may be developed, while there can be no doubt that from the architectural point of view the grouping of the buildings to some extent is almost essential for the production of good street pictures.

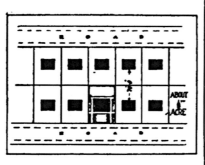

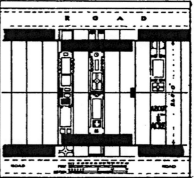

Illus. 269.—*Detached houses in centre of plots.*
Eight houses to the acre.

Illus. 270.—*Plan showing extra depth of garden and distance apart of the houses when they are built in groups, also eight to the acre.*

In residential districts one of the greatest difficulties to be contended with is the constant multiplication of buildings too small in scale to produce individually an effect in the road, and *Illus.* 271. every opportunity should be taken to group buildings so that units may be produced of a larger scale. Even where it is not possible to avoid much repetition of semi-detached or detached houses, they *Illus.* 272. should be so arranged as to give some sense of grouping. The set-back of three or four pairs of houses and the arrangement of *Illus.* 273 *and* 274. a continuous green in front of them, with the proper treatment of the houses at each end, which are set forward again to the *Illus.* 291. building line, will of itself produce some grouping; or the street may be widened and a double avenue of trees planted on this

length ; and in many other similar ways, especially where it is
possible for the site planner to be in touch with the designer
of the buildings, much may be done to produce interest and variety
in the street pictures, while at the same time maintaining the
general sense of unity which is usually so wanting in modern
suburban roads. Also in the spacing of the buildings some
variety may be obtained, the pairs forming the individual group
being kept nearer together and a sufficient break being arranged

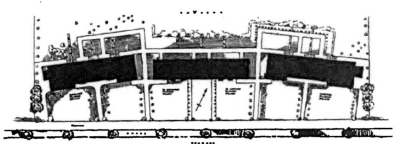

Illus. 271.—Garden City, Letchworth.   A group composed of three blocks of cottages
built in Station Road.

before the commencement of the next group. But the uneven
spacing of the distance between the pairs in an irregular manner
is anything but pleasing, and where detached or semi-detached
buildings stand by themselves some regularity or rhythm in their
spacing is an important matter to secure.

From the groups of houses to be found round old English village
greens, or in our cathedral closes, we may get valuable suggestions. *Illus.* 128,
The tendency of the modern individual has been to build his house 294.
in such a way as to emphasise its detachment and difference from

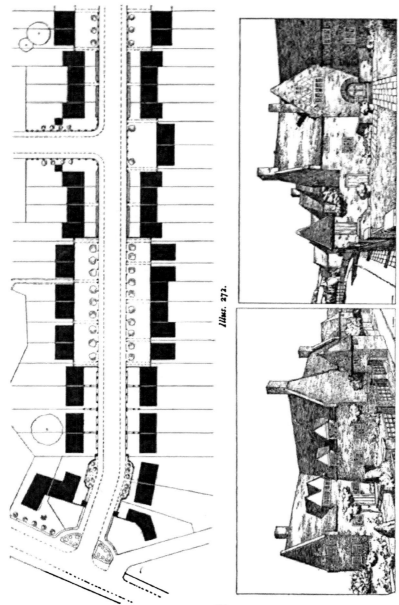

Illus. 272.

Illus. 273.

Illus. 274.

Hampstead Garden Suburb. Plan showing entrance treatment and arrangement of buildings on road already made by Ecclesiastical Commissioners, with different fences used to emphasise the effect, and sketches of houses at each side of the entrance with garden houses as shown on plan, Illus. 272, being built by The Garden Suburb Development Co. (Hampstead), Ltd.

all its neighbours, but no beauty can arise from the mere creation
of detached units.   So long as we are confined to the endless
multiplication of carefully fenced in villas, and rows of cottages
toeing the same building line, each with its little garden securely
railed, reminding one of a cattle-pen, the result is bound to
be monotonous and devoid of beauty.   It must be our effort
to counteract this tendency and to prove that greater enjoyment
to each householder can be secured by grouping the buildings
so that they may share the outlook over a wider strip of green
or garden—in fact, that by some degree of co-operation more
enjoyment of the available land can be secured than by dividing
it all up into individual plots, and railing each in.

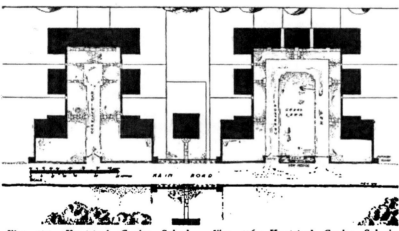

Illus.   275.—Hampstead   Garden   Suburb.   Illus.   276.—Hampstead   Garden   Suburb.
Group of large houses with simple   Group of large houses with carriage
carriage drive access.   drive circling lawn.

In planning groups of houses around greens or subsidiary roads
great variety of arrangement is possible.   In some cases a simple
footpath round the small green is all that is necessary, the
distance from the front door of the most distant house to the
roadway not being greater than one often finds in houses that
are built at the end of a longish garden.
Where a road or carriage drive is used the most economical plan
is to make a single drive with a carriage turn at the head of
it, as shown in Illustration 275.   With this arrangement some Illus. 275.
common tennis-courts may be provided at the back of the houses if

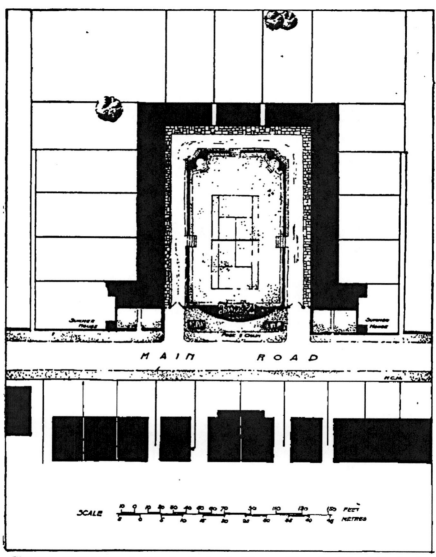

MAIN ROAD

SCALE

Illus. 277.—Hampstead Garden Suburb. Quadrangle of houses with carriage drive circling tennis-court, built for the Hampstead Tenants, Limited. See Illus. 292.

desired ; but although this is the most economical way, it has the
disadvantage that the green or lawn is not available as a decoration *Illus.* 276.
for the street.   Illustrations 276 and 277 show a plan in which
the green forms the centre, and the carriage drive runs round it. *Illus.* 277
Where the length of the cross road is greater the arrangement *and* 292.
shown in Illustration 278 may, if adopted, still secure a public *Illus.* 278.
green in the centre.

Where it is desirable to develop a considerable area of back land
the arrangement shown in Illustration 279 or 280 may be adopted ; *Illus.* 279.
the first being planned for larger houses with two lawns, the second *Illus.* 280
for smaller cottages with two lawns or children's playgrounds, and

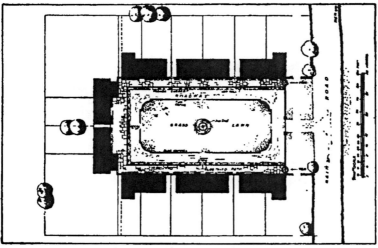

Illus. 278.—*Pairs of houses arranged round a green.*

a bowling-green.   In all these cases the land is developed from
a road on to which the buildings would naturally front, but
examples will occur where it is desirable to develop from a road
at the back of the houses.   One or two examples of this are given. *Illus.* 241.
This method is likely to be useful where the land adjoins an open
space, park, river, or other feature affording a desirable outlook.

In suburban districts the question of fences presents special difficulties.   Few details are more depressing than the masses of new
fencing often seen round a series of little suburban building plots.
The carefully fenced-off front garden patch tends to emphasise the
detachment of the units, whereas, from the point of view of

the street picture, it is of the greatest importance to emphasise their relation and grouping. In America such fences have been largely dispensed with, the front strip of garden being left open to the road ; and even in larger gardens than we are considering at the moment the ground is often left open from plot to plot, without any dividing hedge or fence. In some cases a very fine effect can be produced in this way ; but English people desire some privacy in their gardens, and there can be no doubt that enclosure imparts at any rate a sense of peace, and is almost an essential part of a garden as we understand the word in England.

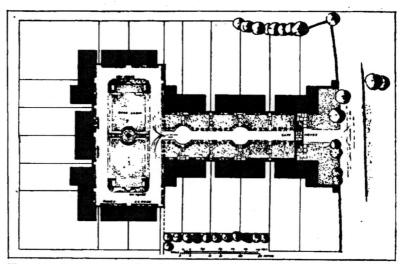

Illus. 279.—Arrangement for developing greater depth of land by means of carriage drive.

The question is whether the privacy obtained by means of the usual 4-ft. wall or fence compensates for the ugliness of the fences themselves. Nothing less than 6 feet in height can really secure privacy from the next garden, and very often this—though enough to give a fair sense of enclosure—would not secure privacy from the upper windows of the neighbouring house. As most of the dividing fences afford little real privacy, it would seem better to await the growth of hedges and shrubberies ; moreover, it is possible by means of these to enclose parts of the garden, without necessarily enclosing the whole space, or following exactly the lines *Illus* 281. of the plot. In laying out a large garden the gardener rarely leaves it all open, but aims at securing separate enclosed spaces, each having its treatment and charm, the whole series so arranged that whether one looks at the whole or at the individual portions the effect is good. There can be no doubt that in the treatment of numerous little garden plots the nearer we can approach to this plan the better. In the front gardens the dividing fences between the plots serve little purpose. It is rarely that any privacy at all can be secured in these small plots; they exist primarily to protect the house from the dust and noise of the road, and its windows from being directly overlooked by passers-by; and, secondarily, as an extended street decoration. For neither of these functions is the dividing fence of any service. Where the houses

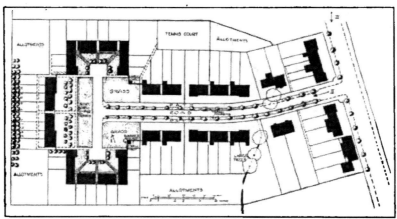

Illus. 280.—*Arrangement for developing greater depth of land planned for groups of cottages, very similar to Asmuns Place, built by The Hampstead Tenants, Ltd.*

stand slightly above the road a retaining wall affords sufficient protection, and the garden may be level with the top of the wall. Divisions may be introduced at the ends of special groups of houses, *Illus. 272.* and may there be marked by a wall or high hedge, which would help to emphasise the group. Where some form of fence is desired, probably the best is a simple trellis, preferably of inter-twined laths, unobtrusive in colour, and up which all sorts of climbing plants may readily twine; by the use of such fence it is possible to secure what would practically have the appearance of a well-grown hedge much more quickly than the hedge by itself could grow; but if people were willing to spend as much

15

money on the planting of the hedges as they usually spend on a
dividing fence or wall, a much better grown hedge than one often
sees to new houses could be secured at once. Trellis is made in

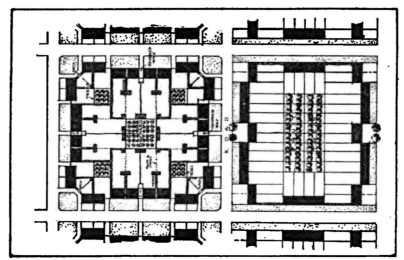

Illus. 281.—Groups of small gardens designed to produce some total effect.

many patterns and styles ; it lends itself to variation in height, so
that special portions of the garden in which privacy is desired can
be screened by higher trellis, without the necessity of having the whole
of the fencing the same height. In this matter of fencing it is,

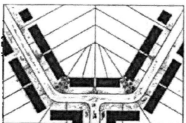

Illus. 282.—Showing converging fences.   *Illus. 283.—Showing an orchard in place of these.*

again, the endless repetition of the lines that is really objectionable ;
many an old garden wall from 6 to 8 feet high forms an interesting
and beautiful feature in a street picture, and the enclosure of a group

of gardens by a high wall may often be rather an advantage than otherwise, while the enclosure of each individual garden by such a wall would produce an appearance which one could not liken to anything but a wilderness of walls.

On sites on curved streets, for example, where the gardens diminish in width almost to a vanishing point, the concentration of fences at such a point is most unpleasing ; but if all these useless strips of *Illus.* 282 ground as they near this point, instead of being separated, could be *and* 283. thrown together to produce a small orchard, a lawn, a hazel copse, a playground for the children, or an allotment garden, a sense of orderly design would at once be given to the ground, and the fences or hedges between the remaining portions of the garden plots would lose much of the ugliness arising from their concentration near the central point.

In all probability there is no way of dealing with these masses of small garden plots without the introduction of some form of co-operative laying out and development, the advantage of which will be referred to later.

X—OF BUILDINGS, AND HOW THE VARIETY OF EACH MUST BE DOMINATED BY THE HARMONY OF THE WHOLE

THE laying out of building sites, whether within the town area or in the residential districts, is so intimately bound up with the nature of the buildings likely to be erected on them that some reference to the general character of these must be made, and some consideration given to the conditions which influence that character, particularly from the point of view of the total effect produced in the street or town. In comparing the architectural results produced to-day with those of earlier periods of our history, we must recognise the great change which has taken place. We may say roughly that at any other period than the modern, there has existed a fairly widespread and consistent style of building; and although this has been a developing and changing style, still, in the main, the development was slow, and the changes spread gradually and evenly over the country, or, at any rate, over large districts of it. No doubt at the period of the Renaissance there was a condition more approaching to what we know to-day, a new style being introduced largely by foreign influence, which for some time was developed concurrently with the old English Gothic, and was developed for certain purposes more thoroughly and consistently than for others. But even this style gradually spread until it became a prevailing one, and nothing parallel to the present condition of affairs was produced. At any of these earlier periods a site planner, laying out his site, would have some fair idea as to what was likely to be erected upon it, and would know that whatever buildings were erected on the different plots would be in the main harmonious in style. No such harmony can be counted on to-day. Buildings are being erected in all conceivable styles, the majority, alas! with little or none; and except where some form of guidance or regulation can be introduced, no harmony or consistency can be counted on by the town planner.

Another change in the character of buildings has been brought about by the development of cheap railway carriage for materials. In former days a general harmony of building in any district was secured by the economic necessity of using mainly local materials. We do, indeed, read of exceptional cases in which building stones were conveyed great distances for special buildings, but in the main each district was built of the materials most readily available there; and in each district there was developed a style suited to these materials, and the skilled handling of these revealed itself in the details of the work. From this fact there resulted, first, a great

Illus. 284.—Siena. View showing general harmony of building materials used.

Illus. 285.—Rothenburg. Standpoint X on Fold Plan III., view showing general harmony of buildings.

harmony of colour and style in each village or town ; and, second, a great variety of colour and style between the different towns and different districts. In spite of the harmony of colour and materials it is seldom that any sense of monotony is produced in the older parts of our villages and towns; while the individuality which the varying treatment of different towns and districts produced is undoubtedly one of the greatest causes of the charm and interest of the scenery of Great Britain.

Cheap railway carriage has, however, upset all this. It has at once destroyed the individuality of our districts and the harmony of their buildings. In place of these it tends to reduce all places to a similar jumble of colours and materials which is fondly referred to as "variety." Is it necessary for us to regard this state of affairs as permanent ? Because we have cheap railway carriage, must we necessarily spend our time and energy in shuffling the materials characteristic of each district over the whole of the country ? Surely it should be possible to check this process, and the first thing required is that both architects and the public should consider their buildings more from the point of view of their effect on the whole town. So long as each architect and each client thinks only of his own building, how individual and how noticeable he can make it, little progress in the total effect can be expected. Architects should *Illus.* 233. be trained to think first of how their building will take its place in *Illus.* 284. the picture already existing. The harmony, the unity which binds the buildings together and welds the whole into a picture, is so much *Illus.* 285. the most important consideration that it should take precedence. Within the limits of this enclosing unity there is plenty of scope for variety, without resorting to that type which destroys all harmony by its blatant shouting. Surely some public opinion could be formed among architects themselves on this point. Certain materials and treatments obviously discordant in a district could be ruled out by common consent of the profession. There is no doubt that in this advertising age some little sacrifice of individual interest might be involved in this course. The business man at any rate believes that he must shout if he is to live, and naturally desires his architect to help him to make his building do some of the shouting for him. The young and original architect, too, must become known if he is to secure commissions, and a little shouting in his earlier buildings may greatly aid him. But, if we are to have beauty of surroundings—and for what does the profession of architecture exist if it is not to produce beautiful surroundings ?—we must set our faces against the development of such incongruities in our buildings as completely

o

destroy the harmony of our street pictures. Harmony does not require monotony, but a proper relation between the different colours and parts.

By all means let the architect revel in colour, let him develop colour schemes. Both in his site planning and in the buildings themselves much may be done in this direction without producing the mere jumble of incongruous colours which marks so many of our streets and suburbs. The external appearance of a building is so much more important to the public at large than it is to the individual occupant or owner, that there would seem to be clear justification for the exercise of some public supervision of the designs of buildings ; and unless an improvement can be brought about by an educated public opinion, there is little doubt that sooner or later definite public control will be demanded. Difficult as it is for any form of artistic expression to be put under arbitrary regulations without its being seriously checked or even destroyed, nevertheless, it is possible by means of suggestion and supervision to obtain a certain minimum standard of design, to secure a certain degree of harmony, and at any rate to avoid the perpetration of such monstrous examples of ugliness as too often disfigure the country to-day. Where building estates are developed by individual owners, or by companies or associations, as, for example, the First Garden City Company, and the Hampstead Garden Suburb Trust, it is clearly both their right and their duty to endeavour, by the supervision of the plans of all buildings to be erected on their estates, to secure some definite scheme of development. They do not make any profession that the scheme which they lay down is necessarily the best or the only good one ; nor need they, in rejecting or criticising plans submitted to them, take up the attitude that these are in themselves bad. It is only necessary that they should state that they would not fall in with the total effect aimed at in this particular suburb or estate. Experience shows that by means of such supervision a considerable degree of harmony of design may be obtained ; that objectionable features may be eliminated ; and that, although it is not possible to secure by criticism really good designs from those who have not the power to make them, still it is possible to improve the designs of such people up to a point where they will at any rate form a harmless background for better buildings, and will not clash with the general scheme.

In all cases where the supervision of plans is attempted it should be by somebody who is either the site planner himself or is thoroughly in touch and in sympathy with his aims ; and it should be carried

Illus. 286.—High School, Edinburgh, showing general grouping of classical buildings.

Illus. 287.—Rothenburg. Standpoint XI on Fold Plan III. St. Jacob's Church; example of Gothic building.

Illus. 288.—Rothenburg. Standpoint XII on Fold Plan III. Irregular gabled street typical of Gothic town.

out, as far as possible, by means of suggestions offered before the plans are prepared. Where the site planner, to complete his street picture, requires even roof lines he should be able to suggest heights for eaves and ridge ; where he desires to maintain definite colour schemes he should be able to suggest materials and treatment in accordance with these schemes.

Where the position of his building requires a symmetrical, picturesque, or other special treatment to complete some effect aimed at, he should be able to suggest this treatment to the architect or builder who is responsible for the building on the plot. By such suggestions, wisely made, very much may be secured that will be helpful to the total effect. Suggestions will often be welcomed when criticisms to the same effect would be resented. Where, to complete some scheme, a special degree of harmony in the style and character of the building is required, it may often be possible to fix on an architect who is to be employed by any one wishing to build within the area covered by the scheme. Or two or three architects may be asked to meet together and agree on a style and treatment for a certain group of buildings, and the lessees of individual plots in this group may then employ any one of these architects. All these methods have been tried on the Hampstead Garden Suburb, and it will be strange if experience will not provide one which may be applicable to the general control of buildings by the public acting through their municipalities or other local bodies.

The difficulties of such public control are undoubtedly very great, but the evils which result from absolute lack of control are even greater. Without touching at all the higher regions of art and design, where differences of opinion might well come in, there is a mass of building erected which architects would be unanimous in condemning. That there may be great difficulty in establishing a criterion for judging hardly seems a sufficient reason for making no attempt whatever to criticise or veto buildings which, to quote Robert Louis Stevenson, " belong to no style of art, only to a form of business much to be regretted."

Other methods might be adopted besides that of direct criticism. Good design in building might be encouraged by means of rewards, both honourable and material, given annually to the architects and builders of the best buildings in the town. Where a specially good building is desirable on account of its prominent position, the building owner might be induced to agree to improvements in his design by means of some reduction in the rating of the building for a short period, or other *quid pro quo* which it might be within the power of the local authorities to offer.

The simplest and most easily enforced regulations of buildings would be such as those requiring the use of certain materials in certain streets, fixing definite roof lines and angles, and in the case of shops perhaps fixing a definite height for the main fascia line of the shop windows. This is not the place to discuss the different styles of architecture except as they affect the town or site planner, but from his point of view there may be said to be two styles of

Illus. 286, 287, 288.

work, the picturesque and the formal or symmetrical. Of the first Gothic is the best example, with its irregularly shaped masses, its gabled and pinnacled roof lines, and freedom of treatment both in balance and proportion. To the second class belongs classical architecture, usually marked by regular cube-shaped masses, symmetry of balance, and simple unbroken roof lines without gables or pinnacles.

To the picturesque style of architecture irregularity of site and lack of symmetry in arrangement offer no difficulty. English domestic architecture very largely belongs to this class. Though many classical buildings have been successfully designed for irregular sites, there can be no doubt that for this type of architecture a regular and formal lay-out is much better adapted ; for it does not lend itself to the production of picturesque irregularities, nor do clusters of such buildings, designed without regard to one another, produce successful groupings, as often happens with similar buildings of the more picturesque types of architecture. Such formal designs, depending as they do on proportion and repetition of the parts and on strongly marked horizontal cornices and roof lines, need space

Illus. 198.

for their development ; and where, as in an ordinary English shopping street, buildings of narrow frontage have to be designed in close proximity to each other without regulations as to heights and styles, the painful breaks in cornices and window lines which have resulted from the use of this style of architecture are destructive of any satisfactory street picture.

On an estate where some opportunity for suggestion and some degree of regulation are to be secured for the town planner, many things may be attempted which might otherwise be out of the

Illus. 227.

question. He will give much thought to his roof and sky lines and on sloping sites will attempt to secure the necessary breaks in

Illus. 289.

the roof lines in such a way that satisfactory grouping at these points may be obtained. He will try to reduce the number of breaks on such roofs by planning his groups of houses so that the taller ones with higher rooms or additional storeys may occupy the lower ground and those with lower rooms and fewer storeys

Illus. 289.—Hampstead Garden Suburb. Quadrangle of cottages built by The Hampstead Tenants, Ltd. Photo taken by Mr. J. P. Steele, Stoke-upon-Trent.

Illus. 290.—Hampstead Garden Suburb. Asmuns Hill. Photo taken by Mr. J. P. Steele, Stoke-upon-Trent.

the higher. Where the difference in level between two sides of a road is slight he may, in like manner, by arranging for higher houses on the low side of the road and lower ones on the high side, secure an even balance between the roof lines.. He will also use the breaks in his building line in conjunction with the breaks in the roof line *Illus.* 290. to help in the effect he is aiming at, which effect may be of various kinds ; either he may seek to disguise the hill or to emphasise it ; *Illus.* 231 or he may concentrate the emphasis at certain points, producing *and* 233. here and there something of a cliff effect in his buildings. Indeed, it is not so much the details of the individual buildings that will concern him as the general masses and roof lines ; for he is attempting to produce a total effect in the picture, he is thinking of the whole rather than of the unit, or of the unit only as forming part of the whole.

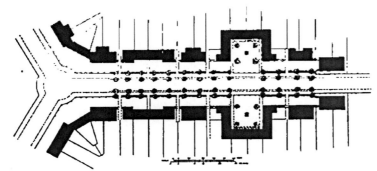

Illus. 291.—*Hampstead Garden Suburb. Plan of Temple Fortune Hill, showing variation in building line and also corner treatment of buildings.*

In the same way he will apportion his materials with a view to some colour scheme. He will avoid monotony, not by an irregular jumble of materials and colours, but by a sufficient though unobtrusive variation in the different buildings, leading up to more definite breaks in colour in certain parts ; treating differently different roads or parts of roads, and so producing interest and variety on his estate, which will be greatly helped by the sense of unity maintained in each individual part, and of harmony over the whole.

In the more suburban areas especially it becomes of great import-ance to group the buildings. Hardly anything is more monotonous than the repetition of detached or semi-detached houses, and this monotony is little relieved by variety in the individual houses,

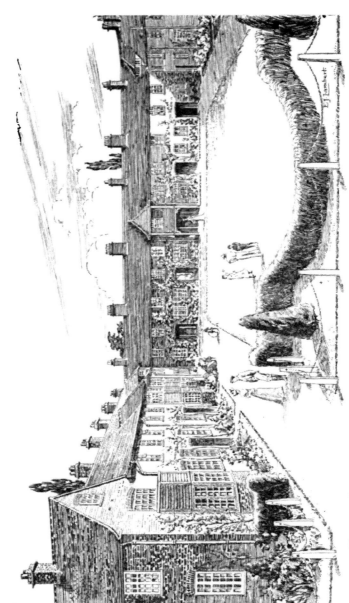

Illus. 292.—Hampstead Garden Suburb. Sketch showing quadrangle of medium-sized houses. For plan see Illus. 277.

372

owing ·to the fact that no total effect in the street is produced.
The variety is, as it were, unrelated variety. A practicable com- *Illus.* 290 .
promise giving most of the real advantages of semi–detached houses *and* 227.
may be made by having passages between every pair, built over on
the first floor, through which access to the gardens at the back
of the centre houses may be obtained.   By this means, on the
ground floor at any rate, complete separation of the two buildings
is secured, while on the upper floor the space over the passage may
often be occupied by bath or box rooms on one side, at any rate, of
the party wall, so that little disadvantage could arise from the noise
passing from one house to the other.   In this way the grouping
of 4, 6, or 8 houses can be attained.   This treatment may be
carried a step farther if two or three of such groups are treated *Illus.* 271.
as one design.   A central feature in the middle block, or pro-
nounced wing features at the ends of the side blocks, may help
to give a degree of coherence to the whole ; while the treatment *Illus.* 291.
of the gardens and even of the street itself may be varied opposite
such an enlarged group to give the needful emphasis.
Care must be taken to maintain a certain relation in the scale of
the different buildings adjacent to one another.   This does not
mean that necessarily larger buildings and smaller ones cannot
be combined, but rather that in their treatment the scale of the
two and the individual features must be kept in such relation that
they will combine satisfactorily.   So long as this comparative scale
is kept in mind great advantage will result from combining buildings *Illus.* 290
of somewhat different size.   In groups of 4 or 6 cottages, for *and* 271.
example, the two at the end may well be somewhat larger, and
will thus materially help the design by giving the opportunity
for breaks in the frontage line and perhaps a different treatment
of the roof.
In planning sites for public buildings many special considerations
should be taken into account ; for instance, one sees in towns
school sites with expensive paved and macadamised roads running
on two or three sides of the playground.   The money wasted in
useless road frontage in such a case would have been far better
devoted to a larger site on which some grass and trees could have
been planted.   It is, of course, important in a school site that
there should be sufficient points of access for the scholars, but
it is an advantage rather than otherwise that the access should
not open out too directly on to the high-roads.   There should,
indeed, be some space for the children to disperse without going
into conflict with the ordinary road traffic.   This applies not only

to school sites but to sites for all other public buildings where people congregate in large numbers. Places of worship, in which special attention is likely to be devoted to architecture, should be so placed as to afford the maximum of decoration to the district. As terminal features at the ends of streets they are well seen, but very often their towers, domes, or pinnacles rising up behind the other buildings would form an equally beautiful decoration to the street, and the site planner should always be on the look-out for opportunities of bringing such decoration into his street views, leaving openings, arranging pathways, or prescribing some low buildings, where helpful for this purpose.

The mistake of isolating buildings with the intention of their being exceptionally well seen has already been referred to when treating of the importance of enclosing *places* in towns. We have indeed in our English villages many beautiful examples of isolated church buildings; in most cases, however, the church itself is of a simple character and is surrounded by ancient trees, which go far to remove any sense of its isolation; but even in these cases, beautiful as they are, it seldom happens that the church produces so great an effect in beautifying the village as where it comes more completely *Illus.* 128. into the street picture, as in the photograph of Astbury.

XI.—OF CO-OPERATION IN SITE PLANNING, AND HOW COMMON ENJOYMENT BENEFITS THE INDIVIDUAL.

THE consideration of site planning can hardly have failed to emphasise still further what appeared so evident when considering the question of town planning, namely, that the features which we deplore in the present condition of our residential areas have been largely due to the excessively individualistic character of their development. We have referred in an earlier chapter to the fact that towns and suburbs are the expression of something in the lives of those who build them. The fact that our town populations have been too much mere aggregations of struggling units, having little orderly relationship one with the other, and little of corporate life, has naturally expressed itself in our street plans and in the arrangement of sites. The absence of any attempt to develop with a view to making the best of the whole site for the benefit of everybody dwelling on it, and of any unity and harmony in the total effect produced, are but too evident.

In feudal days there existed a definite relationship between the different classes and individuals of society, which expressed itself in the character of the villages and towns in which dwelt those communities of interdependent people. The order may have been primitive in its nature, unduly despotic in character, and detrimental to the development of the full powers and liberties of the individual, but at least it was an order. Hitherto the growth of democracy, which has destroyed the old feudal structure of society, has but left the individual in the helpless isolation of his freedom. But there is growing up a new sense of the rights and duties of the community as distinct from those of the individual. It is coming to be more and more widely realised that a new order and relationship in society are required to take the place of the old, that the mere setting free of the individual is only the commencement of the work of reconstruction, and not the end. The town planning movement and the powers conferred by legislation on municipalities are strong evidence of the growth of this spirit of association. To no one can this growth appeal more strongly than to the architect, who must realise that his efforts to improve the design of individual buildings will be of comparatively little value until opportunity is again afforded of bringing them into true relationship one with the other, and of giving in each case proper weight and consideration to the total effect. In the planning of our towns in future there will be opportunity for

the common life and welfare to be considered first ; how are we to
secure that consideration for the commonweal shall also come first
in the planning of our sites and buildings ? To some extent the
planning of sites and buildings will, no doubt, be taken in hand
by the community, as organised in its municipality ; but there seems
no need to wait until the development of corporate life and feeling
has reached the stage at which it would seem natural for the
community to carry out for itself through its own officials the entire
development of its towns and homes ; it may be better that
smaller bodies, more responsive to the initiative of individual
pioneers, should deal with the more detailed work. There is a
wide field for the activities of companies, associations, and co-operative societies, and for what the Germans call Societies of Public
Utility, to develop suburban areas and sites, on lines which shall
place first the good of the whole of their community. The
way has been shown to some extent by individuals. Mr.
Cadbury at Bournville, Mr. Lever at Port Sunlight, and Mr.
Rowntree at Earswick have all as pioneers broken ground, and
demonstrated how great are the improvements possible in the
housing of the people. Others are following their example, as,
notably, Mr. Cory in South Wales and Sir Arthur Paget at
Wolverhampton. The First Garden City at Letchworth and
the Hampstead Garden Suburb Trust are examples of companies
banded together for the purpose of experimenting on a larger scale
in the development of new towns and suburbs, while the various
Co-partnership Tenants' Societies are proving the value of co-operation in the development of the sites themselves, and in the building
of the houses upon them. Many estates have, of course, been
developed in the past by co-operative societies with a view to
housing their members, and in a sense they are co-operatively
developed. Too often, however, co-operation has ceased with the
purchase of the estate, and the development has been carried
out very much on the old lines without a full realisation of the
opportunities which co-operation offers. It is the importance of
these opportunities which I wish to emphasise, and to illustrate
to some extent from the work of those Co-partnership
Tenants' Societies. In some cases, as in the Garden City at
Letchworth and the Garden Suburb at Hampstead, the roads and
the laying out of the land have been carried out by parent
bodies, and the Tenant Societies have developed co-operatively
the sites thus prepared. In other cases, as at Ealing, Manchester,
Birmingham, Leicester, &c., they have taken up sites of 50 to 100

Illus. 293.—Hampstead Garden Suburb. Asmuns Place, showing children's green and garden house. See Illus. 280.

Illus. 294.—The Vicar's Close, Wells.

acres and have undertaken the construction of the subsidiary roads themselves.

Consider how different is the position of the site planner when designing for one of these co-operative societies from his position when planning an area to be let in plots to individuals or speculative builders. In the latter case his first consideration must be the dividing up of the land into well-marked individual plots, avoiding any joint usage or other complications—in fact, securing first of all the absolute separation of each holding from its neighbour. He cannot well provide sites even for minor public buildings, for these will be chosen on individual lines and only after the need for them has arisen. But in working for a co-operative body, such as the Tenants' Society, where the houses when built remain the property of the association, the site planner can approach the problem from a quite different point of view ; *Illus.* 169, he at once begins to think of the good of the whole. Just as 170, *and* 171. in the other case he was bound to concentrate his attention on making individual "sell-able" plots, now he can concentrate it on the creation of a village community ; he can consider the needs of such a community, how far they will be met by outside opportunities already existing or likely to be developed, and how far they will need to be met on the area of the site. The shops, schools, institutes, and places of worship can all be considered, and the most suitable sites for each reserved. Some *place* can be arranged around which many of these buildings can be grouped and a centre point to the plan be thus secured. The designer can then proceed to lay out the buildings as a whole, considering first their main lines and arrangement, with a view to create a good total effect, and to preserve and develop any fine views or other advantages the site may offer. It is not necessary for him to think of the absolute isolation of his buildings ; this point, instead of being his first consideration, becomes his last thought. The whole of the land remaining in one ownership, there is no difficulty in the common enjoyment of footpaths, greens, or other open spaces ; hence he is able to consider the grouping of his buildings with much greater freedom. Where, as may often happen in connection with such co-operative societies, the architect who plans the site also plans the buildings, a most complete opportunity is given for making the best of the site.

Only under some such circumstances is it possible to work up the whole scheme in the right order, taking first the big interests and the main lines, following on with the buildings in their masses

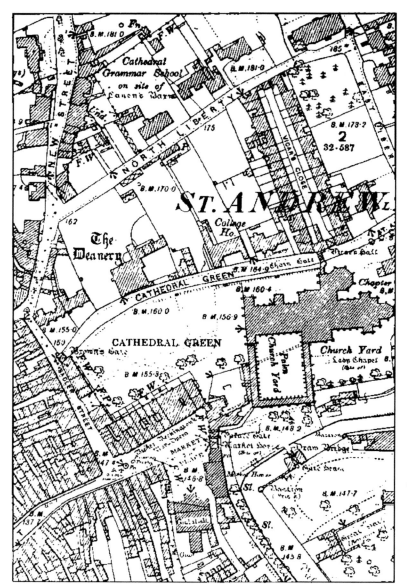

Illus. 295.—Plan showing the Vicar's Close and Market-place at Wells. Reproduced from the Ordnance Survey Map, with the sanction of the Controller of H.M. Stationery Office.

380

and their grouping, working down to the individual buildings themselves, and finally to the details of their arrangement, placing the best rooms where it has been planned to give the best aspect and the best outlook; designing bay windows to take advantage of views which have been kept open, giving special attention and care to those elevations which will most prominently come into the picture, and, indeed, welding the plan of the site, the buildings, and the gardens, more and more into one complete whole.

With a co-operative society it is safe to count also on the common enjoyment of much of the garden space. It is, indeed, possible, even where houses are sold to individuals, to arrange some degree of associated use of gardens, as has often been done in the centres of squares; but difficult problems, both legal and practical, are always

Illus. 296.—Group of cottages with a co-operative centre.

raised by such schemes, which do not arise where the whole of the site is owned co-operatively. Where this is the case it becomes possible to group the houses around greens, to provide playgrounds for the children, bowling greens, croquet or tennis lawns or ornamental gardens for the elders, or allotment gardens for those who wish for more ground than the individual plot affords. It becomes *Illus. 280,* possible also to carry out some consistent treatment of garden land, 292, 293. such as the creation of an orchard; for by a consistent planting of fruit-trees in an orderly manner in a series of gardens, much *Illus. 281,* of the beauty and effect of an orchard may be produced. In this 282, *and* 283. way it seems possible to hope that with co-operation there may be introduced into our town suburbs and villages that sense of *Illus.* 294. being the outward expression of an orderly community of people, having intimate relations one with the other, which undoubtedly *Illus.* 295.

16

is given in old English villages, and which has been the cause of much of the beauty which we find there.

The growth of co-operation among cottage dwellers which will, no doubt, spring from the development of the Tenants' Copartnership and other Societies of Public Utility which are undertaking, and no doubt in future will increasingly undertake, the erection of dwellings, will lead to a need for something in the way of common rooms, baths, washhouses, recreation-rooms, reading-rooms, and possibly eventually common kitchens and dining-halls. These will give to the architect the opportunity of introducing central features in his cottage group designs, like the dining-halls, chapels, and libraries that we associate with colleges and almshouses.

Illus. 296.

However much we may strive to improve the individual cottage, to extend its accommodation, and enlarge its share of garden or public ground, it must for a long time, and probably for ever, remain true that the conveniences and luxuries with which the few rich are able to surround themselves cannot be multiplied so that they can be added to every house. It is possible, however, and indeed easy, by co-operation to provide for all a reasonable *share* of these same conveniences and luxuries ; and if we once overcome the excessive prejudice which shuts up the individual family and all its domestic activities within the precincts of its own cottage, there is hardly any limit to be set to the advantages which co-operation may introduce. Nothing can be more wasteful, alike of first capital cost, cost of maintenance and of labour, than the way in which hundreds and thousands of little inefficient coppers are lit on Monday morning, in small, badly-equipped sculleries, to carry out insignificant quantities of washing. Here, at least, one would think it possible to take a step in the direction of co-operation. Where cottages are built in groups round a quadrangle, how simple it would be to provide one centre where a small, well-arranged laundry could be placed, with proper facilities for heating water, plenty of fixed tubs with taps to fill and empty them, and with properly heated drying-rooms. By two or three hours' use of such a laundry each housewife could carry out her weekly wash more expeditiously and more cheaply than she could do it at home. Perhaps some play-room would need to be attached in which the children could be within reach of their mothers, during the hour or two they would be at work in the laundry. The distance to the laundry from any of the cottages using it must not be too great, and it would be better if it were accessible without passing through the street. In connection with this laundry there might be an arrangement by which, at any time, a hot bath could be obtained at a minimum charge.   Where houses are built in continuous rows it would be easy from such a centre to distribute hot water to all of them, thus effecting a great saving in fuel, boilers, and plumbing systems in the separate houses.   Such an arrangement has been carried out by the Liverpool Corporation in some of their dwellings.   In many other simple ways co-operation may provide for the needs of the individual tenants.   Cloisters or covered play-places for the children ; public rooms of reasonable size, in which the individual may entertain a number of guests, too many for the small accommodation his cottage affords; reading-room, and library at once suggest themselves as obvious and easily managed projects.   More difficult, perhaps, is the question of the common kitchen and dining-hall, and yet it is probably quite as uneconomical, in every sense of the word, for forty housewives to heat up forty ovens and cook forty scrappy dinners, as to do the weekly washing in the usual way. Among the middle class the difficulty of obtaining efficient domestic service is forcing large numbers of people to give up the privacy of family life altogether and to live in boarding-houses and hotels ; but by co-operation it is quite possible to combine all the valuable elements of private family life with the advantages of a more varied diet, less engrossing domestic labour and care, and a greater degree of social intercourse, which are the features that attract so many people to the life of the boarding-house and hotel—a kind of life which is unsatisfactory owing to its entire destruction of family life, just as the individual house is unsatisfactory owing to its oppression of the individual by all the necessary details of that life.

This, however, is carrying us beyond the scope of the present subject.   We should need a volume in order adequately to discuss the advantages and the difficulties of co-operative living.   Along certain directions it is clearly possible, even with the present prejudices, to secure by co-operation very great advantages to the individual ; but such a form of life can only be developed tentatively, and the subject is considered here mainly as it affects town planning and architecture.   One cannot but feel that for successful work to be produced in this field there must be some form of social life, some system of social relationships, which must find expression, and may be the means of introducing harmony into the work.   We see that in the great periods of architecture there have been definite organisations of society, definite relationships, the interdependence of different, clearly defined classes, and the association of large bodies of people, held together either by a common religion, a common patriotism, or by the rules of a common handicraft guild. Many of these uniting forces have been weakened or lost in modern times. One naturally looks around to see in what way the unit members of society, who have secured their freedom from so many of the old restraints and guiding influences, are likely in the future to be drawn and bound together. These units are undoubtedly realising very strongly in the present day how limited is the life which it is possible for them to obtain for themselves under conditions of greater freedom from restraint and organisation. They are seeking more and more to procure an extension of opportunities through the State, the municipality, and other existing institutions, and through numberless voluntary unions and associations. It seems, therefore, likely that we may with some confidence predict that co-operation will recover for society some organised form, which will find expression in our architecture and the planning of our towns and cities.

How far this more crystalline structure of society will be due to the direct effort of the whole body, acting through the medium of its State, municipal, and parochial organisations, and how far it will spring from independent, voluntary societies, only time can show. Experience alone can prove how far our present municipal organisations can advantageously carry the work of town planning, laying out of sites, making of streets, and building of houses. Obvious advantages would be found if the whole of the people living in a limited area could co-operate for its development, for the laying out of their city and the building of their houses. The possibilities are greater and the convenience of the whole community can be more thoroughly considered, the wider the area covered by the unit of association. On the other hand, effective oversight of expenditure and details and effective adaptability to new ideas are apt to decrease in proportion as the magnitude of the unit of organisation increases. The problem may well be worked out from both ends. The municipalities will find how far they can wisely go, working from the town-planning end ; while the smaller societies, beginning with co-operative building, will find by experience how far they can extend their sphere of operations without losing touch with the individual needs. They will prove, also, how far the interests of separate societies will come into conflict, and will need to be harmonised by some federation, controlling in the interests of a wider whole.

The whole question is more one of convenience and form of organisation than of principle. By the present haphazard system we entrust the satisfaction of the community's needs to the individual, who generally acts only when, and in so far as, that satisfaction falls in with his own inclination, and his own limited view of his personal interest. The real opposition of principle lies between this and the organisation on co-operative lines of the spontaneous ministering of the community to its own requirements. The form in which this associated effort will organise itself is of secondary importance. The essential thing is that it shall be as little artificial as possible, that it shall be a spontaneous growth following the traditional lines of development ; for in so far as it is the natural outcome of the past and present life of the community will its foundation be firm and its future assured.

o

XII—OF BUILDING BYE-LAWS

WE have incidentally in an earlier chapter spoken of the good work which bye-laws have done in checking the worst evils of overcrowding and bad building. There is, however, no doubt that the English building bye-laws do not work altogether satisfactorily when considered from the point of view of good architecture. Any one who has been accustomed to building under the various sets of bye-laws which are to be found in different towns is able almost on entering a town to say which of certain bye-laws are in force there, owing to the influence they have on the buildings. Indeed, the abrupt and arbitrary manner in which some of these regulations work has produced a type which is practically bye-law architecture. Forms are distorted ; the roof is exaggerated or depressed ; lines of space and height cut the buildings at awkward angles ; street corners are spoiled by spaces being left between the buildings just where it is important that they should be carried round in a continuous group; and feeble imitations of old styles of building, needlessly prevented from being properly constructed, are encouraged. It is not, of course, to be said that the whole of the responsibility for this ugliness can be attributed to the action of the bye-laws. The general low standard of design, and the lack of imagination in working within the rules laid down, greatly exaggerate the result. Neither must it be assumed from this detrimental influence that restraints on building are necessarily harmful. There are many natural restraints which have no tendency to produce ugliness ; nay, indeed, very much of the beauty of buildings results from working within defined limitations. Questions of cost, strength of material, utility, and stability, all exercise restraint on the builder, and he is constantly feeling these. But there is this great difference between natural restraints and the action of building bye-laws, that with the former the limits, though fairly defined, are flexible in character. The height of the building is strictly limited by the strength of the material of which it is built, but a little increase in the material will allow of a little added height where desired. So also with regard to cost ; the size of a building of a given style is absolutely limited by the cost ; but a little economy may be effected in one part in order to enable a little extravagance to be indulged at another, where the design may seem to require it. On the other hand, the line laid down by the building bye-laws is a rigid and inflexible one. The builder is compelled to conform to it, and in seeking to secure the utmost which the bye-laws will allow him, he pushes his building, as it were, against an unbending line or plane. His building becomes moulded by this, and from this moulding springs what I have called "bye-law architecture." It is the hard-and-fast form of these building regulations, coupled with the want of any sympathy between the building impulse and the restraining action of the bye-laws, resulting in mutual antagonism and suspicion between the builder and the man whose duty it is to enforce the restraint, which leads to so much harm. What is required is that we should give to our bye-laws something of that elastic character which belongs to natural restraints ; so that while the height of a building, for example, may be as strictly limited as at present, a little give and take, a little averaging of one part with another, may be permitted, and the rigid form which results from the present arbitrary rules may cease to be required.

There are many ways in which this can be done, and in certain bye-laws there have recently been introduced new forms, having much of this elastic character. Probably to begin with there may need to be a certain excess of strictness. If, for example, the size and shape of the open space at the rear of the buildings is to be subject to averaging, to give and take, in the first instance the amount of open space must be somewhat larger. So long as 150 superfeet, with a distance across of 15 to 25 feet, is all the open space that the bye-laws require for a building, it may be difficult to relax the rule that the open space shall measure this amount at all points, that it shall, in fact, be practically rectangular in shape. But if the amount of the open space were double in size, its exact form or position would immediately become a matter of less importance for health, and therefore much greater freedom could be given. So also with the height of buildings. So long as streets are narrow and houses are allowed to be erected to the utmost limit of height consistent with the decent lighting of the streets, this limitation may require to be fairly rigid ; but with a less maximum height in proportion to width of street as the general stipulation, a much greater freedom could be allowed in the interpretation of the bye-law, either by permitting, within certain limitations, the average height to be taken, or in some similar manner.

It is well worth the while of the authorities to devote more care to framing and revising bye-laws, so that their action shall be as little arbitrary as possible. So long as some definite standard of building is required, so long will bye-laws in one form or another be necessary. It is not a matter that can be entirely left to the discretion of the building surveyor. It is as necessary to the builder in preparing his plans that he should know within fairly definite limits the standard required of him as it is for the building inspector to have some definite standard to keep his judgments regular and consistent and fair to all. At the same time, it is eminently desirable that certain discretionary powers should be vested in the building inspector on points specially defined in the regulations themselves. Building regulations cover such a multitude of matters, and the combinations of circumstances under which difficulties may arise are so numerous, that it is quite impossible to frame absolute regulations on all these points, without a considerable amount of needless harassment and restriction of really good building. It is the opinion of the Local Government Board at present that in the case of municipal building inspectors the evils arising from the giving of discretionary powers are greater than the benefits. Such powers lay them open to so much undue influence and pressure that they are often placed in very difficult positions, and in addition, are subjected to severe temptations. At present, therefore, it would seem that beyond altering the form of bye-laws, as suggested above, any introduction of elasticity, through leaving individual cases to the discretion of a surveyor, will only be brought about if some outside person, free from local influence but having a sufficient opportunity for securing knowledge of the circumstances of a given case, can be made the recipient of this discretionary power. There must shortly be created some department of the Local Government Board to supervise the town planning work and the extended work in connection with the housing of the people which the Housing and Town Planning Bill will call upon the local authorities to undertake. It would seem that such a department would be exactly suited to exercise the discretionary powers of which we have spoken above. Through its inspectors it would have an intimate local knowledge; it would be in constant touch with the general planning work and building operations carried on in the different localities, and would be in an exceptionally good position for judging as to the fair working of any bye-law in particular instances. Such a department would be entirely independent of the influence of local builders, or landowners connected with the municipality, who might be in a position to exert very unfair pressure upon a local official.

If town planning is to produce the good results that are hoped for, the range of building bye-laws must necessarily be extended; it will not be practicable for a town plan to show everything that needs to be determined. The limitation of the number of houses to the acre; the reservation of sites for probable public buildings or other requirements; the proper distribution of works and factories;

and many other similar matters, will need to be brought under some public control if towns are to be adequately managed, and developed along the best lines. Upon many of these points it will be peculiarly difficult to frame regulations, so difficult that probably it will hardly be practicable, unless some means can be discovered of introducing the element of discretion and affording some opportunity for the individual case to be considered on its merits. Rules may be framed that will cover the majority of cases and work out satisfactorily, but there must arise in a minority of instances circumstances not allowed for in the regulations, where some special consideration is required. It is these few cases that cause nearly all the friction and outcry against bye-laws; except, of course, the general outcry from jerrybuilders, which, unsupported by instances of obvious unfairness, would be a negligible quantity. It cannot be too clearly recognised that for building bye-laws to work successfully they must have the sympathy and actual support of those architects and builders, admittedly many, who are seeking to do good work. So long as the goodwill of those who are trying to build well can be retained on the side of the bye-laws they can be enforced with ease, and are in no danger of being seriously weakened; but as soon as they hamper the operations of those who are trying to do good work they raise against themselves a very powerful opposition which strongly appeals to the public. Architects as a body do not object to reasonable restrictions; they would be the last to desire that the jerrybuilder should be allowed a free hand; but they do strongly resent the arbitrary character of many building bye-laws, and the needless restrictions which their hard-and-fast character imposes. I believe that greater care in their framing along the lines suggested above, and some simple and inexpensive arrangement by which a special case could be referred to an impartial person, who should have the power to decide promptly whether some modification could, without harm to the community, be allowed, would, by removing much of the friction, greatly strengthen the position of the bye-laws.

From the first a greater degree of co-operation and sympathy should be cultivated between the municipal controlling office and the builders and architects working under this control. When new building bye-laws are being framed, instead of their being pushed through with the minimum amount of publicity, every encouragement should be given to those concerned to consider them and bring forward objections. Not so, however. Obstacles are put in the way of people finding out what the proposed bye-laws will contain. In one case the writer had to pay 17s. 6d. for a copy of a few only of the proposed new bye-laws of a district, in which he wished to secure modifications. In another case a copy of the draft bye-laws cost £7 8s. 6d. It is not to be expected that individuals will incur expenses such as these on the chance of finding out something in the proposed bye-laws to which they ought to object, or that they will, in most cases, give the time necessary to consider a complicated set of bye-laws, or will learn up the procedure for lodging objections to them. The result is that the bye-laws are framed almost entirely by the surveyor, who looks at the matter from the point of view of the man who has to administer them, not of the man who has to work under them. They are advertised in the local paper, it is true, but only a few people read such advertisements, and in many cases builders and architects find that new bye-laws, having clauses of the most arbitrary character, have come into force without their having had any effective opportunity to consider them. Surely when a municipality is preparing a new set of bye-laws affecting such an important industry as the building trade, it should be compelled to secure the co-operation of all those interested ; it should be obliged to supply copies of the proposed regulations to all builders and architects, free of cost ; it should be obliged to afford opportunities for the consideration of objections and suggestions from those affected; and generally to secure that the question is thoroughly ventilated. If objections to the bye-laws are lodged, it is generally possible to secure an inquiry by the Local Government Board, and the result of several such inquiries, coming within the writer's personal knowledge, has been that the Local Government Board took a reasonable view and was willing to introduce modifications, and in some cases to compel the local authorities to accept these, even against their wish. But the procedure should be put on a different footing ; the inquiry should not be a last resort, but, on the contrary, those interested in building should be encouraged to come forward with suggestions and objections, and their co-operation in the framing of the best possible set of bye-laws, adapted to the needs of the locality, should be secured.

It may be of interest to refer to some particular instances in which modification of bye-laws has been obtained, and to give the form of some of those which were secured by the Hampstead Garden Suburb Trust in the new bye-laws of the Hendon district, which were being framed at the time that the Trust purchased their estate. As far as possible this work was carried out under agreement with the Hendon District Council, certain matters being left by both parties to be decided by the Local Government Board after hearing both sides. I can only say that in this case the greatest care and trouble were taken, both by the District Council and the Local Government Board, to secure a form of regulation which would effect the ends desired, and hamper as little as possible the general building operations. As the Hampstead Garden Suburb Trust had obtained an Act of Parliament giving them special exemption from certain of the new bye-laws as to the width of streets and roads, it was agreed that no question referring to this should be raised. There are, however, many points that should be watched when new bye-laws on this subject are being made in any district. First of all, some distinction should be made between roads that are likely to be required to carry considerable traffic, and those that are likely to serve only to give access to comparatively few houses or other buildings. The width of 40 or 50 feet, prescribed for all roads exceeding 100 or 150 feet long, is as absolutely inadequate for main traffic roads as it is excessive for roads giving access to a few houses only, and the length of the road is no criterion of the size required. A short road of 100 feet may happen to be so placed that it will become a very important traffic-way ; while a considerable length of road may often serve no purpose that would not be quite adequately provided for by means of a simple carriage drive, such as is found sufficient for a college, a hospital or asylum, or other large building, containing a population sometimes as great as that of a considerable village. No doubt the Town Planning Bill will materially assist in this matter of providing different widths for streets, but the bye-laws also should be so framed as to provide for the necessary variations. The technical definition of a street, taken in conjunction with the common law as to streets, undoubtedly raises difficulties.

Mr. J. S. Birkett, Solicitor to the Hampstead Garden Suburb Trust, has kindly furnished me with particulars of the law in this matter, from which it appears that the Public Health Act, 1875, section 150, enacts that the Local Authority can give notice to the owners or occupiers of the premises fronting on any road to sewer, level, pave, metal, flag, channel, and make good, or to light any street within any urban district not being a highway repairable by the inhabitants at large where such street is not made up or lighted to the satisfaction of such Local Authority, and if such notice is not complied with the Local Authority may themselves do the work. When the work has been done, the Local Authority may, if they think fit, declare such street to be a highway, and thereupon it will become repairable by the inhabitants at large unless a majority of the proprietors object (in other words, the street is taken over by the Local Authority). Where the Private Street Works Act, 1892, has been adopted by the Local Authority, they have power to take over a street if they wish to do so, and are compelled to take it over if the greater part in value of the owners of the houses and land call upon them to do so. Where Part II. of the Public Health Acts Amendment Act, 1907, is by order of the Local Government Board declared to be in force in the district of the Local Authority, the majority in number or rateable value of the owners of lands and premises in a street may require the Local Authority to do the necessary paving, &c., works, and on completion thereof the local authority must take over the street. In all cases the making up of the road by the Local Authority is chargeable *pro rata* on the owners of the houses and land fronting on the roads.

Section 4 of the Public Health Act, 1875, provides that the term "street" includes any highway and any public bridge (not being a county bridge) and any road, lane, footway, square, court, alley, or passage, whether a thoroughfare or not ; a definition sufficiently wide to include pretty well anything in the way of a road or path.

Where, for instance, houses are set back from the road, a common footway is often provided to give access to them, running round the green or margin that may be left between the houses and the road or highway, and such an arrangement is in every way desirable. Under many bye-laws, read in conjunction with the common law, it would be impossible to carry out this arrangement, without making this footway into a complete street 50 feet wide. Provision should clearly be made in the bye-laws for permitting such narrow roads or footways. There is no doubt that the bye-laws as to streets, for want of other powers, have been used as a means of doing away with objectionable courts and narrow alleys, but other and more direct means should be taken for dealing with these evils. The widths between houses should be regulated independently of the width of the roadway. That courts and quadrangles shall be sufficiently large to be airy, or sufficiently open at the ends when small, are matters which can be directly secured ; and it is not necessary, in order to secure them, that we should be prevented from erecting an arched gateway over the end of our street, or carrying our minor or back roads through

a sufficiently large opening in a building ; and yet bye-laws for-
bidding these archways and preventing the picturesque bridging of
streets are often in force.   Provision should also be made for the
construction of cheaper roads, adapted to lighter traffic than main
roads, having grass margins planted with trees to take the place
of part of the width of the kerb, channel, and pavement, required
for main roads.   There seems no sufficient reason why, in the case of
roads running along the slope of a hill, or through a cutting, the
footpaths should not be allowed to be raised above the roadway, as
one often sees in old roads.   Where this is done a more satisfactory
result can be attained, and a better gradient for the road secured,
than would be practicable if the whole of the road, footpath, &c.,
had to be excavated to the bottom of the cutting.

Some bye-laws contain a provision that no street shall exceed a
certain length without a cross road, a regulation reasonable in itself,
but liable in particular cases to work out in a most unfortunate
manner for the convenience of the town.   At Ealing, for example, *Illus.*169.
owing to this bye-law, an estate of some thirty or forty acres would
have been nearly isolated from the remainder of the town, access
only being had through a bottle-neck at one end, but for a happy
accident which brought into the market an additional piece of land,
enabling a cross road (A, B) to be planned within the 600 feet required.
This is a very good example of the sort of case that could with
advantage be submitted to some referee.   Obviously it was the
intention of those who made this bye-law to secure specially good
and convenient point-to-point access, but it worked out in practice
so as to prevent any communication at all from being obtainable
through a very large area.   Another bye-law which is not uncommon is that against roads having no through way, known as
cul-de-sac roads.   This action has, no doubt, been taken to avoid
unwholesome yards ; but for residential purposes, particularly since
the development of the motor-car, the cul-de-sac roads, far from
being undesirable, are especially to be desired for those who like
quiet for their dwellings.

No one is likely to find fault with the rules requiring the damp
course, proper foundations, and a sufficient strength of structure
for buildings.   It is only where these provisions prevent other
legitimate arrangements that some modification is desirable.

In the Hendon bye-laws the following modifications were
secured : —

1. In the bye-law permitting hollow walls, the word " outside " was
omitted, so that hollow walls can now be built where it is specially

desirable to secure a sound-proof party-wall, a matter of no little importance.

2. Modifications were secured in the bye-laws relating to half-timber walls, and permitting tile-hanging on wood-framing of the upper storeys of buildings. The usual clauses render the construction of genuine half-timber work either impossible or so costly that its erection becomes impracticable, and where the effect of half timber is desired cheap and flimsy imitation work is resorted to. The effect of the modifications introduced was to extend the permission for half-timber framing from one building to a block of domestic buildings not exceeding 6 in number, the block to be 15 feet from an adjacent building. Further, the brick backing usually required for half-timber work may be dispensed with in the case of a wall or part of a wall, not exceeding 25 feet in height or 30 feet in length, where the following requirements are complied with—

> "The timbers to be of oak, teak, or other suitable hard wood, to be not less than 6 inches by 4 inches in section, the studs or vertical timbers to be not more than 14 inches apart, measured between, the inner surface to be covered with a sufficient thickness of good hard plaster, or suitable non-combustible material, and any brickwork used in filling the spaces between the timbers to be built in cement mortar."

The projecting of the party wall beyond the face of the timber framing was dispensed with. These rules make it possible to construct half-timber work with the necessary over-hang and other characteristics of old work. They might be still further improved —notably the distance apart of the uprights for work of a certain character is needlessly small. The use of other solid and non-combustible material than brick-work for filling in the spaces is an advantage. The requirement that such framing shall be carried out in hard wood, though adding to the cost, at least secures additional durability and power of fire resistance.

3. In the bye-law concerning framing, tiling or slate hanging to upper storeys was allowed in groups not exceeding 4; cement plaster, not less than 1 inch thick, was permitted in addition to tile-hanging as the outside covering, on condition that the spaces between the timber-framing should be completely filled in with a thickness of 4 inches of brick-work or other non-combustible material. The wording of the requirement was so modified that it was made to apply to the "topmost storey, including any gable above it, and if the topmost storey should be wholly in the roof to the storey next below it."

In addition to the above there was introduced the following bye-law allowing a similar treatment for the space between bay windows which occur over one another, and for the space in the gable over such windows, where it is found difficult to provide an outside wall of the bye-law type, and where its provision throws an unnecessary and unsuitable weight upon the bay window :—

> "That where in a new domestic building an external wall is constructed in the form of a bay for a bay window, and the bay extends through more than one storey in height, but does not in any place exceed *twelve feet* in width, measured externally, or project more than *five feet* beyond the main external wall of the building, the person erecting such new building may construct such part of the external wall of the bay as is above the level of the top of the ground floor window opening, of timber framing covered with tiles, slates, or other suitable incombustible material, subject to compliance with the following condition, that is to say—

> "The timber framing shall be properly put together, with sufficient braces, ties, plates, and sills, and shall be of sufficient strength, and the spaces between the timbers shall be filled in completely with a sufficient thickness of brickwork or other solid and incombustible material."

Further to secure the overhanging of half-timbered walls, words were introduced in the bye-law providing for overhanging walls properly supported, permitting corbels or supports of oak or other hard wood to be used, and in other bye-laws making it clear that such timber-framed walls were to be exempted from the action of certain bye-laws applying to the ordinary outside wall. The definition of fire-resisting material was also modified to include " beams or posts of oak, teak, or other hard wood." Indeed, it is important when examining a proposed set of bye-laws to scrutinise the definitions, as the scope of a bye-law is often very much extended by a definition.

4. There is a common form of bye-law which requires the whole of the walls of the two main storeys to be increased in thickness where any use is made of the attic storey. So long as economy in building requires cottage walls to be 9 inches thick it is clearly only necessary when the attic storey is made use of to increase the thickness of the wall for the height of one storey. This modification was secured.

5. One of the most valuable modifications secured at Hendon was that which permitted a party-wall to be carried up to the under

sides of the slates or tiles only, these to be bedded in mortar; instead of requiring it, as is common in London, to be carried up above the roof and formed into a parapet wall. This, which may be a necessary precaution against the spread of fire in the case of lofty buildings crowded together in the centre of a town, cannot be regarded as a sufficiently necessary precaution against the spread of fire from house to house in the case of ordinary dwellings, in which it very rarely happens that fire spreads to any serious extent. It is, of course, desirable in the interests of the community to reduce this risk, but it is certainly not desirable to disfigure the whole of the buildings in a district with parapet walls to divide the roofs, and projecting corbels to divide the eaves and gutters, for the sake of the infinitesimal degree of additional safety thereby secured.

6. The difficulty and structural weakness of carrying all timbers in 9-inch party-walls on corbels was met by allowing them to rest $4\frac{1}{2}$ inches on the wall, provided that $4\frac{1}{2}$ inches of brickwork was secured at the back of the timber. So long, therefore, as purlins and joists in the two adjacent houses are arranged not to come opposite one another they may get a firm bearing in the party-wall. Here again the necessary protection from the spread of fire is sufficiently secured, while a more satisfactory bearing for the timbers is allowed.

7. Oak or other hard wood was added as a sufficient support for a bressummer, and—

8. In the bye-law dealing with the thickness of 9 inches required at the back of fireplace openings this was allowed to be reduced to $4\frac{1}{2}$ inches in cases where fires are back to back.

9. Some modification was made in the bye-law relating to hearths, allowing these to be above the level of the floor, in order to bring the regulation in harmony with the modern types of fireplace, so many of which require a raised hearth.

10. With regard to the open space rules, the bye-laws already contained a clause allowing for the average measurement across the open space to be taken: thus for a building requiring a space 30 feet across, if rectangular and extending the full width of the building, a triangular site measuring 60 feet to the apex of the triangle would give the average measurement of 30 feet and would be taken to satisfy the bye-law. But the bye-laws contained no provision on corner sites for counting space at the side of the building as part of the open space to be provided, and in the form suggested it was not possible to turn the corner of a street with a continuous group of buildings, nor to build a quadrangular block, or a part quad-

rangle of houses, without omitting the corner houses, and thus causing a gap in the roof line quite destructive of the quadrangular, enclosed effect. The local authorities were unwilling to adopt over the whole of their district a bye-law permitting the erection of corner houses in the way desired, but on account of the large amount of open space in proportion to the houses provided on the Garden Suburb estate, they agreed to bye-laws upon this matter applying to this estate only, and to this the Local Government Board also agreed, so that the following two bye-laws were inserted :—

(*a*) To provide for an internal corner house.

" Provided further that in the case of a new domestic building erected in the Garden Suburb the open space hereinbefore mentioned shall not be required to be provided throughout a frontage of more than *eight feet* if two sides of the building *Illus. 297a.* other than the front shall abut on an open space of not less than *one thousand square feet* exclusively belonging to the building, the distance across which, measured at right angles from each of such sides to the boundary of any adjoining land or premises, shall not at any point be less than *twenty feet.*"

(*b*) To provide for an external corner house.

" Provided that in the case of a new domestic building erected in the Garden Suburb upon a corner site the requirements of this bye-law shall be deemed to be satisfied if the following *Illus. 297.* conditions are complied with—

"(1) There shall be provided at the rear of such building an open space of at least *one hundred and fifty square feet* exclusively belonging thereto. Such open space shall extend throughout not less than *ten feet* of the width of such building, and shall be free from any erection thereon above the level of the ground except a water closet, earth closet, or privy, and an ashpit constructed respectively in accordance with the requirements of the bye-law in that behalf.

"(2) One side of such building other than the front shall abut on a further open space (not being a street) of such an extent as together with the open space provided at the rear of the building will amount to not less than six hundred square feet."

It will be seen from this that a very generous provision of open space was agreed upon in exchange for the permission to arrange it in a different form to that required under the ordinary bye-law, and this would seem to be a useful precedent.

11. The minimum height of 8 feet for rooms was secured in these bye-laws, on the ground that 8 feet is a sufficient height for health, and that it would be wiser to leave it to the public to decide whether they wanted higher rooms or not.

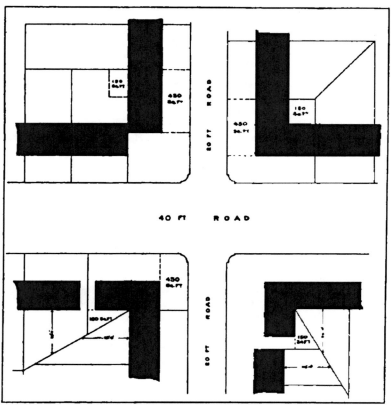

Illus. 297.—Diagrams showing the effect of the modifications in the usual space byelaws permitting the completion of an external angle in buildings showing four different arrangements.

12. That regulation in the bye-laws relating to attics with a portion of sloping ceiling was made to apply to any room in the roof, whether on the first, second, or third floor. This bye-law, as sometimes worded, hampers the design of houses considerably by permitting rooms partly in the roof, only on the third floor.

The above notes on a recent set of bye-laws are not in any sense put forward as covering all the points in which alteration is desirable ; but they may, perhaps, serve both to show that reasonable modifications can be obtained, and to suggest the lines on which such modifications may be introduced into the different building regulations, so as to give them a less arbitrary character. The point aimed at by a bye-law is generally a good one in itself, and attention should be turned to its wording, so that while the point desired is effectually secured, it is not at the expense of needless regulation and hampering of design.

As examples of other points in which some variation might be

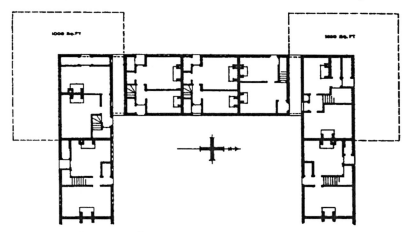

Illus. 297a.—Diagram showing completion of internal angle.

allowed, the regulation as to thickness of walls and use of buttresses may be mentioned. The projection of a buttress beyond one-third of its width is not usually allowed to count as adding to the stability of the outside wall, whereas in the modern type of building, which often resembles a heavy cabinet standing on a few legs, it may be of the utmost importance that these legs should be stiffened by wide buttresses to resist wind pressure and the tendency to buckle under great weight.

Regulations as to soil pipes and ventilating pipes from drains, though no doubt generally required, should be subject to some modification, so that buildings may not have to be disfigured by these pipes being carried up entirely exposed to view. Extra

precautions as to the character and jointings of pipes should enable
them to be placed in a chase in the wall or to be carried up behind
rough-cast, tile-hanging, or half-timber framing.

Provision is also necessary for the utilisation of new materials, such
as ferro-concrete, concrete blocks, and the many fireproof concrete and
plaster slabs which are now made ; while the relatively high fire-
resisting qualities of good beams and hard wood as compared with iron
girders and stanchions should be recognised ; and the use of other
than fire-proof materials for minor features in buildings, and for the
roofs of buildings which are sufficiently isolated, might well be
allowed under suitable restrictions.

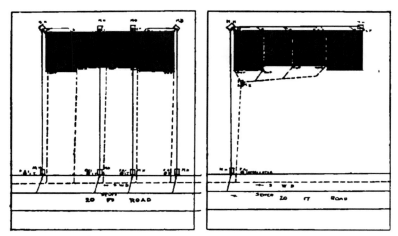

Diagram 1.   Diagram 2.

*Illus. 298.—Diagrams showing the simplicity of combined drainage for groups of cottages as
compared with separate drainage.*

In the question of drainage, particularly that of small cottages, much
needless complication and expense is caused by the requirement that
every cottage shall have a separate connection with the sewer in the
road, and in many places another separate connection with the
surface-water drain also. In some districts this requirement can be
enforced under the bye-laws, in others it is being put forward owing
to the unsatisfactory condition of the common law in relation to
combined drainage. A Bill has already been introduced into Parliament and approved by the Local Government Board to deal with
this matter, and make it clear that the local authorities shall be able,
if they wish, to allow the use of combined drainage for a number of

cottages, without being liable to be called upon to maintain and repair such drain at the public expense. It is obviously important that no needless obstacles should be put in the way of those who are willing to set their cottages back some distance from the road line ; but with this requirement of separate connections to the sewer and surface-water drain for each house, the increased cost of setting back the houses becomes a serious item. Hence this really forms of itself a strong inducement to the builder to build his houses in long rows as near to the street line as may be, because every departure from such an arrangement will add to his drainage expenses. The

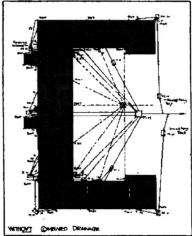 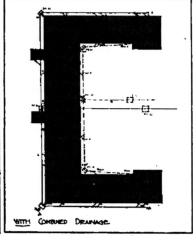

WITHOUT COMBINED DRAINAGE.   WITH COMBINED DRAINAGE.

Diagram 3.   *Diagram 4.*
Illus. 298.—*Diagrams showing the simplicity of combined drainage for groups of cottages as compared with separate drainage.*

diagrams given show the needless complication and expense of providing separate connections, and show further that it is generally necessary in a group of cottages to bring some of these connections under the buildings, an obviously undesirable arrangement even when careful precautions are taken to render the drain secure against damage. Diagrams 1 and 3 show groups of cottages with separate *Illus.* 298. connections, while Diagrams 2 and 4 show the same cottages provided with combined drainage. In the case of Diagrams 2 and 4 the drainage is entirely ventilated as if it were one system. In some cases independent ventilation is required. This is very often a quite needless complication, but even with this arrangement the saving in expense on a group of eight cottages by using the combined system was found to be about £80, and it is only necessary to compare the two diagrams to realise the comparative simplicity of the combined system.

The preparation of town plans should afford an opportunity for adopting another expedient for giving somewhat greater elasticity to building bye-laws. At present, in England, bye-laws are usually adopted for a whole town, and any regulation which is deemed advisable in the most closely built up centre of the town applies equally to the most sparsely built areas on the outskirts. It is obvious that this must mean that either too little is secured for safety in the centre or needlessly much is required on the outskirts. In Germany towns are divided into zones or areas, and certain of the bye-laws apply to the inner zones only, while certain others vary for the different zones. The building plots are further divided into classes according to the use which is to be made of them, and very elaborate regulations are framed for these classes—fixing, for example, the proportion of a site to be left unbuilt-upon, which varies from one quarter of the site in some parts to two-thirds or more in other parts; and in some of the zones and classes, only the land behind the building line is reckoned as unbuilt-upon land for determining this proportion. In the same way the maximum height of buildings is varied both for the different classes of site and in relation to the width of streets, and altogether the system enables the bye-laws to be adapted to the requirements of the particular districts of the towns with much greater exactitude than is possible in our country.

There are some very interesting precautions in the German bye-laws which read oddly to one used only to the English byelaws; for example, plastering work may not be commenced sooner than six weeks after the authorities have made a survey of the rough construction, and a certificate of completion must not be given before six months have elapsed from the date fixed for the commencement of the plastering operations. Thus some steadiness in the rate of building is secured and some opportunity for the building to be dried before occupation.

In addition to fixing zones or areas, and varying the bye-laws in connection with these, it would seem to be a good policy for local authorities to follow and carry farther the precedent created by the Hampstead Garden Suburb Act; where, in exchange for an undertaking embodied in that Act that not more than 8 houses to the acre should be built over the whole estate, certain of the existing regulations as to roads were relaxed. So long as the land-owner is allowed to build 30 or 40 houses to the acre under the ordinary building regulations, it is not to be expected that individual owners will greatly reduce this number, unless some inducement is offered to them by the local authorities. Such inducement could quite easily take the form of transferring their land to a zone or class within which certain of the bye-laws which are chiefly necessary in districts very closely built up are omitted or modified.

BIBLIOGRAPHY

ENGLISH SECTION

The following list of books and papers bearing on the subject of Town Planning and Housing Reform, though by no means exhaustive, contains many works which the student of the subject will be likely to find useful.

For the German section I am indebted to Dr. Stübben, Professor Theodor Goecke, Herr von Berlepsch-Valendas, B.D.A., Herr Zetzsche, Professor Schultze-Naumberg, and others for valuable assistance.

For the French section I am indebted to Mons Augustin Rey.

N.B.—In the German section the most important works and essays of general interest are marked *; those which are chiefly important for the study of the historical development during the last hundred years are marked **; those dealing specially with individual cities are marked ***.

Adams, Thomas, Garden City and Agriculture. 1s. London : Simpkin.

American Cities. Reports on—
> Boston. Society of Architects. Report on Municipal Improvements, 1907.
>
> Charities and the Commons, Feb. 1908. Series of articles on the city plan, edited by C. Mulford Robinson.
>
> City of Cedar Rapids. Civic Improvement Reports. C. Mulford Robinson, 1908.
>
> Columbus, Ohio. Report of the Plan Commission. Charles Mulford Robinson, Secretary.
>
> Crawford, A.W., The Existing and Proposed outer Park Systems of American Cities.
>
> Day, Frank Miles, Municipal Improvement Report. Proceedings of the Annual Convention of the American Institute of Architects, 1904.
>
> Detroit. Reports to the Detroit Board of Commerce, by Frederick Law Olmsted, Jun., and C. Mulford Robinson, 1905.
>
> Honolulu, the Beautifying of; Oakland, The Civic Improvement of; Ridgewood, the Improvement of. Reports, by C. Mulford Robinson.
>
> Massachusetts Civic League Reports.
>
> New York. Report of the City Improvement Commission, 1907.
>
> Philadelphia. The City Parks Association. Numerous Reports.

Anderson and Spiers, The Architecture of Greece and Rome. London : Batsford.

Architectural Record, The, New York—
> August and November, 1908. German City Planning, by Cornelius Gurlitt.
>
> August, September, November, December, 1907, and January, 1908. Series of articles on the Topographical Transformation of Paris, by E. R. Smith.

Art and Life and the Building and Decoration of Beautiful Cities; five essays, by T. J. Cobden Sanderson, Reginald Blomfield, W. R. Lethaby, Halsey Ricardo, Walter Crane.

Association of Municipal Corporations—
> Planning of Suburbs, 1907
>
> Scheme for Town Planning Bill, 1907

Barnett, Mrs., Science and City Suburbs. A Chapter in *Science and Public Affairs*. Edited by J. E. Hand. London : Allen. 5s. nett.

Birmingham, City of, Report of the Housing Committee. Birmingham, 1906. 2s. 6d.

Blomfield, Reginald, Mistress Art, The. 5s. Edwin Arnold.

Booth, Charles, Life and Labour of the People in London. Macmillan.

Cadbury, George, Bournville, Illustrated Papers on.

Co-Partnership Tenants, Ltd., Garden Suburbs, Villages, and Homes. London, 1906. 6d.

Fougères, Gustav, and Mons. Hulot. Sélinonte, R.I.B.A. Journal, Third Series, vol. xv, No. iv.

Frankfurt-on-the-Main, Guide to some of the Public Works of. Published by the City Engineer's Department, 1907.

Garden City Association, Town Planning in Theory and Practice, 1s., and other publications, including Garden Cities and Town Planning (formerly The Garden City.) 1d. monthly.

Geddes, P.—
    City Development. Edinburgh. Geddes and Colleagues. 1904.
    Civics, in Sociological Papers. Vol. i., ii., and iii. Sociological Society, and Macmillan & Co., 1904-7.
    Papers on Town Planning, City Surveys, Chelsea, &c., in *Sociological Review*. Sherratt and Hughes, 1908-9.

Gurlitt, Cornelius, *see Architectural Record, The.*

Harvey, W. Alexander, The Model Village and its Cottages, Bournville. Batsford, London.

Horsfall, T. C.—
    Housing Lessons from Germany, *The Independent Review*, October, 1904.
    The Improvement of the Dwellings and Surroundings of the People : The Example of Germany. Manchester, Sherratt and Hughes, 1904. 1s.
    Translation of Part of Swedish Building Law for Towns, 1874. *The Municipal Journal*, November 8, 1907.

Howard, Ebenezer, Garden Cities of To-morrow. London, Sonnenschein.

International Congress of Architects, 1906. Transactions R.I.B.A. Articles by C. H. Buls, E. Hénard, B. Pollés, Augustin Rey, Dr. J. Stübben, Gaston Trélat, R. Unwin.

Lanchester, H. V., Town and Country : Some Aspects of Town Planning. Paper from the R.I.B.A. Journal, February, 1909.

Lever, W. H., Port Sunlight, Illustrated Papers on.

London County Council—
    Housing Question in London. King & Sons. Report by C. J. Stewart.
    Park Handbooks. King & Sons.

London, Maps of Old. Adam and Charles Black, London. 5s.

London Traffic Branch of the Board of Trade, Report of the. Wyman & Sons. 4s.

London Traffic, Royal Commission Reports.

Marr, T. R., Housing Conditions in Manchester and Salford. London, Sherratt and Hughes. 1s. nett.

Mawson, Thomas A., Carnegie Dunfermline Trust Scheme for Park and City Improvements. London.

Meakin, Budgett, Model Factories and Villages. London, Unwin, 1905. 7s. 6d.

National Housing Reform Council—

    Report of the National Housing Congress. London, 1908, and other publications.

    International Housing Congress, 1907, and other reports.

Nettleford, J. S., Practical Housing. Garden City Press. 1s.

Peabody, Robert S., A Holiday Study of Cities and Ports. Society of Architects, Boston, 1908.

Pite, Professor Beresford, The Planning of Cities and Public Spaces. R.I.B.A. Journal, April, 1905.

Robinson, C. Mulford—

    A Railroad Beautiful. *House and Garden*, Nov., 1902.

    Improvement of Towns and Cities, The. G. P. Putnam & Sons, New York and London. 5s. nett.

    Modern Civic Art. G. P. Putnam & Sons, New York and London. $3.25.

Rowntree, B. S., Poverty : A Study of Town Life. London, Macmillan.

Sennett, A. R., Garden Cities in Theory and Practice. Bemrose & Sons. 2 vols. 21s.

Simpson, J. W.—

    R.I.B.A. Journal, April, 1905, Town Planning.

    The Planning of Cities and Public Spaces. R.I.B.A. Journal, April, 1905.

Smith, Edward R., *see Architectural Record, The.*

Thompson, William—

    Housing Handbook. King & Sons.

    Housing Up-to-date. King & Sons.

Town Planning and Modern Architecture at the Hampstead Garden Suburb. By the Hampstead Garden Suburb Development Company. Published by T. Fisher Unwin. 1s. and 2s. 6d.

Unwin, Raymond, Town and Street Planning, *Royal Sanitary Institute Journal,* September, 1908.

Weather—

    Meteorological Reports. Annual Summary, &c., from the Meteorological Office, Victoria Street, S.W.

    Rainfall Organisation, Reports of the British, London.

    Royal Meteorological Society's Report.

GERMAN SECTION

Baumeister—
   ***Hygienischer Führer durch Karlsruhe.
   **Stadterweiterungen. Berlin, 1876.
   **Stadtpläne in alter und neuer Zeit.
   Zeitfragen des christlichen Volkslebens. Heft 206. Stuttgart, 1902.
***Brentano, Professor, Wohnungszustände und Wohnungsnot in München.
   Ernst Reinhardt, Karlstrasse 4.
**Brinkmann, A. E., Platz und Monument. Berlin, E. Wasmuth, 1908.
Eberstadt—
   ***Das Wohnungswesen. Jena, 1904. S. Lex.
   **Die städtische Bodenparzellierung in England und ihre Vergleichung mit
      deutschen Einrichtungen. Berlin, Carl Heymann's Verlag, 1908.
   ***Städtische Bodenfragen. Berlin, 1894. C. Heymann.
***Fischer, Th., Stadterweiterungsfragen, mit besonderer Berücksichtigung
   Stuttgarts. Stuttgart, 1903.
***Fritz, J., Deutsche Stadtanlage. Beilage zum Programm des Lyceums in Strass-
   burg im Elsass. Strassburg, 1894.
***Gartenstadt—Mitteilungen der deutschen Gartenstadtgesellschaft. Hans
   Kampffmeyer, Karlsruhe.
**Genzmer, Die Entwickelung des Städtebaues und seine Ziele in künstlerischer
   Beziehung. *Technisches Gemeindeblatt*, 1900, Seite 363.
**Goecke, Verkehrsstrassen und Wohnstrassen. Sonderauszug aus den preussischen
   Jahrbüchern. Berlin, 1893. Verlag Walter.
***Gross-Berlin. Ernst Wasmuth, Berlin.
**Gurlitt, C., Städtebau. Sammlung Mathesius, Verlag Bard, Berlin.
***Heimann, Kleinhäuser. *Deutsche Bauzeitung*, 1908, Seite 178, 238.
Henrici—
   *Beiträge zur praktischen Ästhetik im Städtebau. G. Callwey, München, 1904.
   *Die künstlerischen Aufgaben im Städtebau. *Deutsche Städtezeitung*, 1905,
      Seite 271.
   *Von welchen Gedanken sollen wir uns beim Ausbau unserer deutschen Städte
      leiten lassen ? Trier, 1894.
*Lilienthal, Warum enstehen bei uns keine Gartenstädte ? *Bodenreform*, 1908,
   No. 4. Verlag J. Harwitz, Nachfl. Berlin, Friedrichstr. 16.
***Meyer, Prof., Die Haupt- und Residenzstadt. Karlsruhe.
*Neue Aufgaben in der Bauordnungs- und Ansiedlungsfrage. Report of the
   Germany Company of Dwelling Reform. Vandenhoeck & Ruprecht,
   Göttingen, 1906.
***Oehmke, Th., Gesundheit und weiträumige Stadtbebauung, insbesonders her-
   geleitet aus dem Gegensatze von Stadt zu Land und von Miethaus zu
   Einzelhaus, samt Abriss der städtebaulichen Entwickelung Berlins und
   seiner Vororte. Berlin, 1904, Julius Springer.
*Pfeifer, Kon trast und Rhytmus im Städtebau. *Der Städtebau*, 1904, Seite 97.

*Rehorst, Dr. Carl. Über die Möglichkeit der Erhaltung alter Städtebilder unter Berücksichtigung moderner Verkehrsanforderungen. Karlsruhe, C. F. Müllersche Hofbuchdruckerei, 1907.

*Schultze-Naumburg, Städtebau, Kulturarbeiten—

    Bd. I. Hausbau.

    Bd. II. Gärten.

    Bd. III. Dörfer und Colonien.

    Bd. IV. Städtebau.

    Bd. V. Kleinbürgerhäuser.

*Sitte, Camillo, Der Städtebau nach seinen künstlerischen Grundsätzen. Wien, 1909, C. Graeser & Co.

Stübben—

    **Der Bau der Städte in Geschichte und Gegenwart. Berlin, 1895.

    *Der Städtebau (Handbuch der Architectur IV. 9). Stuttgart, 1907, A. Kröner.

*Voigt und Geldner, Kleinhaus und Mietskaserne. Berlin, 1905, Jul. Springer.

***Wohlfahrtseinrichtung in der Guss-stahlfabrik von Fried. Krupp zu Essen a. d. Ruhr (Krupp in Essen on the Ruhr). Buchdruckerei der Guss-stahlfabrik von Fried. Krupp. III. Bd., 1904.

***Wuttke, R., Die deutschen Städte. Leipzig, 1904.

*Zetzsche, C., Das öffentliche Gebäude im Stadtbild. *Architectonische Rundschau*. Seite 73.

FRENCH SECTION

Annuaire de Paris et du Département de la Seine, 1904.

Barras, Notes sur le Bois de Boulogne. Paris, 1900.

Benoit-Lévy, Georges, Publications of the French Garden City Association.

Blondeau, Servitude militaire. Grenoble, 1892.

Bocher, Mémoires à consulter de Édouard Bocher avec consultations de MM. Berryer, Dufaure, Paillet, Odilon, Barrot. Paris, 1852.

Brousse, Paul—

    Rapport sur la suppression du mur d'enceinte de Paris. Paris, 1893.

    A propos de la désaffectation partielle du mur d'enceinte de Paris. 1898.

Bulletin de la Société des Paysages, 1902, 1903, 1904, 1905, 1906, 1907, 1908.

Buls, Ch.—

    De la position et du développement des Rues et des Espaces libres dans les Villes. Cong. Int. Architectes, Londres, 1906.

    La Construction des Villes.

    L'Esthétique des Villes.

    L'Esthétique de Rome.

Des Cilleuls, Le domaine de la Ville de Paris dans le passé et dans le présent. Paris, 1885.

Dezamy, Th., Conséquence de l'embastillement et de la paix à tout prix. Dépopulation de la capitale. 1840.

Dieudonné, Notice pittoresque et historique sur le Bois de Boulogne. Paris, 1855.

D'Andigné—

    Rapport sur la désaffectation des Fortifications. Paris, 1906.

    L'aggrandissement du Bois de Boulogne. *Echo de Paris*, Septembre, 1905.

Forestier, Grandes Villes et système de Parcs. Paris, 1906.

Fougères, Gustav, Sélinonte Colonie Dorienne en Sicile. Essai de restauration d'une ville grecque au VI° et au V° Siècle avant J.C. 110 francs, Charles Schmid, Paris.

Fuster, Édouard—

    La santé publique et les espaces libres. *Revue de l'Aide Sociale*, 1907, 1908.

    Articles dans le journal *Le Figaro* intitulé "L'aide sociale," 1906, 1907.

Guist'hau, Discours sur l'action des Mutualités sur l'amélioration de la santé publique.

Hébrard, Jean, Articles dans le *Journal* sur l'hygiène de la population et l'amélioration des plans de villes, 1906, 1908.

Hénard, Eugène—

    Études sur les transformations de Paris. Fascicule 2, 1903.

    Projet de prolongement de la rue de Rennes avec pont en X sur la Seine. Fascicule 1, 1903.

    La question des fortifications et le Boulevard des grandes ceintures. Fascicule 2, 1903.

    Les grands espaces libres, les parcs et jardins de Paris et de Londres. Fascicule 3.

    Le parc des sports et les grands dirigeables. Fascicule 4, 1904.

    La percée du Palais Royal, la nouvelle grande croisée de Paris. Fascicule 5, 1904.

    La circulation dans les villes modernes, l'automobilisme et les voies rayonnantes de Paris. Fascicule 6, 1905.

    Les voitures et les passants, carrefours libres et carrefours à giration. Fascicule 7, 1908.

    Des Places publiques, la Place de l'Opéra, les Trois Colonnes. Fascicule 8, 1909.

    Paper for the London Inter. Congress of Architects, 1906.

Journal des Débats—La ville rationelle, par Arvède Barine. Septembre, 1906.

Mabilleau, Léopold, Articles et discours sur la santé publique et la Mutualité Française, 1905 à 1908.

Marmottan, Les espaces libres. Paris, 1902 (*Journal des Arts*, juillet).

Meynadier—

    Paris au point de vue pittoresque et monumental.

    Elément d'un plan général d'ensemble. Paris, 1849.

Montet, Eugène, Rapports au Musée Social sur les espaces libres.

Revue Scientifique. Stéphane Leduc, Les conditions sanitaires en France. Février, 1892.

Rey, A. Augustin—

    Les espaces libres, les rues, les cours. Cong. Intern. Tuberc., Paris, 1905.

Rey, A. Augustin (*continued*)—

 De l'action des espaces libres boisés sur la santé publique, notamment dans les quartiers populaires. Cong. Int. Architectes, Londres, 1906.

 Méthodes nouvelles de création des rues modernes.

 La ville et les espaces libres. Cong. Nat. Hyg., Marseille, 1906.

 La santé publique et les espaces libres.

 Les formes nouvelles de l'habitation salubre. Cong. Alliance Hyg. Soc., Lyon, 1907.

 La spéculation sur les terrains et l'hygiène des grandes villes. Cong. Int Hyg., Berlin, 1907.

 Les espaces libres et les plans de formes nouvelles à adopter pour les villes modernes.

 La santé publique et les agglomérations actuelles.

 La spéculation du sol dans les villes modernes et la tuberculose. Comment enrayer le développement croissant de cette speculation. Cong. Intern. Tuberculose, Washington, 1908.

 Une ceinture de parc pour Paris—Un projet exécutable. Paris, 1909.

Sitte, Camillo, L'art de bâtir les villes. (Translated from the German, with additions by Camille Martin). Lib. Renouard.

Souza, Robert de, Le Bois de Boulogne et les fortifications de Paris. Avril, 1907.

Turot, Henri, Le surpeuplement et les habitations populaires. Paris, 1907.

FOLD MAP I

NUREMBERG OLD PLAN

FOLD MAP II

NUREMBERG EXTENSION PLAN

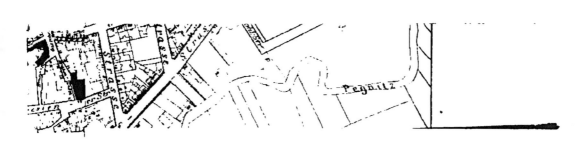

FOLD MAP III

ROTHENBURG

FOLD MAP IV

KARLSRUHE

FOLD MAP V

COLOGNE, DETAILED PLAN OF SMALL AREA

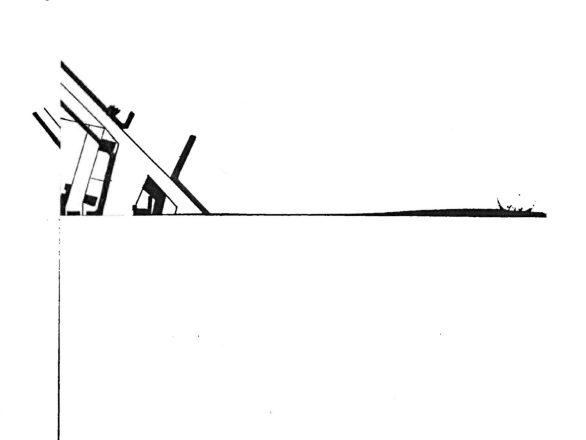

FOLD MAP VI

HAMPSTEAD GARDEN SUBURB

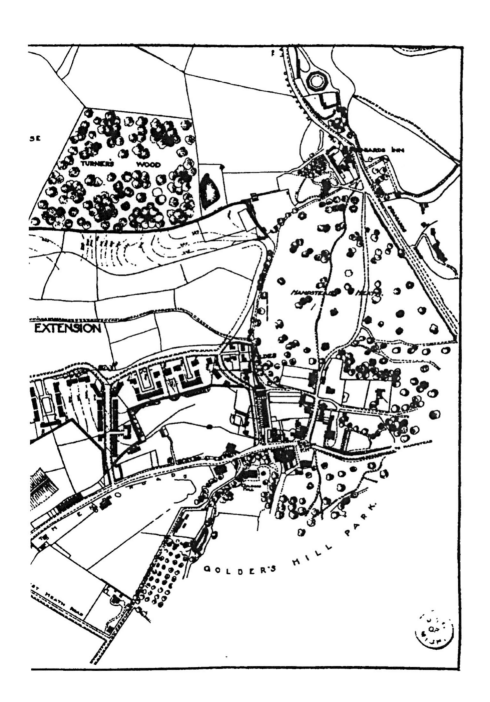

FOLD MAP VII

FIRST GARDEN CITY, LETCHWORTH

19

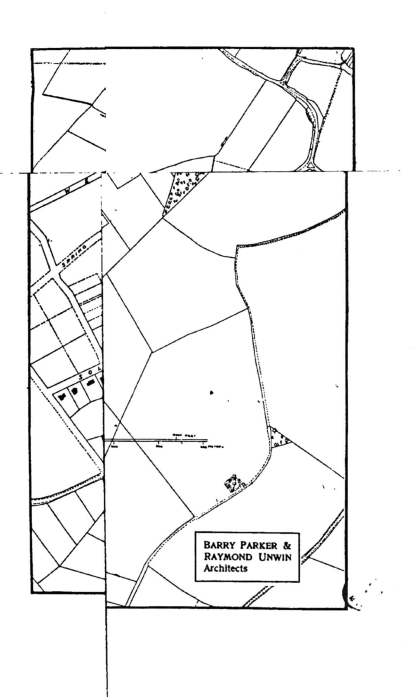

BARRY PARKER &
RAYMOND UNWIN
Architects